Elisha D. Smith Public Library

Menasha, Wisconsin 54952

DEMCO

Simon and Schuster's

GUIDE TO GEMS AND PRECIOUS STONES

Curzio Cipriani
and Alessandro Borelli

Kennie Lyman, U. S. Editor

Translated by Valerie Palmer

Simon and Schuster • New York

ACKNOWLEDGMENTS

The publisher wishes to thank the following for their kind
collaboration: Prof. Pio Visconti from the Centro Analisi
Gemmologiche in Valenza (Alessandria, Italy), the
Associazione Orafa Valenzana, Valenza (Alessandria, Italy)
and Mr. Giancarlo Fioravanti, Rome.

553,8

C 49S

CONTENTS

KEY TO SYMBOLS

HARDNESS

The number inside the rectangle indicates the degree of hardness according to Mohs' scale.

DENSITY (g/cm^3)

light minerals with a density of less than 3

medium-weight minerals with a density of between 3 and 4

heavy minerals with a density of more than 4

REFRACTION

single refraction

double refraction (birefringence)

COLOR

The colored rectangle shows the main color of the stone. The possibilities are: white; colorless; red; pink; yellow; green; dark blue; light blue; violet; brown; black.

Order of Description of Precious Stones

There are many possible ways to order a book on precious stones. One very straightforward method is to arrange the descriptions of the gems in alphabetical order. This has the advantage of making the book quick to consult, but it disregards similarities or even identity of composition between different stones. A second possible basis of organization, color, while useful for distinguishing between different stones of similar appearance, has the same drawback. A third possibility is the classic mineralogical system of organization by chemical composition. Although logical, in that natural gemstones are minerals, this system would be unbalanced. Some classes of minerals (silicates and oxides) would make up the bulk of the book, while others (halides, borates, sulphates, sulphides, carbonates, and phosphates) would be represented scarcely, if at all. This leaves a fourth option: selection of a basic physical property, hardness, which is one of the major qualities of a precious stone. Organization on the basis of a decreasing order of hardness according to Mohs' scale also has the advantage of corresponding very roughly to a descending order of commercial value.

This, then, is the order followed in the section of this book devoted to the description of individual stones. One exception to this rule is the garnets. The various subdivisions of the garnet family have been listed sequentially to emphasize their relationship to one another and to counter the popular practice of using the word *garnet* to refer only to red-colored stones. The reader should keep in mind that this descending order of hardness is only approximate, since experts don't always agree. For ease of consultation, the mineral itself is examined first, then the varieties used as precious or ornamental stones. Gems of organic origin, formed by biological processes, are considered separately, as are synthetic and artificial stones produced in the laboratory.

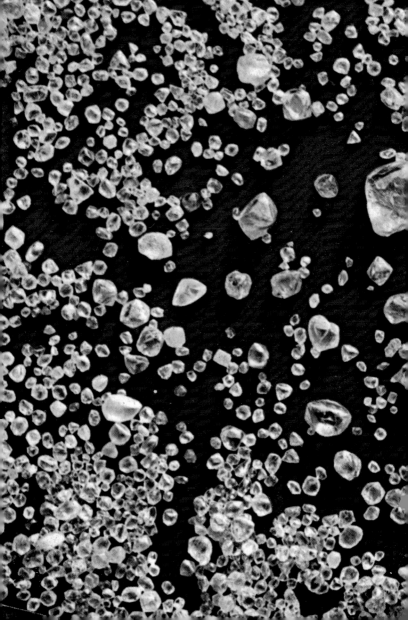

Precious stones and the gems cut from them to highlight their brilliance and color are fascinating objects.
Celebrated in poetry and art through the ages; worn by beautiful women; epitomizing wealth, luxury, and power; obtained by strenuous labor and transformed by skill and experience, a precious stone is a pure and tangible concentrate of

INTRODUCTION

"A precious stone is a small, rare, hard stone which has inherited from Nature the name of beautiful." Thus Piero Aloisi, in his classic treatise on gems of fifty years ago, quoted Anselm de Boodt, seventeenth century scholar and physician to Emperor Rudolf II of Hapsburg.

While the notion of size is debatable (there is no reason why a large stone should not be precious, the other four characteristics—rarity, hardness, natural origin, and beauty—together with chemical resistance, all constitute an acceptable definition of a precious stone. A natural object (and therefore a mineral), beautiful, rare, hard, and resistant. Let us look briefly at these properties:

A precious stone should be a mineral, that is, an object formed spontaneously in nature, without human intervention. This property is essential to our definition, because many modern artificial stones are highly prized, and the synthetic varieties are sometimes virtually indistinguishable from the natural ones. Beauty is essentially a subjective concept, even if the appreciation of precious stones is commonly based on objective criteria, above all optical characteristics, such as dispersive power (the so-called play of colors), color, transparency, and high refractivity. Rarity too is a criterion which has more to do with the beholder than the beheld. It is connected to that part of human nature that prefers things that are hard to come by, partly to arouse in others a sense of envy. Despite their in-

trinsic qualities, no one would wear rubies for ornamentation if they were as common as pebbles on the beach.

The remaining two properties——hardness and chemical resistance——are truly objective because they are physical and chemical. Hardness is fundamental to a precious stone; scratching of the surface or abrasion of the edges would spoil its appearance. Similarly, poor chemical resistance would eventually lead to partial disintegration, depriving the stone of value by destroying its brilliance.

A fabric of subjective and objective properties, fact and fantasy, sensations, fashions, superstition, and reality; celebrated by poets and studied by scientists, depicted by artists and worn by the fair sex, symbol of power and wealth, product of the miner's toil and the craftsman's skill——a precious stone is all this——something which has defied the passage of time and will surely continue to fascinate future generations: a thing of beauty.

Fantastic origins, not to mention magical and medicinal properties, used to be claimed for precious stones; though references were usually prefaced by something like "it is said that," or "it has been observed that," making it hard to determine whether or not the authors believed what they were saying. Ice permanently frozen by intense cold (rock crystal); product of the earth's extreme aridity combined with the sun's powerful action (hyacinth); lynxes' urine and birds' tears (amber): these are just a few of the fantastic notions about the

Opposite page: looking for minerals with a divining rod (pictures taken from *De Re Metallica*, by the Renaissance scholar Giorgio Agricola).

Over the centuries, numerous magical and medicinal properties were attributed to precious stones. Here are some examples of medieval folk medicine, taken from *Hortus Sanitatis* (1483).

The lapidary prepares the stones (top left); bufotenine is extracted from the head of a toad (above right) and is used to treat poisoning (above left); heliotrope is used to stop nosebleed (right).

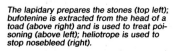

origins of precious stones——not differing very much, truth to tell, from those once claimed for minerals of all kinds.

Innumerable magical and medicinal properties were attributed to precious stones over the centuries: diamond gave immunity to poison and revealed infidelity; amethyst protected against drunkenness; heliotrope stopped nosebleed and conferred invisibility; sapphire enabled the wearer to escape from prison. These are merely a few better known examples, but there are also countless tales of stones with mysterious names, impossible to identify.

We may laugh at all this; but are we ourselves innocent of all trace of superstition? It is worth recalling that at the beginning of this century the Hope blue diamond was alleged to have brought death or economic ruin to its possessors.

The nature of crystals

Observation of quartz crystals, which are mainly of hexagonal, prismatic form or of pyrite, which often consists of perfect cubes, reveals an external regularity, which is verifiable experimentally by measuring the dihedral angles. These are mathematically precise and constant. It is not surprising that this regularity is the reflection of a perfectly regular internal order. This internal perfection, brilliantly perceived at the end of the eighteenth century by the French crystallographer Haüy and verified experimentally some seventy years ago by the German von Laue, using X-rays, is the *crystalline* state, mani-

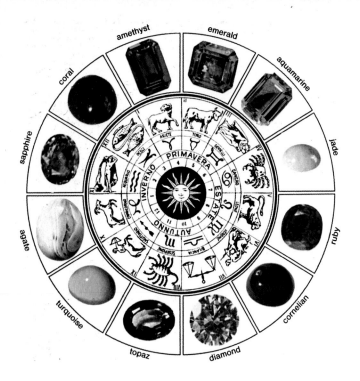

fested in a periodic sequence of constituent particles—atoms or ions—precisely repeated in all dimensions.

Crystalline state is synonymous with solid state, definable not as that which gives actual form and volume—as taught in schools—but as possessing a regular arrangement of atoms, repeated in identical fashion about 100 million times per centimeter. This strict repetition is not found, for instance, in glass, where the order is limited to very few atoms, about 10Å (1Å [angstrom] = 10^{-8} cm) in size, with a random, mosaiclike repetition of differently oriented "tesserae" some 10 million times per centimeter. Clearly the high quality glass that is commonly called crystal is, scientifically speaking, in the vitreous, not the crystalline, state (Fig. 1).

A *crystal* is, in fact "a homogeneous body in the form of a polyhedron, bounded by spontaneously formed faces, whose character is determined by the nature of the constituent substance." A crystal must therefore be formed by a substance in the crystalline state, but a crystalline substance does not necessarily appear in the form of crystals. There are, for example, objects of crystalline substance that have not developed plane faces or others, such as cut precious stones, in which facets have been produced artificially. All precious stones are in the crystalline state, with the exception of opal, which is in the vitreous state.

Opposite: At one time, gems were believed to be of celestial origin, whence the belief that they possessed magical powers and brought luck to those born under the sign of the zodiac with which they were associated. Such superstitions are of course no longer believed, yet many people still choose to wear the stone of the month, or rather of the zodiac sign under which they were born.
Below: The external regularity of these crystals of pyrite, consisting of perfect cubes, is an expression of a perfect internal order——the crystalline state.

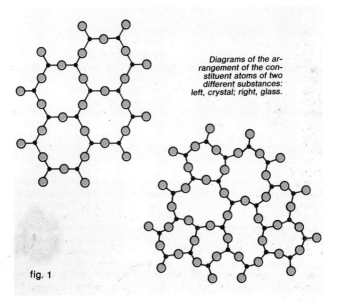

Diagrams of the arrangement of the constituent atoms of two different substances: left, crystal; right, glass.

fig. 1

Elements of symmetry (shown in red): a. plane of symmetry; b. axis of symmetry; c. center of symmetry.

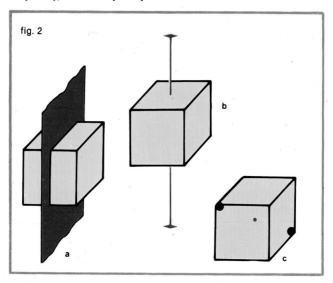

fig. 2

Symmetry

Crystals display a certain degree of *symmetry*, depending on the ordered arrangement of their atomic particles. Symmetry operates in three ways: by reflection, rotation, and inversion. *Reflection*, exactly like that produced by a mirror, entails the existence of a *plane of symmetry*, or a plane dividing the crystal into two specularly equal halves. *Rotation* takes place about an axis. As the object rotates around this axis, it occupies the same position in space every $\frac{360°}{n}$ where n is the order of the *axis of symmetry*, which in crystals can only be 2, 3, 4, or 6. In contrast, polygons display axes of symmetry from 1 (scalene triangle) to 2 (rectangle), to 3 (equilateral triangle) and so on for regular polygons up to infinity for the circle. *Inversion* takes place in relation to a *center of symmetry*, or a point on opposite sides of which identical faces and edges occur (Fig. 2).

In crystals, these elements of symmetry can be variously combined. There are in fact thirty-two different possibilites, known as *crystal classes*. These thirty-two classes can in turn be allocated to seven *crystal systems*, which bring together classes having certain elements in common. Without entering into a description of the thirty-two classes, it is worth mentioning the seven crystal systems, as their effects on physical properties are important.

Triclinic system: three unequal crystal axes with mutually oblique intersections.

Monoclinic system: three crystal axes of unequal lengths

All crystals belong to classes of symmetry, which are grouped into 7 systems. Left, top to bottom: 1. cubic crystals of pyrite (cubic system); 2. crystals of smoky quartz (trigonal system); 3. prismatic crystal of phosgenite (tetragonal system); 4. prismatic crystals of apatite (hexagonal system). Right, top to bottom: 5. prismatic crystals of stibnite (orthorhombic system); 6. tabular crystal of gypsum (monoclinic system); 7. tabular crystal of kyanite (triclinic system).

Crystals are further subdivided into three groups depending on the arrangement of their atoms in the three dimensions: a. monometric; b. dimetric; c. trimetric.

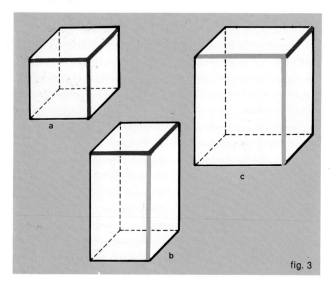

fig. 3

having one of their intersections oblique, the other two intersections being at 90°.

Orthorhombic system: three crystal axes at right angles to each other, all of different lengths; three unlike planes of symmetry meeting at 90°.

Trigonal system: three like planes of symmetry intersecting at angles of 60° in the vertical axis.

Tetragonal system: three crystal axes at right angles to each other; two of them, taken as the horizontal, being equal; the third, the vertical, being longer or shorter than the other two.

Hexagonal system: four crystal axes, three of which are equal and lie in the horizontal plane making angles of 60° and 120° with each other, while the fourth axis is vertical and has a different length (shorter or longer) from that of the horizontal axes.

Cubic system: three crystal axes at right angles to each other and of equal lengths.

Finally, there is a further, more general subdivision of crystals into three *crystal groups: trimetric, dimetric,* and *monometric,* formed respectively by the first three systems, the second three, and the last (cubic system only). The meaning of these groups is implicit in their names: trimetric denotes three measurements or a different arrangement of atoms and therefore a diversity of crystalline form in the three dimensions; dimetric meaning two measurements or equality in two directions, and monometric equality in all three directions (Fig. 3).

Some stones are *twinned,* i.e. with two or more crystals which have grown together according to precise rules of orientation. Twinning produces an additional element of symmetry (one two-fold axis) compared with the typical symmetry for the crystal substance in question. Twin crystals are often, but not always, recognizable by the presence of reentrant dihedral angles, which are impossible in single crystals. In the case of precious stones, twinned forms of corundum are of particular interest, above all in the ruby variety. These are very occasionally seen in the shape of an arrow, consisting of two welded individuals, or more often as a series of close striations on the faces of a single crystal, parallel to the twinning plane.

Physical and chemical properties
Objects in the crystalline state have a different sequence of atoms in the various directions of the crystal, which as a rule also involves a difference in physical and chemical properties, or *anisotropy,* a word of Greek origin meaning diversity in different directions. Glass, to the contrary, always displays *isotropy,* or equality in all directions.
This difference in behavior can be demonstrated by subjecting a spherical piece of glass and another of quartz, to two simple experiments. The first, a chemical test, consists of immersing the two items for a few seconds in hydrofluoric acid, which acts as a solvent, and examining their behavior as they dissolve. The other experiment, concerning a physical property,

Illustration of the different behavior of a sphere of glass (a) and one of quartz (b) subjected to a test of chemical solubility. The glass sphere retains its spherical shape, while the quartz one assumes the form of an ellipsoid of rotation.

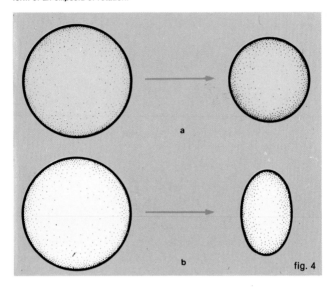

a

b

fig. 4

thermal expansion, can be performed by heating the two spheres. In both cases, the glass will maintain its spherical shape, despite becoming smaller in the first and larger in the second, while the quartz will assume the form of an ellipsoid of rotation, demonstrating that the crystalline substance behaves differently in various directions (Fig. 4).

Density
This property concerns the crystal as a whole, so that direction is unimportant. *Density* is defined as weight per unit volume and is expressed in g/cm^3, the figures for which basically coincide with those for *specific gravity* (s.g.), represented by a pure number, corresponding to the ratio of the weight of the substance to that of an equal volume of distilled water.
The density can be determined by one of the following methods. The *hydrostatic balance* uses Archimedes' principle, according to which a body immersed in a fluid experiences an upward force equal to the weight of the fluid displaced. Accordingly, if the substance is weighed first in air (W_1) and then in water (W_2), its specific gravity, according to the definition, will be:

$$s. g. = \frac{W_1}{W_1 - W_2}$$

There are various ways of determining the specific gravity. Fig. 5 shows a pycnometer; Fig. 6, a Westphal balance.

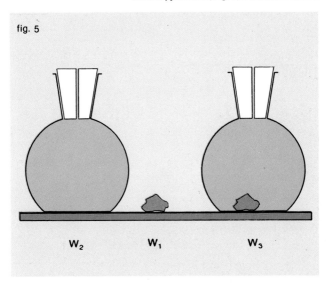

fig. 5

W_2 W_1 W_3

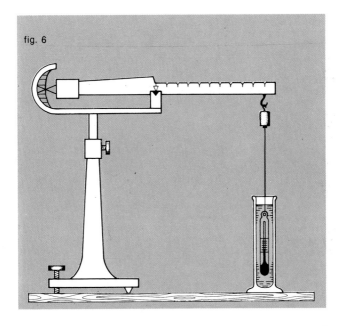

fig. 6

An example of cleavage according to crystal shape: the rhombohedral cleavage of calcite.

An example of cleavage according to crystal shape: the rhombohedral cleavage of calcite.

The *pycnometer* (from the Greek, measurer of density), is a bottle with a ground glass stopper pierced by a capillary channel (Fig. 5). The procedure consists first of weighing the substance (W_1), then the bottle filled with distilled water (W_2), and finally, the bottle, containing the substance, after having eliminated the excess water (W_3).
The specific gravity will be:

$$s.g. = \frac{W_1}{W_1 + W_2 - W_3}$$

The comparison with *heavy liquids* is based on the elementary fact that a body immersed in a fluid floats to the top, sinks or remains in indifferent equilibrium, depending on whether its density is lesser, greater or equal to that of the fluid. This test can be conducted with one of the heavy liquids, so called because they have a much higher specific gravity than that of water. The most commonly used are bromoform (s.g. 2.9), acetylene tetrabromide (3.0), methylene iodide (3.3), and Clerici's solution (4.2), which is an aqueous solution of tallium malonate and tallium formate. The first three liquids can be diluted with benzene or toluene, the last with water.
The density of the liquid (d_l) is varied until the body under examination remains in indifferent equilibrium (d_x), accordingly:

Cleavage traces (left, seen under a microscope; right, shown diagrammatically in a prismatic crystal) are narrow cracks corresponding to incipient cleavage and are most often found in minerals which cleave readily.

 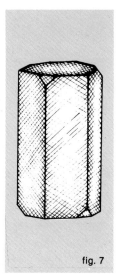

fig. 7

$$d_x = d_l$$

The problem then is to establish the exact density of the liquid. This is much easier and can be done either by using a pycnometer—weighing it first empty, then full of water—or by means of a special *Westphal balance* (Fig. 6), which is basically a hydrostatic balance suitable for liquids, in which the equilibrium of a plunger, calibrated with water, is reestablished using a series of weights which slot into the nine notches on the balance arm.

Cleavage
A mineral subjected to powerful mechanical stress can break. The breakage may occur along irregular conchoidal surfaces—in which case it is an example of *fracture*—or along planes corresponding to crystal faces, when it is known as *cleavage*. This particular type of breakage is only found in crystal substances, indicating a clear difference in cohesion in different directions. When cohesion is much the same in all directions, fracture can occur, even in a crystalline substance.

According to the facility with which it occurs, cleavage can be described by adjectives such as perfect, easy, good, or imperfect. It can also be described in terms of crystal shape, e.g. cubic, octahedral, rhomb dodecahedral, prismatic, rhombohedral, pinacoidal (i.e. along two parallel faces), and so on. Nar-

The hardness of a stone can be determined by scratch tests, since a harder material will scratch a softer one.

row cracks corresponding to incipient cleavage may often be observed in crystal substances. These are known as *cleavage traces* and always occur parallel to the planes of symmetry (Fig. 7).

Cleavage is a very useful characteristic in precious stones. Not only is it an aid to recognition, but it makes it easier both to fashion the stones (e.g. it facilitates cutting of diamonds) and to guard against breakage by a suitable choice of setting.

Hardness
Hardness is the result of the greater or lesser cohesion of minerals, or the strength of their chemical bonds. It is definable in terms of resistance to external stresses in one direction (scratching), in two (abrasion) or in three (penetration). Crystallography and mineralogy are mainly concerned with the first. Given the difficulty in measuring hardness precisely, it is expressed in terms of an empirical scale consisting of ten sample minerals of increasing hardness, each of which is capable of scratching the preceding mineral, and being scratched by the subsequent one. This is known as Mohs' scale and consists of the following:

1. talc	5. apatite	9. corundum
2. gypsum	6. orthoclase	10. diamond
3. calcite	7. quartz	
4. fluorite	8. topaz	

When a light ray R encounters a surface SS' separating two different media, part of it is reflected back into the first medium (R'), with the result that the angle of incidence i and the angle of reflection I (i.e. the angles which the incident and reflected rays form with the perpendicular P at the point of incidence O) lie in the same plane and are equal; this is the phenomenon of reflection. If part of the ray (R'') enters the second medium, it undergoes a change in direction compared with the incident ray, known as refraction. The resulting angle r will be greater or smaller than the angle of incidence, depending on the nature of the two media.

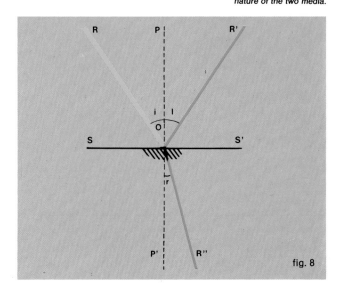

fig. 8

As examples, the first two items can be scratched by a fingernail (and are therefore "soft"), while a steel point, depending on its type, can scratch the following three or four (known as "hard"), so that the remaining four or five must be "very hard."

Hardness, like optical properties, is one of the most important characteristics of a precious stone. Considerable hardness, in fact, enhances optical features from luster to refraction——the play of light——since it enables the surfaces to be kept perfectly smooth and the corners clear-cut.

Given the importance of this property, the sections on individual stones in this volume have been arranged in descending order of hardness. Hardness, commonly associated with something that is unbreakable, has nothing to do with lack of brittleness. Brittleness, or the tendency to break easily, is really related to cleavage——the tendency to break along precise crystallographic planes. Diamond, the hardest material, is in fact quite brittle, owing to its easy octahedral cleavage.

Optical properties

When a light ray encounters a surface separating two different media, such as air and a mineral, part is reflected, or sent back into the first medium, part is refracted, entering the second medium, and part is absorbed (Fig. 8). Depending on the nature of the substance in question, one or other part can prevail. For example, in metals, a high proportion is absorbed (*opaque*

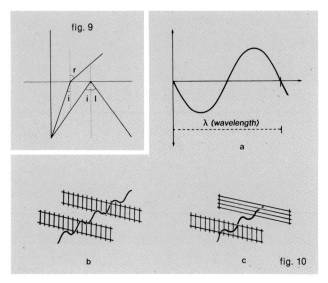

material) and in many cases a high proportion is also reflected,
whereas none is refracted. Conversely, in *transparent* materials, the refracted portion prevails, while the reflected and absorbed portions both vary (slightly if the mineral is *colorless*,
appreciable if it is *colored*).

Reflection is governed by two very simple laws: (1) The incident ray, the reflected ray, and the perpendicular to the surface lie in the same plane. (2) The angle of incidence *i* (formed
by the incident ray and the perpendicular) is equal to the angle
of reflection *l* (formed by the reflected ray and the perpendicular):

$$i = l$$

There are also two laws for refraction. The first is identical
to the one indicated for reflection: incident ray, refracted ray,
and perpendicular to surface lie in the same plane. The second
states that the ratio of the sine of the angle of incidence *i* to
that of the angle of refraction *r* is a constant, that is:

$$\frac{\sin i}{\sin r} = n$$

If the incident ray comes from a vacuum (in practice, the air),
the constant *n* is defined as the *refractive index* of the second
medium. In refraction, therefore, a deflection takes place due
to the reduction in velocity of the light as it enters a different
substance from air and it can be demonstrated that the refractive index *n* corresponds not just to the quotient of the sines of
the angles but to the ratio of the velocity of the light in the two

media——the air and the substance under examination. For crystal substances, which have a diverse arrangement of atoms in different directions, the reduction in velocity of the light generally varies with the direction, so that there is more than one refractive index. Thus monometric crystals and vitreous substances have a single index n, but birefringent crystals have a whole series, whose extremes are $n\omega$ and $n\epsilon$ for dimetric crystals and $n\alpha$ and $n\gamma$ for trimetric ones.

The paths of the rays in the two media do not change if the light ray passes from the second medium (the mineral) into the first (the air), traveling away from the perpendicular. The maximum possible departure is 90°, at which point the refracted ray becomes parallel to the boundary between the two media. This angle of refraction is matched by an angle of incidence inside the mineral, known as the *critical angle*, above which refraction can no longer occur. This is known as *total internal reflection*, because the entire incident ray is reflected by the boundary into the mineral (Fig. 9).

Two very important instruments for gemstone recognition, associated with the phenomenon of total internal reflection, are the total reflection meter and the total refraction meter, both of which consist basically of a glass hemisphere with a known, very high refractive index. The stone to be examined is placed on the smooth, flat surface of the glass, optical contact being maintained with a drop of highly refracting liquid. In the total reflection meter, the object is lit through the hemisphere. The rays at small angles will be refracted into the stone, but once the critical angle is exceeded, total internal reflection will occur. By using a rotating eyepiece with a dial, a clear separation may be observed between a light zone (for angles of reflection in excess of the critical angle) and a dark one (for smaller angles, which give rise to refraction). In the total refraction meter, the same result is achieved with grazing light. In this case, the separation between light and dark areas occurs for the refracted ray produced by an incident ray of 90°.

The refractive indices of crystal substances generally vary with the direction of propagation of the light rays. If one were to take three very thick but transparent crystals——rock salt (cubic system, monometric group), calcite (trigonal, dimetric), and gypsum (monoclinic, trimetric)——and observe a dot drawn on a piece of paper through them, in the first case, one would see a single dot, in the second two dots, one of which would be still and the other rotating as the crystal was rotated and in the third case, two dots again, but both rotating as the crystal was rotated. Because one would normally expect to see a single, still image, the conclusion to be drawn from this is that monometric crystals, and for that matter glass, behave normally, i.e. an ordinary ray is propagated in them. In dimetric crystals, there is an ordinary ray plus an extraordinary one, which does not follow the normal laws of refraction. When the ordinary ray

The phenomenon of double refraction is shown in this Iceland spar variety of calcite crystal. Note the double image of the word "calcite."

has a higher refractive index than the extraordinary ray, the crystal is called positive and vice versa. Finally, in trimetric crystals, there are two extraordinary rays. Thus all crystals, with the exception of cubic ones, display the phenomenon of *double refraction,* the formation of two polarized light waves traveling in different directions, i.e. the production of two rays of polarized light.

Every motorist knows the eyestrain caused by the sun's glare on a smooth surface, such as a tarmac road. This glare can virtually be eliminated by the use of special "polaroid" glasses. The rays that cause the glare normally consist of light waves free to oscillate in all possible planes, intersecting one another according to their direction of propagation. Polarization curtails this freedom as the light waves are forced to vibrate in a single plane (Fig. 10 a,b,c).

To understand how polarization works, an analogy can be made with a stick, which can only pass through the bars of a gate if placed parallel to them. The polaroid lenses in glasses may be compared to the gate, in that the minute crystals of which they are composed, all equally oriented, only let through light rays oscillating in one direction (that of the "bars"), blocking the ones perpendicular to that direction.

Returning to the different behavior of different crystals, we may conclude by saying that monometric crystals and glass are *singly refractive* (a single ray, consisting of a single light

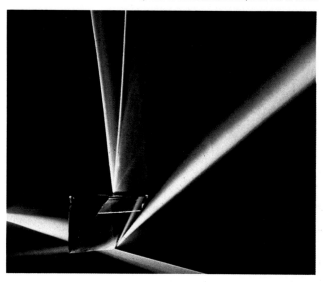

wave is propagated in all directions) and therefore they have just one refractive index. The other crystals are *doubly refractive or birefringent.* A light ray entering these crystals is, generally speaking, split into two polarized light waves, each with its own refractive index. The exception occurs when the light enters the crystal in particular directions, called *optic axes,* at which time the crystals are only singly refractive. The significance of the crystal groups is further demonstrated by the fact that dimetric crystals have only one optic axis, whereas trimetric crystals have two.

It is evident, therefore, that a stone can be assigned to one or other crystal group and, in some cases, even to a crystal system (two valuable aids to recognition) by its behavior in relation to polarized light. This behavior can be analyzed by using a polarizing microscope, or one with two polarizing filters in which the "bars" or directions of vibration are set crossways to each other, and placed one above and one below the rotating stage. Under these conditions, light cannot pass through the microscope, because the light waves coming from the first filter are blocked by the second. The same thing happens if a monometric or vitreous stone is placed on the stage. But if a dimetric or trimetric substance, i.e. one that is birefringent, is examined, it will appear lit up on a dark ground, and then, as the stage of the microscope is rotated, merge with the background in four positions. These are the positions of *extinction,* in which light cannot pass, due to the coincidence of the directions of vibration of the polarizing filters with those of the birefringent crystal, which can thus be identified. In these positions of extinction, it is possible, keeping only the polarizing filter beneath the stage, to determine the refractive indices for the crystal in that position.

Color and dispersion
Color is extremely important in gemology. A stone looks colored because it absorbs a greater or lesser portion of the rays of the visible spectrum that constitutes white light. Thus a red stone appears red because it absorbs part of the green radiation, and so on. This absorption can affect wide bands of the visible spectrum, or be confined to just a few, corresponding to precise radiations generated by particular types of atoms in the stone. For example, when a sodium chloride crystal is held over a gas flame or more simply, when a drop of salt water boils over from a pan onto a gas ring, the flame turns bright yellow, corresponding to a precise band of the visible spectrum characteristic of sodium.

A given color can be produced in various ways, even by wavebands in different parts of the visible spectrum. It is this very diversity that makes it possible in some cases to distinguish between different stones of similar color and in a few, rare instances, even between natural and synthetic stones of the same type. This is done with an instrument called a spectroscope, which is basically a prism that separates out the colors of the spectrum, emphasizing the bands of absorption, which look black against the colored background.

A distinctive type of coloration, produced virtually only by opal, is due to the *diffraction* of light. This physical phenomenon occurs when a light ray encounters a material possessing an ordered internal structure, with intervals of the same order of magnitude as its own wavelength. This might happen with objects shaped like a comb or a row of identical balls, the teeth of the comb or the balls being spaced about $1/1000$ mm, or one micron, apart. Under these conditions, rays are deflected in various directions in relation to the incident ray and these will appear colored due to the disappearance of some radiations by mutual annihilation.

Light absorption can vary enormously according to the nature and thickness of the substance. A substance which, even for minimal thicknesses, absorbs the light completely is called *opaque*, whereas one that lets through nearly all the light even at considerable thicknesses is called *transparent*. Between these two extremes there are, of course, various intermediate types of stone, generally described as *translucent,* because they allow light to penetrate, though not sufficiently for the outline of an object to be distinguished through them. Different behavior in terms of light absorption basically depends on the

The color of precious stones depends on the extent to which they absorb light rays. Top, the iridescence of labradorite; center, "cat's-eye" chrysoberyl; bottom, the "Star of Asia," 330 carats, the second largest star sapphire in the world. Asterism is due to light reflection by minute needlelike inclusions.

Australian black opals, 44 carats (left) and 30 carats (right). The patches of color are due to light diffraction.

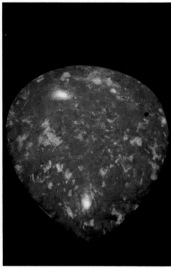

nature of the substance; thus metals are wholly opaque, as are sulphides and some oxides, while the remaining minerals are generally transparent, above all in single crystals. In fact, one of the most common causes of lack of transparency, apart from the presence of inclusions and minute cracks, is the aggregation of tiny crystals.

Apart from varying in quantity, light absorption can vary in quality, because of the different radiations of the visible spectrum. A substance may appear *colorless* if there is modest absorption, equal for all colors, but if the absorption is appreciable and affects some colors in particular, the substance will assume a color depending on the mixture of light rays not absorbed.

Light absorption, like refraction, varies in crystals according to direction. Thus, dimetric and trimetric colored crystals exhibit a greater or lesser degree of *pleochroism,* i.e. display more than one color due to the different absorption of light in different directions. This phenomenon, which does not apply to monometric crystals and glass, is easily observable under a type of polarizing microscope known as a Haidinger dichroscope. It is possible in this way to observe separately the two colors of a section of pleochroic crystal which, viewed with the naked eye, would merely reveal a mixture of colors.

The refractive index is different for each of the colored radiations which, when superimposed, form white light. Thus, when a beam of white light from the air enters the mineral, it breaks up into many colored rays, with different angles of refraction.

This phenomenon is called dispersion of the refractive indices or simply *dispersion,* and can readily be observed in a transparent substance with nonparallel corners which, when illuminated, produces the sequence of colors of the rainbow: red; orange; yellow; green; blue; violet. The degree of dispersion varies a great deal from one substance to another, as do the mean refractive indices. Dispersion is commonly expressed in terms of the difference in refractive indices for violet and red:

$$n_v - n_r$$

The *luster* a stone can acquire is also very important to its value. This property depends both on objective criteria, such as the amount of light reflected, and subjective ones, such as the sensation of warmth or coldness it produces. Luster is commonly indicated by a set of adjectives associated with familiar substances:

adamantine	diamond, zircon
vitreous	ruby, emerald, quartz
waxy	turquoise
pearly	moonstone
silky	gypsum
metallic	hematite

Greasy and *dull* are also sometimes used to describe luster. The type of luster is obviously due to the nature of the stone, but its degree is related to surface polish which, of course, is greater the harder the material.

The play of light and color is one of the most important qualities of colorless or faintly colored stones. This sparkle of colors is seen mainly in cut diamonds, where the artificial formation of many facets, combined with a very high degree of dispersion, produces a distinct separation of the various colors of the visible spectrum, as a result of a series of refractions inside the stone.

Chatoyancy, or the cat's-eye effect, is due to the presence of minute inclusions of fibrous minerals, such as asbestos, but also to the existence of infinitesimal channels. When the filiform inclusions are so oriented that they are parallel to more than one crystal face, *asterism,* a four- or six-pointed star effect, is produced; this is shown to advantage by the cabochon cut.

Labradorescence is due to a mosaiclike arrangement of minute tesserae of different compositions, typical of the stone called labradorite, and consisting of a distinctive type of blue-green iridescence.

Chemical properties

The chemical properties of precious stones are generally less important to the gemologist than their physical properties. As already mentioned, it is essential that precious stones should be resistant to chemical attack. Tests to determine the chemical properties of stones are not commonly used for purposes of recognition, for the simple reason that any such tests are destructive to the gemstone.

Chemical structure can, however, be of interest, and not only for laboratories wishing to reproduce the stones artificially. Many stones have very simple compositions; e.g. one element (carbon for diamond) or oxides (of aluminum for ruby and sapphire, iron for hematite, silicon for quartz and its different varieties); others are quite complex, containing silicates (emerald, zircon, topaz, garnets) or phosphates (turquoise). This chemical diversity has completely refuted old ideas about precious stones being similar in composition to one another, but quite different from other minerals because of their physical properties.

For the sake of completeness, it is worth mentioning two somewhat opposed phenomena relating to the physical and chemical properties: isomorphism and polymorphism. *Polymorphism* (from the Greek, many forms) applies to substances that develop different crystal structures according to their environment (temperature, pressure, chemical environment), with the result that their external appearance and properties differ, sometimes considerably. Carbon, for example, exists in nature as diamond, cubic, colorless, transparent, and very hard (H=10), or graphite, hexagonal, blackish, opaque, and very soft (H=1). Obviously only the diamond form is used as a pre-

cious stone or a very high-quality abrasive, while graphite has completely different applications, exploiting its specific properties such as very low hardness combined with color (pencil) or very good electrical conductivity and chemical resistance (electrodes for chemical processes). Some polymorphous forms are stable under certain environmental conditions, others are always unstable and therefore tend to transform themselves into the stable varieties. It is very important to establish, where possible, which are the correct environmental conditions for the various forms of a polymorphous substance, not just out of scientific interest, but for the practical effects this can have on possible synthesis of the form desired (for example, diamond from graphite). This phenomenon involves different crystal *structures,* as distinct from different *varieties* of the same crystal type, e.g. ruby and sapphire, which differ in color but have the same structure and chemical composition——those of the mineral corundum.

Isomorphism (from the Greek, same form) occurs when two or more chemical substances have identical crystal structures and are chemically so alike that they can form solid solutions, or in other words, mixed, homogeneous crystals in which the corresponding atoms change places at random and in varying proportions. Examples of interest to gemologists are garnets and olivines. Take, for example, pyrope $Mg_3Al_2Si_3O_{12}$ and almandine $Fe_3Al_2Si_3O_{12}$ in the case of garnets, and forsterite Mg_2SiO_4 and fayalite Fe_2SiO_4, the two basic constituents of olivine. In both instances, the close crystallochemical resemblance between magnesium (Mg) and iron (Fe) causes these atoms—or rather ions—to change places at random, acting like a single chemical element in the crystal structure. In fact, nearly all pyropes can be given the formula $(Mg, Fe)_3Al_2Si_3O_{12}$ and periolots the general formula $(Mg, Fe)_2SiO_4$. These are known as crystallochemical formulae, the comma in parentheses signifying "or" and denoting a substitution, according to the following, straightforward chemical ratio Mg+Fe:Si:0= 2:1:4. More complex cases can involve the simultaneous substitution of several atoms, even by groups of different elements. Examples of this are pyroxenes (including jadeite) or plagioclases (e.g. sunstone and labradorite). With the latter in particular, sodium (Na) is replaced by calcium (Ca) at the same time as silicon (Si) is replaced by aluminum (Al), thus their crystallochemical formula can be written $NaAlSi_3O_8=CaAl_2Si_2O_8$.

Crystal structure

As is well known, X rays are very penetrating radiations which are differentially absorbed by various substances. Radiology, which is mainly practiced on the human body for diagnostic purposes, is based on this principle. Slight individual differences in chemical composition or in thickness within the body show up as different shadows on a photographic plate. The same thing happens with crystal substances which, however, also display another, more complex phenomenon known as *diffraction.*

A crystal struck by an X ray, apart from causing a more or less marked reduction in intensity of the incident ray passing through it, gives off a series of deflected rays, called diffracted rays, the direction and intensity of which depend on the reciprocal arrangement of its constituent atoms. These atoms form a three-dimensional motif which is repeated millions of times in identical fashion throughout the crystal; this motif is known as the *crystal structure.*

The crystal structure of different substances is established by highly specialized scientists called crystallographers, who make complex calculations after examining the diffracted rays. Such calculations are of little concern to the general public, or even the majority of students, who are interested, at most, in the effects such structures have on the properties of substances.

X-ray diffraction, however, is very commonly used for recognition of various crystal substances, because the pattern of diffracted rays is specific to each substance, virtually like a "fingerprint." Although by far the most common means of identification in mineralogy, it is hardly ever used in gemol-

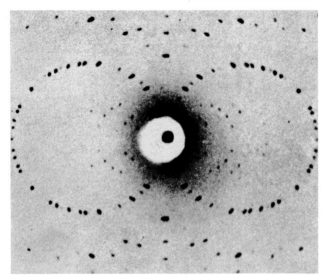

ogy, for two reasons. The first is that the easiest and best technique requires dust specimens of the substance in question, obtainable by grinding, which is clearly inappropriate for precious stones. The second problem with X-ray diffraction techniques is that X ray interaction with substances within the specimen can cause fluorescence, which may permanently alter its color, On the other hand, such variations in color are sometimes deliberately produced in laboratories, to simulate the more valuable varieties of natural stones.

Genesis

The processes whereby minerals are formed are related to the origins of rocks in general, which are in fact associations of minerals. For the sake of convenience, rocks are divided into three groups corresponding to the way in which they were formed, magmatic (or igneous), metamorphic, and sedimentary, although the different categories inevitably overlap.

The *magmatic* or *igneous process* depends on the existence of original magma, a molten silicate mass containing many volatile compounds in solution (water, hydrochloric acid, hydrofluoric acid, carbon dioxide, etc.). This molten mass, which is presumed to exist in certain areas within the earth's crust, can rise to the surface through volcanic pipes to form lava, releasing its volatile components into the atmosphere. But in the absence of a passage to the outside, the magmatic mass cools very slowly, leading to the formation of crystalline rocks (at temperatures in the order of 800°–1000° C) similar in composition to lava, but with the constituent minerals present as larger crystals. The volatile components, unable to escape into the atmosphere, tend to accumulate, increasing in quantity due to crystallization. This growth causes a powerful increase in pressure, resulting in the formation of a fluid with particular characteristics; it is mobile like gas but dense like water, and can infiltrate the surrounding rocks, often making chemical exchanges with them. As the pegmatitic fluid cools, crystals of large, sometimes gigantic proportions, are deposited. With progressive cooling, this phase passes into hot water or hydrothermal phases containing many chemical constituents in solution, which will be deposited during the cooling process, sometimes forming fine crystals. To make a simple analogy, the magma can be compared to soda pop in a bottle. If the cork is removed (the volcanic pipe opened up), there will be a rapid discharge of gas, both as such and combined with the liquid as foam. If, on the other hand, the bottle is placed, unopened, in a freezer (slow cooling of the magma inside the earth's crust), the water will turn to ice, unable to dissolve the gas, which will collect near the cork with a buildup in pressure.

The *metamorphic process* is related to an increase in temperature (from 300° to 600° C), often combined with an increase in pressure, to which existing rocks that are formed at different (greater or lesser) temperatures may be subjected. This increase in temperature can be due to proximity of a magmatic mass of very high temperature but also—and this is more usually the case—to the rock's sinking in the earth's crust, obviously leading to an increase in pressure. These changing environmental conditions, sometimes combined with circulation of fluids of particular chemical compositions, produce a rearrangement of the mineralogical groups, and the formation of new minerals, characteristic of these new conditions. An everyday comparison to illustrate the process is a flour and water dough which, baked in the oven, turns to bread.

The third process is the *sedimentary process*, the easiest to understand because it takes place under our very eyes. Existing rocks are not stable in our environment, which is characterized by low temperatures (from −50° C to +50° C), low pressures, and a plentiful supply of water and oxygen. The rocks physically disintegrate into boulders, pebbles, and sand and undergo chemical changes as well, some components dissolving in water, other, more resistant minerals remaining unaltered. The parts in solution can be deposited at various stages of their journey (by streams, rivers, the sea). Thus, the

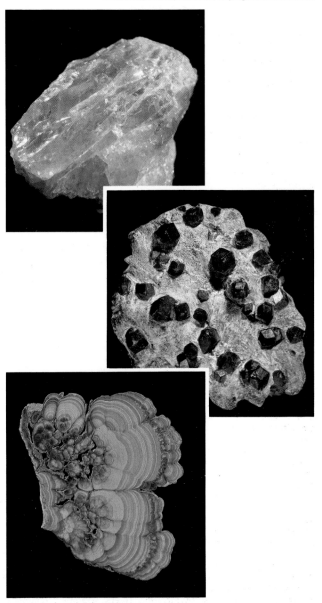

Examples of minerals formed in different environments: top, beryl (magmatic environment); center, almandine garnet (metamorphic environment); bottom, malachite (supergene environment).

crumbling of a loosely compacted stone into sand, the deposition of travertine by a calcareous spring, and the crystallization of rock salt in a pool on the seashore are all part of the sedimentary process.

Any of these processes, which together roughly account for all the rocks of the earth's crust, can lead to the formation of precious stones, many of which are attributable to more than one such process. For example, because of their hardness and chemical resistance, precious stones are nearly always found in sedimentary deposits. These are known as *secondary deposits* because they are derived, through the physical disintegration and chemical alteration of the country rock, from *primary deposits* where they were first formed by crystallization from magma, pegmatitic fluid or aqueous solutions, or by metamorphic recrystallization.

It is well worth knowing the origins of stones not just out of scientific interest, but for practical reasons as well, because any attempt at synthesis of gemstones should obviously aim to reproduce in the laboratory the conditions which led to their formation in nature. Clearly, however, such conditions can only be approximated, partly because natural processes are always much more complex than artificial ones, and mainly because of the vast time-scale at Nature's disposal.

On the other hand, as we shall see in due course, man, apart

40

from attempting the synthetic reproduction of precious stones, can go Nature one better by producing in the laboratory precious artificial stones not found naturally because they are made up of chemical components that are rarely available in sufficient quantities or are outnumbered by other elements.

Units of measurement

The common unit of measurement for precious stones is weight, expressed in carats and decimal parts thereof. A *carat* is equal to 0.200 g, a standard value fixed at the end of the nineteenth century to unify the traditional values of individual markets (in Italy, for example, they varied from 0.188 g in Bologna to 0.216 g in Livorno). Similarly, subdivision of the carat into a hundred *points* has replaced the old binary system according to which a *grain* was worth a quarter of a carat.

The reference to a grain of wheat seems clear enough, but the derivation of the word *carat* is less certain. It probably came from the carob seed (*qirat* in Arabic) which, being quite constant in weight, once served as a counterweight on the market for precious stones.

Some confusion is created by the system of subdivision into carats that is applied to gold-working. This referred to the ownership of a merchant vessel, which was traditionally divided into twenty-four shares. Thus pure gold is 24 carat, or 24k, the gold commonly used in jewelry is 18 carat, or an alloy which is $^{18}/_{24}$ or 75 percent gold, and so on.

Diameter measurements expressed in millimeters and fractions thereof are sometimes used instead of carat weights for synthetic stones of modest value and for necklace beads.

Methods of analysis

Probably the first question one tends to ask sbout a gem, as of a mineral, is "What is it?" Some look quite similar, so much so that before their chemical composition was known (i.e. before the eighteenth century) they were easily confused and given the same names. The answer to the question "What is it?" is primarily mineralogical, if, for example, a ruby needs to be distinguished from a garnet or spinel of similar color but, among other things, of different value, or a green tourmaline from an emerald; but it is also gemological and commercial, whenever a natural ruby or sapphire has to be distinguished from its synthetic counterparts or from doublets which, as we shall see, are particular types of imitation.

Chemical methods are not normally employed to answer this question, as they involve the destruction of at least part of the object, and of the physical methods, only those forms are used that do not cause appreciable changes or, at any rate, damage to the gems in question.

Establishment of the density

One of the basic physical properties used for identification of precious stones, and one of the easiest to establish, is density. As mentioned earlier, two main methods are employed to determine this: heavy liquids (the two variations of which we shall examine) and the hydrostatic balance. The first method in its simplest version, most often used with gems, calls for a limited number of glass bottles containing liquids of known densities, which form a scale. As each bottle normally contains a mixture of two chemicals, one of which may be volatile, a fragment of a mineral of known density, appropriate to that of the liquid, is kept in each bottle by way of control. If the liquid has the proper proportion of each of its constituents, the mineral should remain in indifferent equilibrium. A suitable series of liquids that can be bought already prepared is shown in the table opposite, along with the respective indicators (Fig. 11). It should be noted that these chemicals can be extremely dangerous. Anyone using them should take appropriate precautions, including the use of a chemical hood and gloves.

If a gem under examination is put, for example, into bottle No. 2, one will note: $d>2.71$ g/cm^3 if it sinks; $d<2.71$ g/cm^3 if it floats: $d \cong 2.71$ g/cm^3 if it remains in indifferent equilibrium or sinks or rises very slowly. In the first or second cases, the operation will be repeated with a liquid of greater or lesser density, depending on the initial result. Let us suppose, for example, that $d>2.71$ g/cm^3. One tries bottle No. 3, which gives the result $d<3.06$ g/cm^3; therefore, $2.71<d<3.06$. In most cases, this combined with other observations will be sufficient to identify the gem.

Where a more precise figure is required, two pairs of liquids are used: methylene iodide diluted with toluene, and Clerici's solution diluted with water. Each pair of liquids can be mixed in

Below: A series of heavy liquids with their respective densities and the mineral indicators used with each.
Bottom: A series of bottles containing heavy liquids for rapid establishment of the density of gems. The density in g/cm³ is shown on each bottle.

Liquid	Density	Indicator
bromoform, diluted with bromonaphthalene up to	2.65	quartz
bromoform, diluted with bromonaphthalene up to	2.71	calcite
methylene iodide diluted with bromonaphthalene up to	3.06	green tourmaline
Clerici's solution diluted with distilled water up to	3.52	diamond
Clerici's solution, diluted with distilled water up to	4.00	synthetic ruby

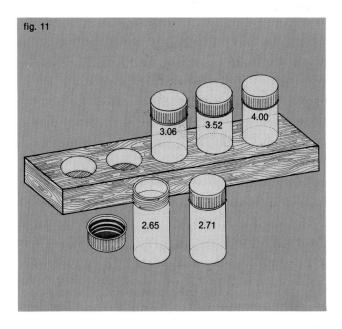

fig. 11

Graph giving the refractive index and density of methylene iodide diluted with toluene.

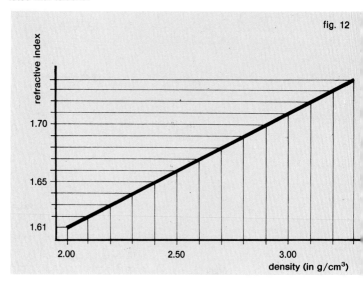

fig. 12

variable proportions until it equals the density of the object under examination. The first pair cover a range of 2.00 to 3.30 g/cm³ and the second pair a range of 3.00 to 4.02 g/cm³. Each of these mixtures shows a linear relationship between density and refractive index, as can be seen from the graphs in Figures 12 and 13. Therefore, if the refractive index of a drop of liquid from a mixture prepared to equal the density of a given gem is measured with an ordinary jeweler's refractometer, one can determine the density of the liquid and consequently of the gem remaining in indifferent equilibrium in it. Failing a refractometer, a pycnometer or balance can be used to determine the density of the liquid, as noted previously.

The heavy liquid method (especially the first version) is quite straightforward and works very well even with stones of very small volume, but the abovementioned liquids, i.e. the ones that are easiest to use, cannot determine densities in excess of about 4.10 g/cm³. The hydrostatic balance method can be used whenever a reasonably precise balance is available, as is generally the case where gems are dealt with. To transform the balance into a hydrostatic balance, all that need be done is to place a "bridge" with a transparent container of distilled water on top of it over one of the pans. A small wire basket to contain the gem is suspended from the arm of the balance by a thin

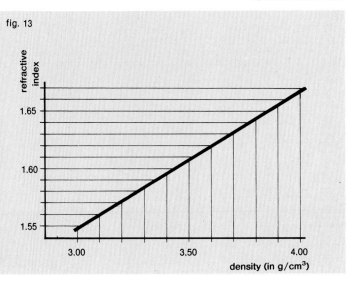

fig. 13

piece of wire, in such a way that it is fully immersed in the water (Fig. 14).

The specific gravity of a stone, which is also its density, equals the weight of the stone divided by the weight of an equal volume of distilled water. To obtain this figure, the following procedure is followed: the stone under examination is weighted in air (W_1), and then, using the apparatus described above, it is weighed immersed in distilled water (W_2); the difference between the two weights ($W_1 - W_2$) represents the loss of weight due to Archimedes' principle and this, assuming that distilled water always has a density equal to that of 1 g/cm^3 (which is not strictly correct, but is near enough for our purposes), corresponds numerically to the volume of the stone. Thus, using the formula sp. gr. $= \dfrac{W_1}{W_1 - W_2}$ one can calculate the specific gravity of the stone.

The chief complication is due to the fact that the weight of the stone in immersion must, in turn, be calculated as the difference between two weights: that is, one must read how much the balance registers with the equipment for specific gravity measurement and the basket immersed in water, then how much it registers with the stone in the basket. The difference is the weight of the stone in immersion.

With the hydrostatic balance, one can determine the specific

Balance adapted for operation as a hydrostatic balance using the accessories illustrated below: "bridge"; flask; basket.

fig. 14

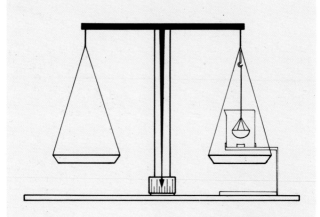

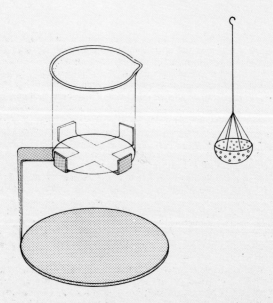

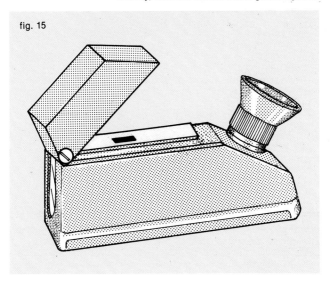

Gemological refractometer. With this instrument, one can establish certain optical characteristics (refractive index, single and double refractivity) which are valuable aids to gem recognition.

fig. 15

gravity of a gem even when it is more than 4, provided the gem is not of too limited weight or rather, too small volume. In the case of artificial diamond simulants, for example, which have a specific gravity of between 5 and 7, or thereabouts, it is difficult to obtain acceptable results with stones of less than 0.5–1 carat, depending on the precision of the balance. The necessary lack of absolute precision is not usually a serious problem with gemstones, as one is concerned with no more than a hundred different minerals at the outside, of which only about twenty are very common.

Establishment of the optical properties

Certain optical properties are a valuable aid to identification and are readily established by means of a gemological instrument called a refractometer (Fig. 15), which is a simplified version of the total refraction meters used in mineralogy. With this instrument, if a yellow filter is placed over the eyepiece or a sodium light employed, the refractive index (or indices in the case of a doubly refractive mineral) can be read straight off, as can the value for birefringence of which the optic sign can also be established. In this way, for example, in the case of a red stone with a specific gravity of 4.0, one can readily distinguish between a negative, uniaxial, birefringent ruby corundum with indices of about 1.761–1.770 and birefringence of 0.009, and a garnet of the pyrope-almandine series, which has only one index, of between 1.775 and 1.790 when the specific gravity is 4.0, proving that it is singly refractive, with an index just enough higher to make a distinction possible (see final synoptic tables).

It is important when using a refractometer for the specimen to have a flat, polished surface. This is always possible in the case of gems. The reading is taken by placing the refractometer in front of any type of strong lamp, with a yellow filter fitted over the eyepiece, or in front of a sodium discharge lamp in the absence of a filter. A drop of special contact liquid is put on the prism of the refractometer, one facet of the gem under examination being placed on top of this. The calibrated scale is visible through the eyepiece (Fig. 16). The point at which the dividing line between the areas of light and shade falls on the graduated scale indicates the refractive index, or, where two lines are visible, indices. The stone is turned on the refractometer glass, and the values of the two indices are read when the greatest distance between the lines is achieved. This maximum distance is the value of the stone's birefringence.

In the case of a uniaxial, birefringent gem, one of the two shadows (that of the ordinary ray) will remain stationary during rotation, while the other will move away from it and then return. The crystal is optically negative if the index of the extraordinary ray is lower than that of the ordinary ray and optically positive if the opposite is the case. In biaxial, birefringent gems, both shadow edges, marking the two indices, are seen to move, and the reading is given by the top figure legible for the higher one and the bottom figure legible for the lower one. The maximum birefringence is indicated by the difference between the two indices thus established. One need not usually be concerned with the optic sign (positive or negative), or with uniaxial, birefringent stones.

In the case of singly refractive stones, everything is much simpler, as only one shadow edge is visible (Fig. 16a); this edge remains stationary when the gem is rotated.

With the refractometer, one can measure refractive indices of between 1.40 and 1.80. All told, this excludes diamond, zircon, some garnets, rutile, some synthetic diamond simulants, and a few rarities, for which other methods have to be used. But the inability of the refractometer to measure the refractive index of a given gem is in itself a clue to identification, corresponding to $n > c.1.80$, which greatly reduces the area of uncertainty.

There are various other ways of determining the approximate refractive index of a gem and whether or not it is birefringent, but only the simplest ones are listed here. These are based on elementary observations not calling for any special equipment.

Obvious pleochroism is always a sign of birefringence. But the opposite is not the case: absence of clear pleochroism does

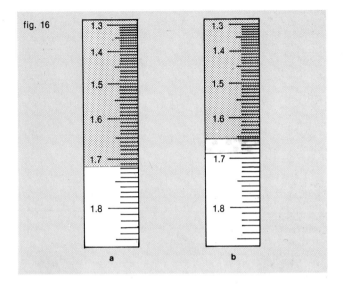

a. Refractometer reading of the refractive index of a singly refractive stone: 1.715.
b. Refractometer reading of the refractive indices of a doubly refractive stone: 1.655, 1.690.

fig. 16

not mean that a stone is singly refractive. Pleochroism is particularly evident in some sapphires and rubies, in tanzanite, cordierite, intensely colored tourmalines, andalusite, and aquamarine; it is very useful for rapid identification of these gems. Marked birefringence can be established by looking through a stone from a flat facet with a 10x lens. The birefringence will be manifested by a double image of the opposite facet edges. This phenomenon is easily detectable in zircons, peridot, and synthetic rutile; a bit less so in tourmaline, kunzite, hiddenite, and diopside. It can also be visible in quartz, corundum, and topaz, but only in fairly large stones. This is a very simple method, for example, of distinguishing a singly refractive diamond from a strongly birefringent colorless zircon, or synthetic rutile, without further investigation. It also makes it possible to distinguish zircons of various colors from other stones, except peridot.

One means of judging the approximate refractive index of a gem is to observe it in transmitted light, immersed in a highly refracting liquid in a transparent container. If the refractive index of the stone is equal to that of the liquid, it will be barely, if at all, distinguishable from the surrounding liquid. If the index of the stone is higher than that of the liquid, it will be clearly visible, standing out the more clearly, with dark edges, the stronger the difference in index. This method can be useful if there is no flat facet to permit reading of the index by means of

Table giving a complete series of liquids with their respective refractive indices, used to establish the refractive index of gems where this cannot be done with a refractometer.

Liquid	Refractive index
toluene	1.50
ethylene dibromide	1.54
bromoform	1.59
monoiodobenzene	1.62
monobromonaphthalene	1.66
monoiodonaphthalene	1.705
methylene iodide	1.74

a refractometer. A complete series of liquids for determination by this method is listed in the table below. But often just two or three liquids with different indices are enough.
If necessary, the refractometer can be used to determine the index of the liquid or liquids used.

Spectroscopy
The light transmitted or reflected by a body can be "analyzed" with an instrument consisting basically of a glass prism, by observing which rays are transmitted and which absorbed. The result is what is known as the *absorption spectrum* of an object, in our case a gem, and this can to some extent be quantified by superimposing a graduated scale from 400 to 800 nanometers on the path of the light rays.
In idiochromatic minerals, the color of a gem (and its spectrum, with possible areas of absorption at different wavelengths) depends on the basic composition of the mineral. In allochromatic minerals, it depends on the presence of very small quantities of other, color-producing elements in certain clearly defined structural positions, or simple structural anomalies. In either case, the various minerals generally have characteristic absorption spectra.
Spectroscopy is used less often than measurement of the spe-

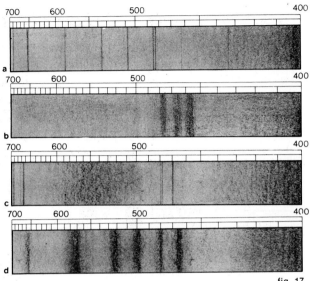

Absorption spectra of two green stones (a. green zircon; b. green sapphire) and two red ones (c. ruby; d. almandine garnet).

fig. 17

cific gravity and refractive indices to identify gems, perhaps because it is less intuitive. But it is extremely useful in the case of rough stones without any flat facets suitable for the refractometer, gems with a refractive index in excess of 1.80, those devoid of significant inclusions, and instances where spectroscopic differences can clearly distinguish between a natural gem and its synthetic counterpart. Furthermore, it is normally a very rapid means of identification.

An optical spectroscope, however, only reveals lines or bands of absorption in areas where there is a significant jump in absorption of the respective wavelengths. Areas of weak absorption, with very hazy edges, affect the color of the gem, but are only detectable by apparatus that is more sensitive than the human eye and is equipped with amplification systems. Therefore the eye is not capable of detecting the absorption spectrum of all gems, but only those in which it is most pronounced. Conversely, some gems have a clearly delineated spectrum, despite being colorless, because of the complementarity between different zones of absorption.

Two of the most typical spectra are shown in Figs. 17a and 17b; they are those of zircon and green sapphire, respectively. The stones can look very similar externally but have clearly different absorption spectra. Figs. 17c and 17d give the spectra for ruby and almandine garnet, which are also of similar color.

Examples of inclusions visible under a binocular microscope:
1. color zoning angled at 120° (Cambodian sapphire, 10x);
2. healed crack known as a "feather" (Sri Lankan sapphire, 20x);
3. characteristic curved striae emphasized by numerous gas bubbles in a Verneuil synthetic sapphire (15x); 4. healed cracks known as insects' wings and transparent euhedral crystal in a pink sapphire from Sri Lanka (10x);

1   2

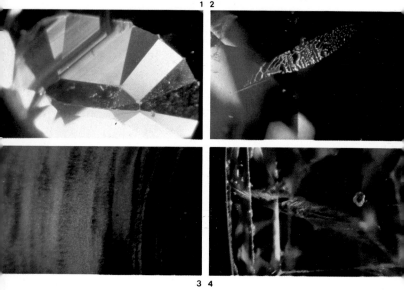

3   4

Here, too, rapid inspection can immediately distinguish them, given the marked difference in their absorption spectra.

Observation under a binocular microscope

A lot of information useful for gemstone recognition can be obtained by meticulous observation under a stereoscopic microscope of low magnification (from 10x to 40x).

The illumination of the object observed is very important. The possible methods of illumination are:

- Transmitted light, with a light source beneath the stage of the microscope, preferably capable of producing polarized light;
- "dark field" illumination, in which the light reaches the object laterally, from all sides, in such a way that the only light entering the microscope is that sent back to it by the inclusions contained in the object, which stand out like dust lit up in a dark room by a ray of sunlight;
- reflected light coming laterally from above, for instance, by placing the stone in a container of highly refracting liquid, normally monobromonaphthalene ($n = 1.658$). Immersion cancels out the reflections produced by the upper facets, which would make the internal details hard to see.

Observations carried out in this manner can reveal certain important aspects of the specimen:

5. rutile needles oriented 120° apart in a Sri Lankan ruby; together, they produce the silk effect (25x); 6. characteristic elongated cavities due to lamellar twinning (Thai ruby, 15x); 7. well formed pyrite crystal in a Colombian emerald from Chivor (20x); 8. bundles of acicular (needlelike) crystals of tremolite in an African emerald (15x).

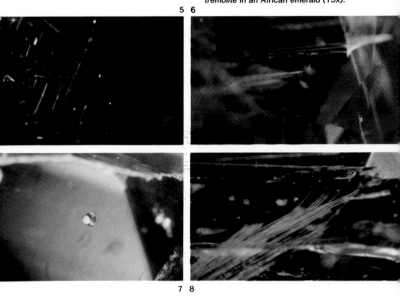

- *Crystallography*——Crystallographic striae which are faint or emphasized by bands of color or areas of inclusions can give an idea of the crystal system to which the stone belongs. Sometimes, multiple twin structures are also visible, and these are particularly evident in polarized light. They are frequent in rubies, but also in some sapphires.
- *Crystallographic optics*——One can detect birefringence or areas of anomalous birefringence in a singly refractive crystal, or pleochroism, which is also a sign of birefringence. If stones are observed in immersion, one can also obtain approximate information on the refractive index, by comparison with that of the liquid.
- *Inclusions*——Many gems are at least five to six millimeters in size, and often ten or fifteen millimeters or more. Hence they are quite well developed crystals which took a very long time to grow. During this time, other crystals were forming in the same environment, but the ones that began crystallizing first and/or grew less will sometimes have been incorporated in the larger ones. Residues of the liquids and gases that constituted the fluid from which the crystals were formed may also have been trapped inside them. These partially crystalline, liquid residues sometimes penetrated a crack in the ready-formed crystal at a later stage, helping to "heal" it to some extent, as long as the necessary material

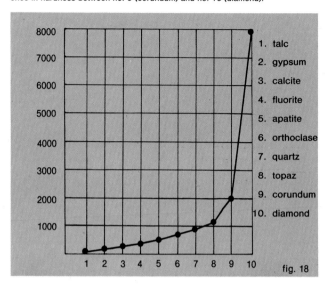

The graph gives the hardness, in Knoop hardness numbers, of the ten minerals on Mohs' scale. The Knoop numbers indicate the depth to which a special point can scratch the minerals. Note that the interval between them is not constant and there is a very great difference in hardness between no. 9 (corundum) and no. 10 (diamond).

1. talc
2. gypsum
3. calcite
4. fluorite
5. apatite
6. orthoclase
7. quartz
8. topaz
9. corundum
10. diamond

fig. 18

to "rebuild" the broken crystal was present in solution. There can also be inclusions which have separated out from the engulfing mineral during cooling, such as the needlelike crystals of rutile found in many corundums, which separated out from the corundum as the temperature fell.

From the overall picture of inclusions, corresponding to a precise chemical and physical environment of formation, one can often recognize not only the crystal species of a gem containing them, but also, the locality in which it was deposited. Thus the type of inclusions found in a Burmese ruby are generally sufficient to identify it as ruby and distinguish it from, say, a ruby with the inclusions typical of rubies found in Thailand. Both of these, moreover, are usually readily distinguishable, under a microscope, from a red garnet and normally from red tourmaline and red spinel as well. The same applies to emerald: observation of the inclusions usually makes it possible not only to identify the stone as emerald, but also to distinguish a Colombian gem from a Zimbabwean specimen.

Synthetic products with the same chemical and physical characteristics as those of their natural counterparts can pose problems. But the inclusions and structures visible inside synthetic products are related to a much faster pattern of growth, which is often quite different from the natural one. Thus, observation of inclusions and possible noncrystallographic growth lines is the principal means of distinguishing them.

Finally, some natural stones are treated in a variety of ways to heighten their desirable characteristics. These procedures will be discussed in more detail in the descriptions of individual stones. Many of these treatments are clearly fraudulent, but some have been accepted as legitimate. The standard accepted by the jewelry trade is that any treatment that cannot be detected under magnification or through testing and that is irreversible is acceptable. Treatments that can be identified or that will deteriorate over time must be revealed whenever the gem is sold.

Having covered the basic methods used to distinguish precious stones from one another we describe below some minor tests which can sometimes help with identification where the principal procedures are inconclusive or cannot be applied. These are basically hardness tests and observation of fluorescence under ultraviolet light.

Hardness tests

We have already seen briefly what is meant by hardness in mineralogical terms and how it is expressed in terms of the Mohs' scale, consisting of ten sample minerals arranged in increasing order of hardness so that each can scratch the preceding one and be scratched by the following one. Hardness tests on cut stones are avoided, whenever possible, in order not to compromise the luster and integrity of the facet edges; however, such problems do not arise when one is dealing with rough stones.

In any case, the results cannot be expected to be very significant (except for diamond), because the majority of precious stones have a hardness of between 7 and 9 on Mohs' scale. Furthermore, if the tests are carefully performed, in order to leave as little trace as possible, they are hard to interpret. For this reason, they are nearly always done under a binocular microscope, using a series of points consisting of very small fragments of minerals from Mohs' scale, which are inserted into the tip of a metal rod roughly the size and shape of a ballpoint pen.

Starting with a point presumed to be less hard than the object, an attempt is made to scratch the outer edge of one facet, generally near to the girdle (the band at the widest part of the stone) or even on the girdle, if it is not too rough. If the gem cannot be scratched, for example, by a point with a hardness of 7, the conclusion is that H>7. This can be sufficient information if all one needs to know is whether it is a gem with a hardness of 8, or another one like it, with a hardness of 6. If this is not sufficient, a point with a hardness of 8 can be tested and according to the result one will note H>8 or 7<H<8.

In the case of an object that could be diamond, or an imitation

thereof, one is normally less scrupulous, using a point with a hardness of 9. If the specimen is diamond, the very great difference in hardness between it and 9 (clearly visible from the graph in Fig. 18) will cause the point to be visibly abraded. If it is not diamond, there is no need to worry unduly about causing damage, as all imitations or substitutes for diamond are of low value. In the specific case of diamond, therefore, a hardness test can be useful, because the results will be very distinctive. Clearly, there is no sense in carrying out hardness tests with a number 10 point, which can cause unwarranted, serious damage to any substance, including diamond.

Examination of fluorescence under ultraviolet light
One last, simple test used for gem recognition, particularly when other methods are hard to apply, consists of observing their fluorescence (and possible phosphorescence) by exposing them to ultraviolet light. Fluorescence basically means the reemission of radiations of greater wavelength by an object struck by any type of radiation. In this particular case, we mean the reemission of light waves by a stone subjected to ultraviolet rays. Reemission of light waves after the incident radiation has ceased is known as phosphorescence.

Many different types of lamp can be used, but the commonest is one that was invented for mineral prospecting. It has two

Willemite in natural light (opposite); in ultraviolet light (below) it turns blue, due to fluorescence.
Examination of fluorescence can sometimes help identify gems.

Willemite in natural light (opposite); in ultraviolet light (below) it turns blue, due to fluorescence.
Examination of fluorescence can sometimes help identify gems.

tubes, with filters to provide radiations with wavelengths of 254 nanometers (SW or short wave) and 365 nanometers (LW or long wave), which can be operated separately by a switch.

Various stones react by displaying quite striking fluorescence, which in some cases can identify them, mainly by a process of elimination. For example, strong red fluorescence on LW and greenish blue fluorescence on SW are seen in light blue synthetic spinels used to imitate aquamarine, which is not fluorescent; ruby and red spinel, which display red fluorescence, can be distinguished from garnet and red tourmaline, which never do (but this test will not distinguish ruby from spinel). The apricot yellow fluorescence of the pale yellow sapphires from Sri Lanka immediately distinguishes them from the corresponding synthetic product and from citrine quartz. Synthetic blue sapphires have a soft, opaque greenish blue fluorescence (on SW only), which normally distinguishes them from the natural varieties. Kunzite sometimes has pink fluorescence, which readily distinguishes it from morganite and synthetic pink corundum. Finally, opals have characteristic fluorescence and phosphorescence, different from their synthetic counterparts. Such data, however, are qualitative and always require interpretation by the operator, who must avoid hasty conclusions.

Apart from these, which are the most usual tests, various other means of investigation are occasionally used for gemstone recognition. Of these, the reflectometer (an instrument for determining the reflective power of a flat, polished facet) and the thermal conductivity tester are two instruments employed almost exclusively in gemology; but their use is very limited and confined to the distinction of diamond from its imitations.

Cutting of gemstones

Cutting is the operation whereby a rough stone is made to assume a certain shape, which brings out its luster and color and enables it to be set in an item of jewelry.

In the old days, most precious stones were used with the natural facets of their crystal structure or were summarily rounded and polished into a convex shape known as a *cabochon*, from *caboche*, an old Norman French word for head (Fig. 19). This type of cut is now only used for stones of limited transparency, either by nature (e.g. turquoise, jadeite, malachite), or as a result of too many inclusions (e.g. some relatively opaque sapphires, rubies, and emeralds). Or else, it is used for gems in which curved surfaces bring out certain special characteristics (e.g. opal, star sapphires and rubies, adularia, and "chatoyant" stones).

Over the last 300 years, however, the faceted type of cut has become increasingly well established. This best displays the beauty of transparent stones because of the fact that light is reflected both by the upper facets and, through the stone, by the lower ones. The faceted cut has been most important in highlighting the qualities of diamond, which for a long time was less appreciated than other gems and only used when found as natural, octahedral crystals. Faceting could display diamond's extraordinary ability to reflect light, even breaking it up into the colors of the rainbow, because of its high power of dispersion.

The earliest record of cut diamonds dates from the mid-fourteenth century. Initially, cutting probably only served to enable rough diamonds of an unattractive, irregular shape to be used as gems, and involved the creation of one or more series of facets arranged in a radiating pattern around the gem, the base of which was left uncut or reasonably flat. Some famous Indian diamonds were also cut into these radiating shapes, known as rose or rosette cuts, only used nowadays for small stones (Fig. 20).

Subsequently, around the middle of the fifteenth century, the shape of octahedral diamonds also began to be modified, creating a flat, upper facet instead of a point and smoothing a few corners into other, flat facets, in an effort to make the stones more brilliant (Figs. 21, 22, 23).

When it was realized that the angles of the octahedron were not ideal for producing light reflection and refraction, the cut was modified in such a way that only the general outline of the

Below: Profile drawings of a flat convex cabochon (left) and a biconvex one (right); photo of two emeralds cut en cabochon.
Bottom: Two examples of highly elaborated rose or rosette cuts, little used nowadays: a. Dutch rose; b. cross rose.

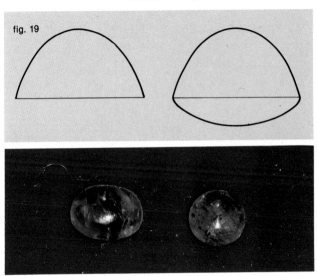

fig. 19

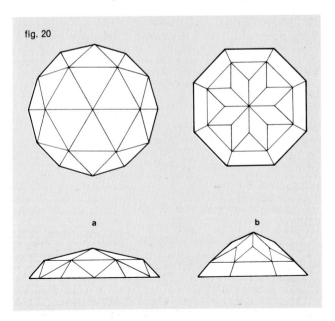

fig. 20

a

b

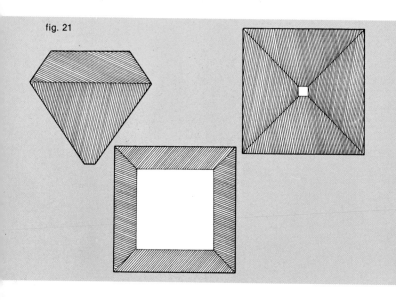

fig. 21

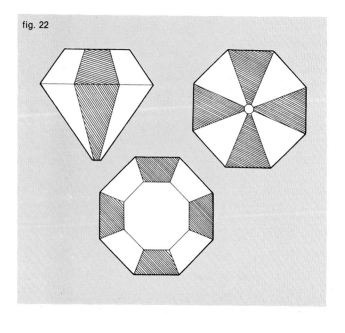

fig. 22

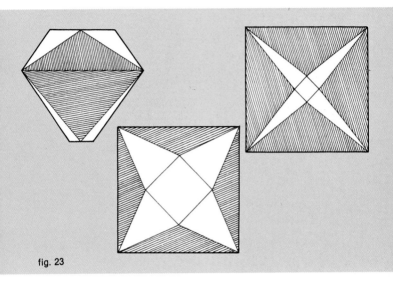

fig. 23

original octahedron was left. By the early eighteenth century, diamonds were already being given what is known as an old-mine cut with facets corresponding to those of the modern brilliant cut (Fig. 24), with a more or less octagonal table facet on top, 4 main facets and 4 corner facets, plus 8 star facets and 8 pairs of cross facets, connecting the table to what is known as the girdle to form the crown. The girdle was almost square (Fig. 24), or almost rectangular (Fig. 25) in shape, with convex sides and rounded corners (cushion-shaped, not circular, as it is today). The lower portion, called the pavilion, terminated by a small facet parallel to the first, had 4 main facets plus 4 corner facets and 8 pairs of cross facets opposite the crown facets.

Only later was the practice established of turning stones on a lathe, using another diamond, to give them circular symmetry before faceting. In this way, the corner facets became similar in appearance to the main ones. Finally, at the beginning of the twentieth century, the brilliant cut was given its present shape and proportions, the facets being of the number and arrangement already described, but angled in such a way as to obtain the maximum degree of light reflection and dispersion (Fig. 26). Nowadays, most diamonds are in fact given a brilliant cut. Although the proportions of the cut stones are usually not ideal, they depart very little from the norm. The (round) brilliant

Old-mine cut: The almost square outline with rounded corners is known as "cushion" shape. The crown, girdle, and pavilion are clearly visible, as are the characteristic facets of the modern brilliant cut: 1. table facet and culet (1+1); 2. main facets (4+4); 3. corner facets (4+4); 4. cross facets (16+16); 5. star facets (8).

fig. 24

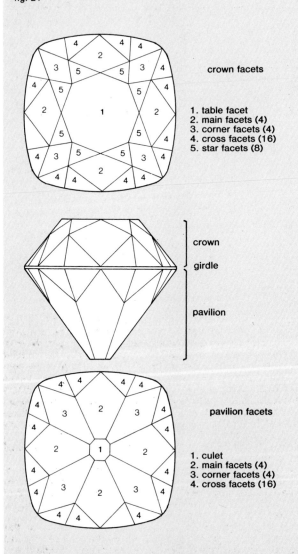

crown facets

1. table facet
2. main facets (4)
3. corner facets (4)
4. cross facets (16)
5. star facets (8)

crown

girdle

pavilion

pavilion facets

1. culet
2. main facets (4)
3. corner facets (4)
4. cross facets (16)

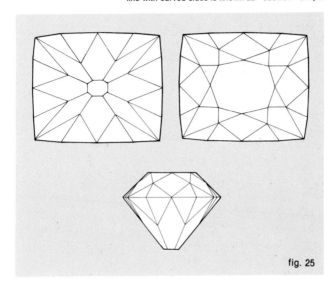

fig. 25

cut is the most common, but diamonds are also cut into oval,
pear or marquise shapes, in which the number and shape of
the facets is the same as those used for the brilliant cut (Fig.
28). Alternatively, some diamonds are cut into rectangular
shape with truncated corners, and a crown and pavilion consisting of successive series of trapezoidal facets. This is
known as the step, trap, or "emerald" cut (Fig. 29). It gives a
less lustrous effect, with lower dispersion, but reduces weight
loss when the uncut crystal is in the shape of an elongated octahedron. The problem of weight loss during cutting is very important, given the rarity and value of diamond: as a rule, a
brilliant-cut stone weighs only 40 percent or so of the original
rough stone.

When the faceted cut is used for stones other than diamond,
the rules followed are less precise. The main aim is normally to
reduce loss of weight as much as possible, and in colored
stones with distinct pleochroism to have the most attractive
color visible from the table facet.

In most faceted stones (as in Fig. 24), one can distinguish the
main, table facet, which is generally larger than the others, and
forms the topmost part of the stone; the crown, consisting of
numerous facets linking the table to the girdle; the girdle,
which is the band at the widest part of the stone, onto which a

63

Modern brilliant cut: the proportions and angles are designed to give the best luster and dispersion.

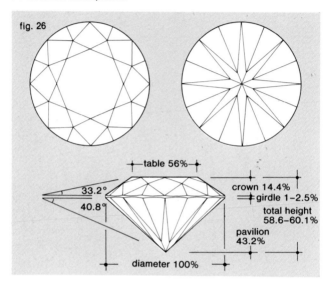

fig. 26

table 56%

33.2°

40.8°

crown 14.4%
girdle 1–2.5%
total height
58.6–60.1%
pavilion
43.2%

diameter 100%

setting can be fitted; and the pavilion, which is the lower, convex portion, of roughly conical shape, sometimes terminated by a bottom facet (the "cutlet") parallel to the main one, but generally much smaller. Depending on the type and arrangement of the facets, the most common cuts are as follows:

- brilliant, when the shape and number of facets are as prescribed;
- step or trap, if both the crown and pavilion consist of successive series of trapezoidal facets (the "steps");
- mixed, if they have a more or less brilliant-cut crown and step-cut pavilion.

Depending on their general outline, they may be round, oval, marquise, pear-shaped, rectangular, emerald (rectangular with truncated corners), cushion (vaguely rectangular, but with curved sides), triangular, and even star-shaped. The most common shapes are shown on pages 69–72 (Figs. 28–31).

The methods used for cutting stones have not changed essentially over the centuries, although the details have been greatly improved. The normally quite small stones are fixed to the tip of a mushroom-shaped support called a *dop* stick, by means of a very strong cement or low melting point solder. Nowadays, dops are also made with a special clamp that grips the stone

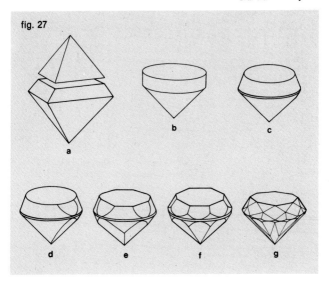

fig. 27

a b c

d e f g

firmly, but allows just enough play for cutting operations. For the cabochon cut, grinding machines not very different from the types used for sharpening knives are employed, firstly with a coarser grain to remove any rough surfaces and give the future gem its shape, then with a finer one to polish the surfaces. The final polishing is usually done on a felt, leather, or fabric-covered revolving horizontal lap, onto which very fine, abrasive powder has been sprinkled.

The cutting of faceted stones is more complex and is carried out in several stages. A revolving horizontal metal lap dressed with a paste of very fine abrasive powder plus oil or water, is used for grinding.

For diamonds, if the rough stone is fairly irregular in shape, advantage is taken of its easy cleavage to reduce it to the typical octahedral form or, at any rate, obtain more easily workable pieces. If the rough stone is already octahedral, part of one pyramid is removed (Fig. 27a), using a sawing disc charged with diamond powder in oil, or by working it against another diamond, in the position where the table facet will be produced (Fig. 27b). It is then rotated on a lathe, bringing it into contact with another diamond, to give it a conical-cylindrical shape (Fig. 27b, c). These two stages are collectively known as "bruting."

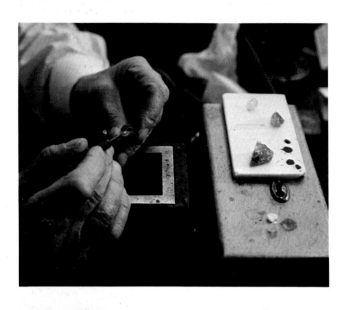

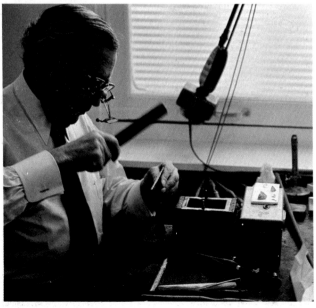

These two pages show some stages of cutting. Opposite: Marking the cleavage planes of a diamond with India ink (top); cleaving the diamond (bottom). This page: Dop sticks with the stones soldered to them; cutting the crown; polishing the table.

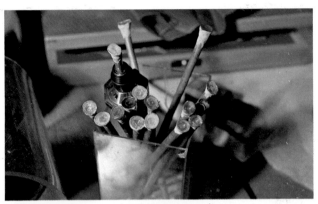

The facets are then cut on a cast iron lap dressed with a mixture of diamond dust and oil (because of its exceptional hardness, diamond is only appreciably abraded by another diamond), starting with the 4 main top facets for the crown and the 4 main back facets for the pavilion (Fig. 27d, e). The exact position of the first 4+4 main facets is very important, and this stage is carried out by highly skilled personnel. The subsequent facets (Fig. 27f, g) are less difficult to produce. This stage constitutes the cutting proper. The cutting and polishing of the facets can be done in a single operation, or in two stages. In the latter case, a slightly coarser diamond powder is used to begin with, to save time, then a finer one, for polishing.

With gems other than diamonds, if the rough stone is large and irregular in shape, it is first sawn into pieces of a suitable size for cutting, although few precious stones (topaz and spodumene are among them) have strong enough cleavage for this to be done advantageously. The operation, which also serves to eliminate any badly flawed areas of the rough stone, can also be done with a small hammer—wielded, of course, with suitable care.

The subsequent stage, which is normally carried out on a rotating, flat-disc, metallic (steel, copper or tin) lap, using fairly coarse abrasives, serves to give the rough stone the required shape and dimensions, but leaves surfaces which are translucent due to lack of polish. As with diamond cutting, this is known as bruting. The final stage, which is performed on a horizontal lap with very fine abrasives, serves to polish the individual facets. Many different abrasives are used, the commonest being emery, garnet, chromium oxide, and iron oxide.

Cutting is an operation that requires time (especially for diamonds), precision, and relatively simple tools. For these reasons, less valuable stones and small diamonds are only worth cutting nowadays where labor is cheap and in plentiful supply.

Important centers for diamond cutting are: Antwerp, Amsterdam, New York, Tel Aviv, Bombay, and Cape Town, while other stones are normally cut in the countries where they are extracted, e.g. Sri Lanka, India, Thailand, Brazil, but also in Israel (Tel Aviv) and Europe (Idar-Oberstein).

Automated faceting machines have recently been introduced but at present they have a relatively limited application.

Main Types of Faceted Cut

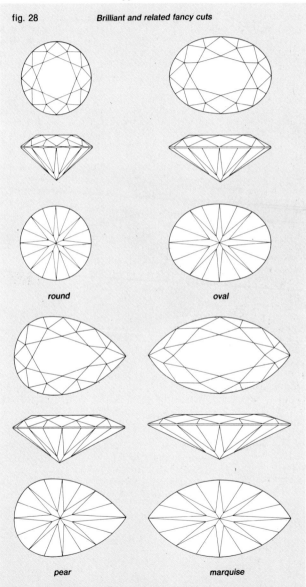

fig. 28   *Brilliant and related fancy cuts*

round

oval

pear

marquise

fig. 29

Step or trap cuts

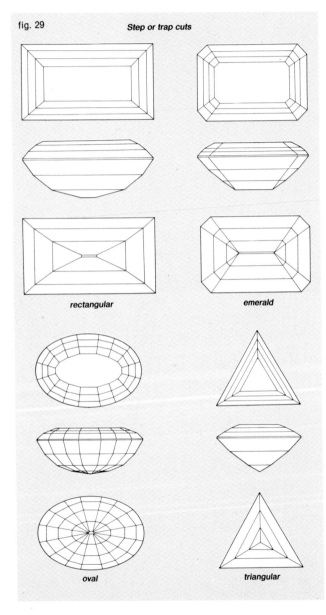

rectangular

emerald

oval

triangular

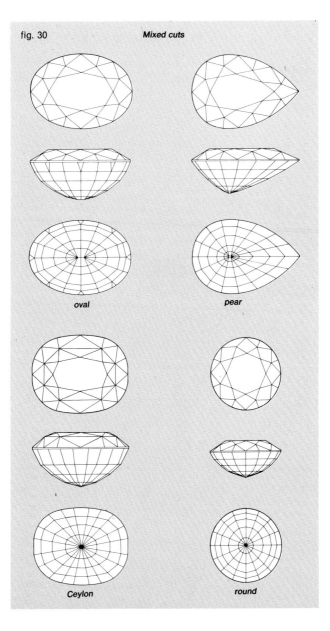

fig. 30

Mixed cuts

oval

pear

Ceylon

round

fig. 31 *Variants of the foregoing and special cuts*

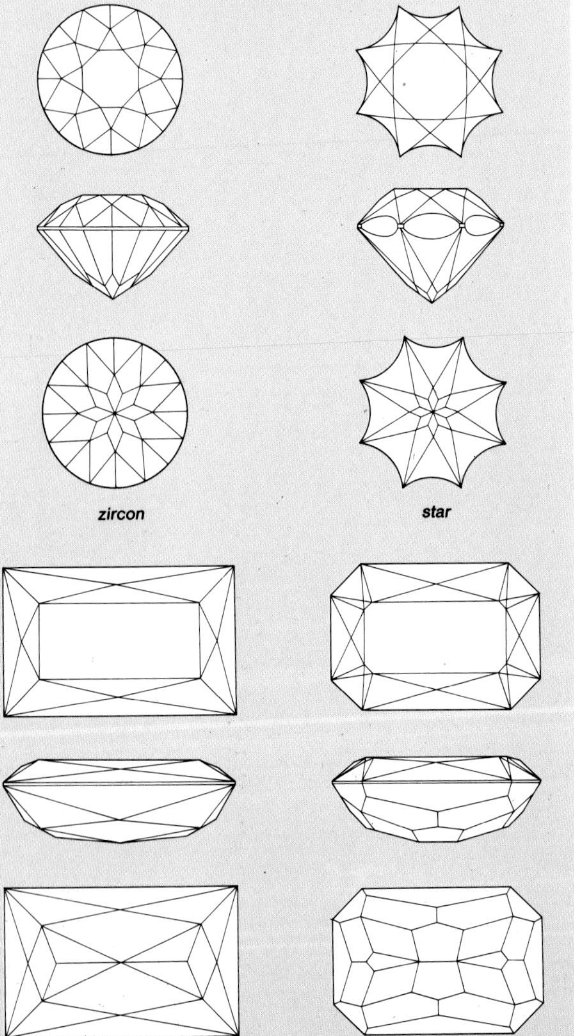

zircon   star

scissors cut   scissors cut with truncated corners

Gem Descriptions

1 DIAMOND
C

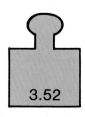

Native carbon. The same element also occurs naturally in the form of graphite, another mineral with completely different characteristics and appearance.

Its name comes from the Greek *adámas,* meaning "invincible," in recognition of its exceptional hardness, which makes it resist any form of abrasion by other minerals.

Crystal system   Cubic.

Appearance Diamonds most commonly occur as isolated crystals, which may be in the form of a more or less perfect octahedron, an octahedron with curved faces, or sometimes an icositetrahedron or hexoctahedron, which are more complex forms somewhat similar to an octahedron. The crystal can also be in the form of a rhombic dodecahedron or a tetrahexahedron with rounded corners and slightly curved faces, to the point of being almost spherical. Certain flattened, basically triangular twinned forms are also frequent. More or less cubic forms are rare. Rough-looking surfaces characteristically display superficial irregularities either in the form of fairly large cavities or hundreds of smaller irregularities, only recognizable under a lens, the extreme hardness of diamond generally ruling out the signs of abrasion seen on rough surfaces of other minerals that are found in secondary deposits. Pieces of diamond are often found that are clearly cleavages of other larger stones. Less typical, but quite frequent, are forms consisting of agglomerations of crystals, with concentric zoning and numerous impurities. Generally of irregular or globular appearance, with a rough or almost smooth surface, they are called *bort* (or *boart*). Another microcrystalline form occurring as irregular aggregates of roughly octahedral, cubic or rhombic dodecahedral appearance, is called *carbonado,* on account of its blackish color. Bort and carbonado are used for industrial purposes only. Diamond's microcrystalline structure compensates for its brittleness due to easy cleavage. Crystals with flat faces can be transparent, with strong luster, but blackish carbon inclusions, cloudy patches or fractures are often visible on the inside.

When the faces are curved or fairly rough, the crystals are generally merely translucent, even though it may be evident from cleavage surfaces that these imperfections are in an outer "skin," and that the crystals are transparent on the inside. Transparent stones are usually more or less colorless, but can be various shades of yellow-to-dull-yellow or more rarely, yellow with a brownish tinge. But bright yellow and clear brown are possible; and, as an extreme rarity, there are diamonds that are blue, pale green, pink, violet, and even reddish. The translucent stones with a skin often look grayish white (like ground glass); or dull yellow, yellow-brown, pale green, or pink. But they are often different on the inside: fairly clear, tinged with yellow or, more rarely, brown. The strongest colors are usually confined to the less transparent, outer layer. The *bort* varieties can often be yellowish, yellow-brown or grayish, while *carbonado* is blackish.

Physical properties   Diamond is rated 10 on Mohs' scale

Above: Octahedral diamond crystal (7 mm) in kimberlite matrix. Kimberley, South Africa.
Below: Variously colored rough diamonds.

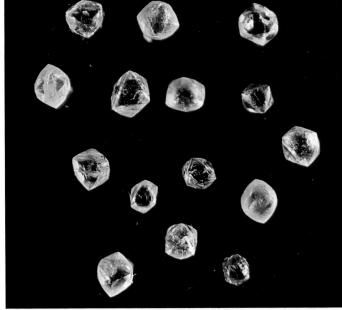

of hardness. It is the only mineral with this degree of hardness, although such a property is difficult to quantify. Depending on the methods of measurement, it is estimated to be from 10 to 150 times harder than corundum, the only mineral with a hardness of 9. Because all the remaining minerals have a hardness of less than 9, clearly there is a vast difference between them and diamond. But diamond has fairly easy cleavage parallel to the octahedral faces, which can make it brittle. The density is 3.52 g/cm^3. The refractive index of n 2.417 is well in excess of the measuring capabilities of the average refractometer. Singly refractive, diamond crystals can display areas of anomalous birefringence. It has fairly high dispersion, equal to 0.044, which is the highest for colorless minerals (the effect of dispersion is not appreciated in colored stones, so it is not considered).

Genesis There is still considerable uncertainty as to the origin of diamond. The most widely accepted theory is that it was formed at great depths in the earth's crust, at very high pressures and temperatures. Explosive types of volcanic phenomena would then have been responsible for driving it to the surface, with such a rapid drop in temperature that it was impossible for the diamond to be transformed into graphite, which is the carbon phase stable at low pressures. It would presumably have been carried to the surface in breccia of the peridotitic type known as kimberlite, which constitutes the infill of diamond-bearing pipes (structures with the appearance of explosive volcanic vents).

Its outstanding resistance to physical and chemical erosive agents means that crystals are found in a variety of environments, in secondary deposits where they have arrived unchanged after two or more cycles of erosion and sedimentation, making it impossible to establish a relationship between present deposits and places of origin.

Occurrence For many centuries, the only place where diamonds were found was India, where, however, very small quantities were mined. Early in the eighteenth century, diamonds also began to be mined in Brazil, which shortly afterwards became the principal world supplier. In the second half of the nineteenth century, they began to be mined from deposits in South Africa, which in turn, soon became the chief world source. Since the beginning of the twentieth century, diamonds have also been found in Angola and Zaire (responsible for up to 60 percent of annual world production, mainly for industrial uses), Ghana, Guinea, Ivory Coast, Tanzania (which has one of the largest primary deposits in the world), and the Soviet Union (which is currently the second largest producer in the world). Diamonds are also found in Guyana, Venezuela, and, in very limited quantities, Borneo. They have recently begun to be mined in China (in the province of Hunan), and considerable quantities have been discovered in Australia, where extraction has already begun. Bear in mind, however, that diamonds are only said to be worth exploiting where they occur in average concentrations of one part in twenty million, or in other words, where twenty tons of rock have to be worked for each gram of diamonds.

Above: Photographic reconstruction of the discovery (in 1866) of the first South African diamond; young Erasmus Jacobs finds a 21.7 carat sparkling "stone."
Below: Map of "Big Hole" in Kimberley, the largest excavated crater in the world.

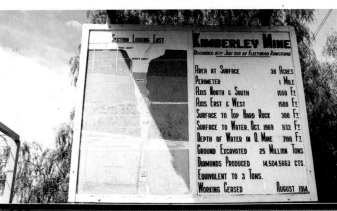

KIMBERLEY MINE

Discovered 15th July 1871 by Fleetwood Rawstorne

Area at Surface	38 Acres
Perimeter	1 Mile
Axis North & South	1550 Ft.
Axis East & West	1500 Ft.
Surface to Top Hard Rock	300 Ft.
Surface to Water. Oct. 1969	512 Ft.
Depth of Water in O. Mine	788 Ft.
Ground Excavated	25 Million Tons
Diamonds Produced	14,504,566½ CTS.
Equivalent to 3 Tons.	
Working Ceased	August 1914.

Section Looking East

1.1 Diamond

Ancient civilizations were fascinated by the exceptional hardness of diamond, although colored gems were regarded as more aesthetically pleasing. Diamond was extremely rare up to the eighteenth century and was only fully appreciated after the modern type of brilliant cut, which shows it in all its glory, was developed at the beginning of the twentieth century. It is the most important gemstone today. Statistics a few years ago showed that diamonds accounted for eighty percent of the movement of money generated by gemstones. About two million carats of cut diamonds are issued on the market each year (it is the only gemstone for which reliable statistics are available), equal to a volume of little more than 110 liters.

Appearance   In most cases it is almost colorless or, to be more precise, ranges from perfectly colorless (infrequent) to yellow-tinged or, sometimes, brownish. Diamonds with a definite color are extremely rare. This can be yellow, yellow-brown, or predominantly brown or, very occasionally pink to reddish, blue, blue-gray, pale green, or violet. Its luster, depending on reflection from both the inner and outer surfaces of the light incident on the table and crown, is greater than that of other gemstones, due both to its high refractive index, which facilitates total internal reflection and its exceptional hardness, enabling it to acquire a similar degree of polish.

By far the most widely used cut is the round, brilliant type, which best displays the gem's unique characteristics. But oval, marquise, pear and, more rarely, heart-shaped fancy cuts are also used. Most of these have a girdle consisting of a series of small, polished facets, while in brilliants, a girdle cut this way is uncommon and is reserved for stones treated with particular care. The special, rather elongated forms often show a dull area along the minor axis. Obviously, the better the cut, the less this band will show. The so-called emerald cut is also quite common. This has a rectangular table, stepped and chamfered. Unfortunately, this cut, which is used to reduce wastage when the stone is fashioned, is more often than not given the wrong proportions. The crown is usually too shallow (even less than 10 percent of the smaller side of the girdle) and the pavilion too deep (50–55 percent of the smaller side). The result is a stone with a lot less fire than one with a brilliant cut, or even than the rare examples of gems with correctly proportioned emerald cuts.

Diamonds are also found on the market with unusual, antique or specially designed cuts. Old mine cuts are not normally circular, but squarish, with rounded corners, or almost rectangular with rounded corners (some people call these polygonal shapes with slightly curved sides and smoothed corners "cushion" shape). The proportions of the height of the crown, the pavilion and the diameter vary a great deal in these cases, depending on the creativity of the cutter. It is still possible to find what are known as "rose" cuts, with a flat base, both in stones of some size, which are usually old or antique, and in small, shallow stones one or two millimeters in diameter, generally used in old-fashioned jewelry.

Top: Open-cast diamond mine in the Namaqualand desert in South Africa.
Center: Diamond prospectors in Venezuela.
Bottom: Examining diamond-bearing gravel in Brazil (left); a Venezuelan Indian shows his find to the camera (right).

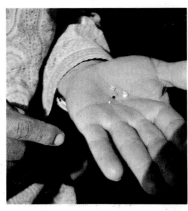

Distinctive features   Hardness can be an important factor in distinguishing diamond from other stones. It is in fact the only gemstone capable of scratching corundum. The best modern imitation, cubic zirconia, is less hard than corundum, so the two can easily be distinguished by comparing them with corundum, although the results of the tests must be observed under a binocular microscope or at least a lens. Diamond's exceptional hardness is also displayed by the facet edges, which are sharper than in imitations. This is best appreciated in relation to zircon, which has brittle, easily damaged edges, and the less hard imitations such as synthetic rutile and strontium titanate. If the stones are turned between the thumb and forefinger, the two softer substitutes feel more slippery, almost oily, compared with diamond, because of this difference in the edges.

Another characteristic can be seen in the girdle, but only when it is not faceted. Due to the procedure used in turning brilliant cuts, the girdle of a diamond will have a satiny finish, similar to that of finely ground glass (in recent years a similar effect has been achieved with cubic zirconia, but no other imitation displays this). Also, when there are numerous flaws like minute cracks extending from either side of the girdle (these are known as "bearding" and are due to inexpert turning of the rough stone), it is bound to be diamond. A brilliant cut can display small facets on the girdle or extending from the girdle toward the pavilion (or more rarely, toward the crown). These are the remains of the outer surface of the uncut octahedron (nearly always with minute, crystallographically oriented shallow triangular cavities), or of the faces of octahedral cleavage. In the latter case, small steps can be observed between contiguous, specular plane surfaces. However, these details are only readily visible if magnified at least 10–20 times. Sometimes small triangular facets alone are seen extending from the girdle. Called extra facets or supplementary facets, these are produced by polishing of the facets just described or by the elimination of some small, almost superficial flaw. Although very similar to the foregoing and not usually found on imitations, these facets are less distinctive in that they could be produced on any other stone.

Other distinctive features are related to the fact that the most frequently used, brilliant and emerald cuts, are designed to make the most of the high refractive index of diamond and obtain the maximum possible total internal reflection of the light coming from the table facet. Therefore if a diamond is placed with the table facet against tiny written characters, nothing will be visible through it, unless the pavilion is extremely flat. With imitation diamonds of a much lower refractive index, such as YAG (Yttrium Aluminum Garnet), something will be visible through the stone and still more will be seen through synthetic spinel and colorless sapphire. The difference is more obvious with emerald cuts than with brilliants. A similar effect, but confined to brilliant-cut stones, can be seen through the table facet. By steadily tilting a stone of lower refractive index than diamond, and looking through the table, a nonreflecting transparent triangle can be seen to appear in the pavilion, with its apex at the center and its base toward the edge of the

Copies of some famous diamonds (left to right, from the top): Star of the South; Hope; Orloff; Regent or Pitt; Cullinan; Florentine; Koh-i-Noor; Great Mogul.

table opposite the observer. The lower the refractive index of the stone, the smaller the angle at which this will appear. In diamonds, this effect is very difficult to see, except in poorly cut stones with very shallow pavilions.

Single refraction is another characteristic that distinguishes diamond from zircon, which is strongly birefringent and from an infrequent imitation of diamond: synthetic rutile, which is even more strongly birefringent. The famous dispersion in diamond, although considerable, is much less than that of synthetic rutile and strontium titanate; but these now uncommon imitations look positively iridescent when viewed through a lens and even to some extent with the naked eye.

Given the constancy of shape and proportions, at least within certain limits, of stones with a round brilliant cut, a given weight can be said to correspond to a given diameter. If the diameter of a stone presumed to be a diamond can be measured with some precision, one can check to see whether it has a suitable weight (in which case it will either be diamond or a stone of comparable specific gravity), or whether the weight immediately rules out the possibility of its being diamond. Generally simulants are too heavy, as in the case of cubic zirconia, GGG (Gadolinium Gallium Garnet) or, to a much less obvious extent, zircon or YAG (Fig. A.). This method could not be used to distinguish diamond either from synthetic spinel, colorless topaz, or colorless sapphire, as their relative densities are too similar, although all of them have other characteristics unlikely to deceive any but the most casual observer.

It was mentioned in discussing physical properties, that the very high refractive index of diamond is outside the range of normal refractometers and the same can be said of many of its imitations. In compensation, however, diamond has other characteristics, such as reflectivity and thermal conductivity, which are quite different (because much higher) than those of its present substitutes. Small instruments the size of a pocket calculator have been produced to measure these characteristics, making a rapid distinction possible.

Occurrence Gem quality diamonds are found in about twenty different countries, a dozen of which are in Africa, three in Asia, one in Oceania, and three in South America. By far the largest producer is South Africa, including the neighboring Lesotho, Botswana, and Namibia. Next come the Soviet Union, Angola, Zaire, and Sierra Leone. Other important areas are the Central African Republic, Tanzania, Ghana, and Venezuela, with Australia and Brazil further behind, and India now one of the last.

Value Diamond is one of the most valuable stones, together with ruby and emerald. The market value of diamonds is determined by complex grading systems that divide them into a wide range of different categories. The basic characteristics considered are weight, color, and purity. Less crucial factors are the proportions of the cut and surface finish.

The influence of weight Although a diamond weighing over 3000 carats has been found, rough diamonds of considerable weight are extremely rare. Still rarer are heavy cut diamonds, given that the average loss of weight in the cutting process is more than 60 percent. All else being

Above: Other famous diamonds: Briolette, left; Dresden green, above; Tiffany, below. Below: Fig. A gives the diameter in millimeters and weight in carats for diamond and some imitations thereof.

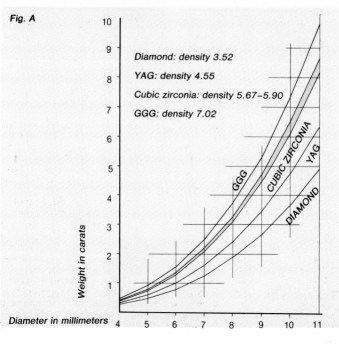

Fig. A

Diamond: density 3.52

YAG: density 4.55

Cubic zirconia: density 5.67–5.90

GGG: density 7.02

GGG

CUBIC ZIRCONIA

YAG

DIAMOND

Weight in carats

Diameter in millimeters

equal, a diamond twice the weight of another is much rarer and therefore much more precious and will have a higher price per carat. Weight also has psychological as well as scarcity value: a diamond of 1 carat or slightly more is worth more weight for weight than one of 0.9 carats because it exceeds the conventional limit of the complete carat. The same applies at the dividing line for 2 carats, 3 carats, and so on (Fig. B). In short, the price per carat increases by stages with each complete carat number, up at least to a weight of about 10 carats, after which the effect is negligible, although such large diamonds are extremely uncommon.

The influence of color The vast majority of diamonds are colorless, or yellowish, ranging from a barely perceptible tinge to straw-yellow. Perfectly clear stones, however, are comparatively rare, but the effect of dispersion in diamonds is more pleasing on a clear ground than on a yellowish one. For these, plus psychological reasons, the more or less perfectly colorless stones are in greater demand; and value diminishes with an increase in yellow (or more rarely, brown) coloration.

In an effort to quantify this, scales of colors of different intensities were established, with names of the color categories relating to the principal localities in which diamonds of that color were found, or to other factors. Thus the main diamond trading centers evolved roughly similar color codes matched by approximate sets of values. A very precise scale has more recently been introduced in the United States, with grades distinguished by letters of the alphabet (beginning with D, not A) and referring to data supplied by special measuring instruments rather than the naked eye. Over the last few years, European scales have been adapted to that of the United States, a series of sample diamonds being used for purposes of comparison. The four scales most widely used today and in the recent past are shown in Fig. C (4b is the same as 4a, but with the old nomenclature of 1). The correspondence between scales 1 and 2 is approximate, as is their relationship to the others, whereas 4a and 4b were designed to be cross-referenced. As a general guide, color H (white) is very good and few diamonds can boast such quality. Color I (the old "commercial white") is much better than this name would imply, with a barely perceptible yellow tinge; and many stones on the market, particularly medium- or large-sized ones, come under categories J, K, L, or M. By contrast, "rare white" stones are much less frequent. A very rough idea of the visibility of coloration in diamonds of different grades (seen from above only, in conditions of "use," rather than the ideal conditions according to which they are classified) can be obtained from Fig. D, which uses the classifications of the CIBJO scale. Naturally, the larger the area over which any coloration is viewed, the easier it is to see. All else being equal, the price of diamonds varies quite sharply with color. Again, as a rough guide and obviously depending on the state of the market, if a diamond with certain characteristics and weight of color H were worth 100, another with the same characteristics of color F could be worth 130, while one of color J would be worth 80, and one of color M, 40.

Above: brooch with brilliants.
Below: Fig. B shows the way in which the price per carat of diamonds increases by stages.

84

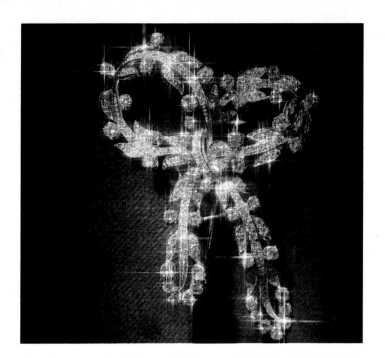

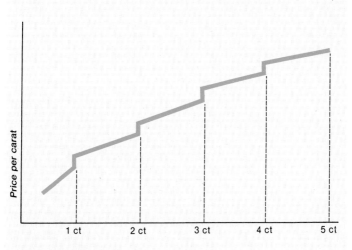

Fig. B

Price per carat

| 1 ct | 2 ct | 3 ct | 4 ct | 5 ct |

Weight in carats

The influence of purity   Many diamonds contain crystalline inclusions or discontinuities (even just fractures) which reduce their transparency, by interrupting the paths of the light rays. Stones free of inclusions or visible discontinuities are described as pure, and value diminishes as visible imperfections increase.

Classification is based on visual criteria and detailed diagrams are available to establish a basis of comparison. Stones are conventionally examined under a 10x lens. The grades of the scale of purity are shown in Fig. E and are referred to by internationally accepted sets of initials, according to the English terminology. Pure stones of IF grade are uncommon; VVS and VS grades are of a good level of purity, SI and PI grades are not so pure and P_2 and P_3 are the lowest categories. Naturally, stones combining perfect purity with excellent color are rare, especially those weighing several carats. If one is prepared to compromise over a single characteristic such as color, it will be easier to find stones of good purity and weight. Similarly, it will be easier to find a stone of good color and weight but mediocre purity; and those of middling color, medium purity, and small size are obviously the most common.

The above should give some idea of the complexity and also the degree of organization of criteria used for the valuation of diamonds. In addition to these fundamental criteria there are others based on the proportions of the cut (when not ideal, they reduce the stone's powers of light reflection and refraction) and surface finish, which are taken into account in establishing value. Proportion and finish are judged as ''very good,'' ''good,'' ''medium,'' or ''poor.'' Sometimes these judgments are based on measurement, but usually they are established by the visual evaluation of experts.

Simulants and synthetics   Diamond has been imitated by glass and special glass with a mirror backing to increase reflection, called ''strass.'' It has been imitated by colorless, synthetic spinel and corundum ever since these began to be produced. Over the last few decades, moreover, it has been imitated by a whole range of synthetic and artificial products:

- strontium titanate or fabulite, which has much higher dispersion than diamond, with striking iridescence, low hardness, considerable brittleness and density;
- synthetic rutile or titania, which has very high dispersion with striking iridescence, marked birefringence, high density, and low hardness;
- YAG (Yttrium Aluminium Garnet), which has a slightly lower refractive index than diamond, a hardness of less than 9, and greater density;
- GGG (Gadolinium Gallium Garnet), which has a fairly low hardness and double the density of diamond;
- cubic zirconia (cubic zirconium oxide), djevelite or phianite, the most recent and hardest to distinguish from diamond. Its density, however, is much greater, and its hardness is less than 9.

Many other artificial substances are similar to diamond, but are not used as imitations because their cost is generally much higher and their characteristics no better than those simulants already mentioned. Diamond has been and still is

Above: Fig. C gives the four color grading systems most widely used today or in the past.
Fig. D gives the approximate visibility of color in diamonds, viewed from above (through the crown) according to size.

C

1	2	3	4a	4b
Old names	**United Kingdom**	**GIA***	**CIBJO***	**Provisional reissue with old names**
Jager	Blue white	D	Exceptional white +	River
River	Finest white	E	Exceptional white	
	Fine white	F	Rare White +	Top Wesselton
Top Wesselton		G	Rare White	
Wesselton	White	H	White	Wesselton
Top crystal	Commercial white	I	Slightly tinted white	Top crystal
Crystal	Top silver Cape	J		Crystal
Top Cape	Silver Cape	K	Tinted white	Top Cape
	Light Cape	L		
Cape	Cape	M	Tinted color — Tinted color 1	Cape
Low Cape		N		
Very light yellow up to	Dark cape	O	Tinted color — Tinted color 2	Light yellow
		P		
		Q		
		R		
		S–Z	Tinted color 3	Yellow
Fancy yellow		Fancy yellow	Fancy yellow	Fancy yellow

* GIA = Gemological Institute of America. CIBJO = Confédération Internationale de la Bijouterie, Joaillerie, Orfèvrerie, des diamants, perles et pierres précieuses.

	< 0.5 ct.	> 1 ct.
Exceptional White (River)	more or less colorless	more or less colorless
Rare White (Top Wesselton)		
White (Wesselton)		
Slightly Tinted White (Top crystal Crystal)		with a very faint yellow tinge
Tinted color 1 (Cape)	with a very faint yellow tinge	with a visible yellow tinge
Tinted color (Light Yellow)		
Tinted color 3 (Yellow)	with a visible yellow tinge	with a pale yellow color

D

manufactured synthetically, in minute crystals, only suitable for industrial purposes. It has also been produced experimentally for use as a gemstone and a few gems of about 0.25–0.45 carats have been cut. But it is so hard to make the crystals grow that the cost would be much higher than that of natural diamonds obtained from known deposits.

Above: Fig. E gives the terms used for purity grading of diamonds.
Below: A handful of sparkling diamonds; a fortune that fits into the palm of the hand.

Grades	Meaning	Visibility
loupe-clean	Pure under a lens or internally flawless	No inclusions better visible than a pinpoint under a 10× lens
VVS	Very, very small inclusions	Very hard to see under a 10× lens
VS	Very small inclusions	Visible under a 10× lens, but not easily so
SI	Small inclusions	Easily visible under a 10× lens, but not to the naked eye, at least from above
P1	With visible, not too small inclusions	Visible with difficulty by the naked eye through the crown of the diamond
P2	Large and/or frequent inclusions	Easily visible to the naked eye
P3	With obvious inclusions	Very easily visible to the naked eye

2 CORUNDUM

Al_2O_3

9

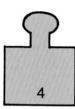

4

1.77 1.76

Aluminium oxide. The name is probably derived from an old Indian word, *corund*, which referred to an unknown mineral or gem.

Crystal system Trigonal.

Appearance It occurs in semiopaque masses similar to whitish or grayish vein quartz, but also in distinct, prismatic or tapered crystals, with close transverse striations, some of which resemble elongated bipyramids. Often opaque or translucent, corundum can be partially or perfectly transparent. All the colors of the spectrum are possible, from red to yellow, green, blue, and violet; in addition, the stones may be pink, gray, black, or colorless and all the shades between. Brightly colored, transparent, translucent, or semiopaque varieties make highly aesthetic and valuable gems. Because of its hardness and resistance to chemical attack, corundum is often found in alluvial deposits in the form of pebbles that retain clear indications of their original crystal shapes.

Physical properties Corundum has a hardness of 9, the highest in the mineral world after diamond. The density is approximately 4.0 g/cm^3. The refractive indices are about $n\epsilon$ 1.760, $n\omega$ 1.769. Parting parallel to the basal plane is sometimes visible, with an appearance of cleavage.

Genesis It is formed by contact metamorphism between alumina-rich magmas (and related pegmatites) and limestone, or by regional metamorphism of alumina-rich, silica-poor rocks.

Occurrence The least attractive variety of corundum, known as emery (usually a corundum-magnetite mixture) and used as an abrasive, is mainly found in Greece, the United States, and Australia. The gem varieties come chiefly from Sri Lanka, Thailand, Cambodia, Burma, and Australia, with smaller deposits in India, Tanzania, and the United States.

2.1 Ruby

The most valuable variety of corundum is ruby. The name comes from the Latin *rubrum*, "red." Like other red stones, it has also been called *carbunculus*, or carbuncle, meaning a small coal or ember.

Appearance The color varies from fiery vermilion to violet red, but because rubies are pleochroic, different colors are also found in the same stone; bright or sometimes brick red in one direction, tending to carmine in the other. The color is also accompanied by marked fluorescence which is stimulated by ordinary, artificial light and above all, by the ultraviolet rays of direct sunlight. Thus rubies turn brighter red under such light and the purplish ones look "redder." If the color is too pale, they are no longer called rubies, but pink sapphires; if it is more violet than red, they are known as violet sapphires. But it is hard to establish precise limits, as all the intermediate shades are possible. The brightest red and thus the most valuable rubies

Above: Rough corundums of various colors.
Below: A ruby in the form of a water-worn pebble from Sri Lanka.

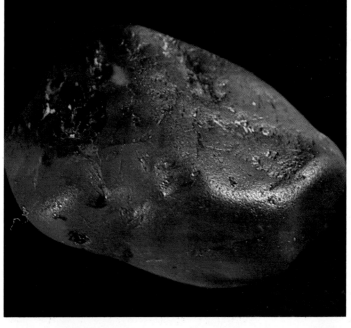

(usually from Burma) often have areas full of inclusions in the form of minute rutile needles (or straws), which interfere with the light, producing a distinctive silky sheen known, in fact, as silk. When the silk is not heavy, the stones are clearer, more attractive, and even more valuable. Other, mainly crystalline inclusions are normally found as well. Rubies of this type are not usually more than a few carats in weight. The rare exceptions generally contain copious inclusions. Violet red, sometimes quite dark, rubies come principally from Thailand. The type most often found on the market nowadays, they can be several carats in weight. They are normally clearer, without patches of silk. While good-sized clear stones are found, specimens with many inclusions are commonly sold as well. Rubies are usually given a mixed cut, which is generally oval, but can be round or, more rarely, other shapes. In the past, they were given a cabochon cut, like all stones outstanding for their color. Today, however, this cut is reserved for less transparent stones with numerous inclusions.

Distinctive features Rubies can often be distinguished by their immediately visible characteristics: a fairly obvious pleochroism, a distinct brightening of color in strong light, the silk effect (where present), and a considerable luster. While spinel can be a similar color and has a similar luster, it is not pleochroic, turns much less bright in strong light, and never displays the silk effect. Red garnet is not pleochroic and the color does not brighten in strong light; it has a similar luster, but when given a faceted cut often displays dark, blackish areas within the stone. Red tourmaline is usually a completely different shade, but can be very similar, with a pleochroism comparable to that of ruby. It does not, however, brighten in strong light, and this can be sufficient indication to warrant testing its physical properties, which are quite different. The other red gemstones mentioned also differ physically from ruby. Some caution is needed with garnets, which show wide variations in both density, which in some cases coincides with that of corundum, and refractive index, which can coincide with one of the figures for corundum. Garnet, however, is singly refractive, and examples with an index in the region of 1.76 have a lower density than that of ruby.

Occurrence The rubies with the finest color come from the Mogok region in Burma. These are most truly vermilion, though they still have a touch of carmine. Thailand, however, is today the main source of rubies. Thai rubies are usually slightly less attractive, a bit darker with a violet tinge, but they often have fewer inclusions. Rubies are also found in Sri Lanka, but in very small quantities. Often pale, almost pink, they can be attractive, with an appearance that is both brilliant and lively. Small quantities of very fine rubies also come from the area of Cambodia on the border with Thailand, while rather opaque specimens, mainly of inferior quality, are found in India and Pakistan. Tanzania and neighboring countries have also been mining rubies for a few years. Some of the rubies found in these countries are almost as finely colored as those from Burma, with inclusions similar to rubies from Thailand, while others are semiopaque and of very limited value.

Value The highest quality, best colored and most trans-

*Above: Ruby.
Below: The silk effect in a ruby, caused by minute rutile needle inclusions (photomicrograph).*

parent stones (usually from Burma), weighing, for example, 3 to 5 carats, can be as valuable as diamonds, or even more so. Very good quality rubies of even greater weight are extremely rare and fetch exceptionally high prices. Good quality stones of at least 2 carats (a bit more violet in color and usually from Thailand) are still quite valuable (particularly the more transparent ones). The price falls considerably for stones of less than a carat, which are too dark in color, and have inclusions clearly visible to the naked eye.

Simulants and synthetics Ruby has very occasionally been imitated by glass, which has a rather different, less lively color and an inferior luster. It has sometimes been imitated by doublets, with the top part consisting of garnet, to provide luster, hardness, and natural-looking inclusions and the bottom part of red glass, fused rather than cemented to the garnet layer. But such imitations are uncommon. Synthetic ruby has been produced from the beginning of the twentieth century and was the first synthetic gemstone to be manufactured on an industrial scale. To make these synthetic stones harder to distinguish from some natural rubies with numerous inclusions, they have sometimes been fractured internally by heating and rapid cooling. More recently, doublets imitating rubies have also been produced in the Orient. The top part of these doublets consists of poorly colored (usually pale green or yellow) natural corundum with obvious, typical inclusions; and the lower part is synthetic ruby, held to the corundum by transparent cement. The effect is highly deceptive: the reassuring presence of natural inclusions and characteristic luster combined with a color which is not perfect, but is normal for the majority of rubies, can be much more convincing than a synthetic ruby.

2.2 **Sapphire**

This is the blue variety of corundum. The name is probably derived, through the Latin *sapphirus* and Greek *sápheiros,* from a Sanskrit word. As with other gem names, however, the Latin *sapphirus* did not originally denote the gem it is associated with today. Judging by the description of Pliny the Elder, it almost certainly referred to what is now known as lapis lazuli, rather than corundum.

Appearance Sapphires can be a very dark blue, to the point of seeming dense and blackish from a distance, sometimes accompanied by a blue to dull green pleochroism, which is only visible from the side in cut stones. They may also be a strong, but not too bright blue, easily recognizable from a distance, this being the ideal color. Other possibilities are light, usually bright, blue, with the color unevenly distributed; palish blue or, finally, blue with a violet tinge, at least in bright light. Like all corundum, sapphire always has good luster.

Some sapphires display clearly defined streaks of paler color, in contrast to a dark ground. Others have areas with a slightly silky sheen, which are not clearly delineated. Still other, uncommon varieties assume a distinct, milky appearance in strong light, with a marked increase in color

intensity. Inclusions are, as a rule, less obvious in very dark stones, due to their general lack of transparency, whereas medium to large, pale stones often show distinct "veils" or "feathers" caused by very fine inclusions and foreign crystals, which are sometimes transparent, sometimes dark, submetallic, and opaque, and, very occasionally, bright red. Sapphires are usually given oval or less frequently, round, mixed cuts, but rectangular or square, step cuts, with or without trimmed corners, are also possible. The cabochon cut is used as well, although less frequently than in the past. Nowadays it is generally reserved for stones full of inclusions or those in which the color is concentrated in a few streaks on a light ground. In the latter case, in fact, the cabochon cut gives the color a more uniform appearance. Stones weighing several carats or even 10 to 20 carats in the case of light-colored specimens, are not uncommon.

Distinctive features   Like other types of corundum, sapphires have a striking luster. The color is also quite distinctive, whether or not clear blue-green pleochroism is visible. The overall appearance is very important. For example, a deep blue color with distinct blue-green pleochroism and internal streaks straight across or at an angle of 120°, combined with the powerful luster of corundum, indicates a sapphire of Australian origin. A slightly patchy, blue color with imperceptible pleochroism and strong transparency showing veillike inclusions and a slight silk effect, still with excellent luster, denotes a sapphire from Sri Lanka. Cornflower to deep blue in a stone without obvious inclusions but of slightly milky appearance, acquiring a distinct fullness of color in bright light, is characteristic of the rare sapphires from Kashmir. Of the other blue stones, tanzanite always shows a hint of violet, fairly obvious pleochroism, and less luster than sapphire. Cordierite, apart from being less lustrous and violet or gray blue, has striking pleochroism from blue to an unmistakable drab yellow. Strongly colored specimens of indicolite tourmaline are often an attractive greenish blue, with a pleochroism ranging from blue to green, but the green is very different from that of sapphire which, when it is present, is always dull or yellowish. Still on the subject of pleochroism in tourmaline, the direction corresponding to the blue color shows a characteristic lack of transparency. While blue zircon has a luster similar to that of sapphire, it is an electric blue or blue-green unlike that of any other gemstone. Furthermore, its strong birefringence, seen in a clear duplication of the facet edges when viewed through the stone with a lens, would remove all trace of doubt; sapphire is doubly refractive as well, but to a much lesser degree. In the rare cases when blue spinel is not cloudy blue or violet gray, but a vivid mid-blue, it can look very much like sapphire, partly on account of its strong luster. In this case, it can only be distinguished by its physical characteristics; establishment of single refractivity, or measurement of the density or refractive index should suffice.

Occurrence   The best sapphires were discovered in a small deposit in Kashmir in 1880, in a remote mountain area which has now probably been exhausted. Very fine sapphires are also found in Burma, but in limited quantities.

Above: Sapphires in various shades of blue.
Below: Sapphire from Sri Lanka.

Appreciable quantities of light- and bright-blue sapphire are found in alluvial deposits on the island of Sri Lanka. These are always attractively (if sometimes patchily) colored, the richest versions being very similar to the Burmese sapphires and equally valuable. The sapphires of Sri Lanka are also famous for the variety of inclusions they display: long, thin rutile needles, like very fine silk; soft, liquid inclusions arranged in the form of veils, lace, and feathers; striking inclusions with a moving bubble, like a spirit level; zircon crystals with small stress cracks radiating from them, and various other types of transparent crystals.

Sapphires are also mined in Thailand and neighboring Cambodia. These are generally pleasing to the eye, though often rather deeply colored. But most sapphires come from Australia, which has numerous deposits of deeply colored stones, sometimes too dark, in most cases with blue-green pleochroism. These are the least valuable, but most widely available on the market. Less important sources are the United States (Montana), Tanzania, and Malawi.

Value   The finest stones, weighing at least several carats, are almost as valuable as diamonds and rubies and are hence very highly priced. This is particularly true of most sapphires from Kashmir, many from Burma, and some from Sri Lanka, Cambodia, and Thailand. But when the color is too dark, blackish or greenish blue or a bit too pale, the value falls sharply, to that normal for secondary gems. Inclusions obvious to the naked eye also lower the price. Small stones (of a fraction of a carat) are modestly priced and readily available. Large ones (from more than ten to several tens of carats), although not common, are much less rare than rubies of this size.

Simulants and synthetics   Sapphire has been imitated by dark to cobalt blue glass, but particularly by doublets with a top part consisting of red almandine garnet, which is very hard and lustrous, with natural inclusions, and a bottom part of dark-to-cobalt blue glass, welded together, not glued. It has also been imitated in the past by synthetic blue spinel, which is brightly colored but emits strange red gleams in bright light. Synthetic sapphire has likewise been produced for many years now, mainly by the Verneuil flame fusion method. Recently, doublets have been produced consisting of a top portion of light green or yellow-green natural corundum with visible inclusions and a lower portion of synthetic sapphire, held together by transparent cement. The visible inclusions and typical corundum of the top part, along with the color, make these doublets very convincing at first sight.

Since the end of the 1970s, greater knowledge of the nature and causes of color in gemstones has enabled the modification of this feature by various procedures. The most recent and important techniques, in fact, relate to the blue coloration of sapphire. One method is to subject very pale blue, almost colorless stones with numerous silklike rutile inclusions to prolonged heating at temperatures in the region of 1500–1600°C. in a reducing environment. This "reactivates" the titanium in the rutile, which reacts with the traces of iron in the sapphire. In this way, the silk is absorbed, while the trivalent titanium and iron thus formed,

Above: Jewelry with sapphire.
Below: Liquid inclusions in a sapphire (photomicrograph).

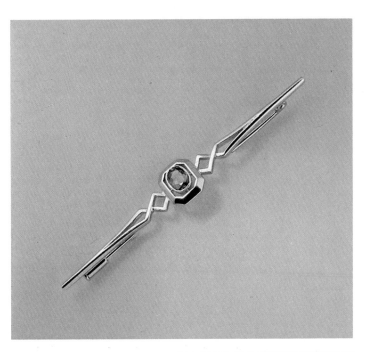

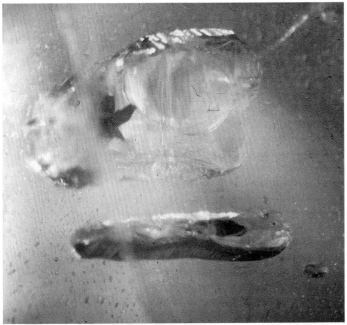

which are responsible for the blue coloration of sapphire, greatly intensify the color of the stone. This treatment is now very widespread and more or less reproduces the sequence of events that occurred when many sapphire crystals were formed. As a result, it is not always possible to distinguish a completely natural sapphire from one whose color has been intensified in this way, and they are treated as one on the market. According to another procedure, however, colorless, pale yellow or pale green stones are covered in a paste consisting of iron and—mainly—titanium compounds. The specimens are then heated to a temperature of about 1700°C. for perhaps several days. The iron and titanium oxides slowly infiltrate the stones to a depth of about one millimeter, producing a deep blue coloration. The stone then has to be repolished (the surface having been damaged by heating to near melting point). Hence part of the colored layer is removed, leaving a very small thickness. This procedure is surprisingly common and involves the introduction of additives as colorants. It is universally regarded as fraudulent if the treated stones are then offered for sale as natural stones, as is often the case.

Inclusions in the shape of a butterfly's wing in a blue sapphire (photomicrograph).

2.3 Pink sapphire

This is the name given to the pink variety of corundum, red corundum generally being known in English-speaking countries as ruby, blue corundum as sapphire, and any other shades as sapphire combined with the appropriate color: pink sapphire, yellow sapphire, green sapphire, etc. Pink sapphire and ruby are regarded as two different varieties, despite the fact that the only difference is their depth of color. The same does not apply to tourmaline, both the pink and red forms of which are known as rubellite, or to sapphire and emerald, which keep their names even for paler specimens.

Appearance Pink sapphire may range from a very delicate, pleasing, lively pink, without any overtones, to pink with a slight violet tinge; but all gradations of color are possible, from those tending toward ruby to those tending to)ard violet sapphire. Like all forms of corundum, it has very good luster. It is normally given a mixed, oval cut and sometimes has fine inclusions and liquid veils in lacelike formations, characteristic of the corundum of Sri Lanka, from where most pink sapphire comes. Stones of several carats are normal, but specimens of 10 carats or more are rare.

Distinctive features Pink sapphire's most striking characteristic is its luster, common to all corundum and most noticeable in light-colored specimens. It is usually, though not always, a livelier, more attractive color than tourmaline; and as is often the case with paler stones, the physical characteristics generally have to be measured to tell them apart. In the case of pink stones, measurement of the density by means of heavy liquids may be sufficient.

Occurence Pink sapphire comes almost exclusively from Sri Lanka; much more rarely from Burma.

Value Although the ''minor'' varieties of corundum are always a lot less val'uable than rubies and sapphires, pink sapphire is more highly prized than the yellow, green, and violet varieties, as it is so attractive. It is one of the most valuable secondary gems.

Simulants and synthetics Pink sapphire has not really been imitated, but it has been produced synthetically by the Verneuil flame fusion method. The synthetic form, like that of yellow sapphire, is extremely well disguised and it is very hard to distinguish it from the natural varieties.

Above: Blue, yellow, pink, etc. sapphires. Below: Pink sapphire, 0.54 ct. Sri Lanka.

2.4 Violet sapphire

This is the name now given to the violet variety of corundum. It was formerly known as "oriental amethyst," on account of its color; but this name has now been abandoned in favor of the debatable, but mineralogically more precise, term used for all minor forms of corundum.

Appearance The typical color is a definite violet, like amethyst, which is very attractive and tends to turn reddish violet in the sun or bright light. But all gradations of color are possible from the violet blue of some sapphires to the violet red of some rubies and the violet pink of some pink sapphires. Whatever the exact shade, it is always a very pleasing color, and has perhaps been less appreciated than it deserves because of the association of violet with mourning and sorrow in the West. As always with corundum, it has very good luster, most evident in lighter gemstones. It is usually given a mixed, oval cut. Stones weighing a few carats are often found, but those of 10 carats and more are rare.

Distinctive features When the color of the sapphire tends to be blue-violet, red-violet or pink-violet (the first turning more violet, the others, redder, in sunshine or bright light), it is fairly distinctive, but not so when it is a true violet or violet with a slight hint of red. Some very fine amethysts look very similar to such sapphires, even to the reddish tinge. The characteristic luster of corundum is another distinctive feature, but here too, care is needed, as amethyst can bear a close resemblance.

Violet sapphires are easily distinguished, however, by their physical characteristics. If the density is measured with a heavy liquid such as methylene iodide, corundum rapidly sinks, while amethystine quartz floats.

Occurrence Many violet sapphires, particularly the paler, pinker ones, come from Sri Lanka. Much smaller quantities are also found in Thailand and Burma.

Value Despite its considerable aesthetic qualities, violet sapphire is not widely appreciated. It is accorded much the same value as other, secondary gemstones, being somewhat more valuable than yellow sapphire (which is more plentiful).

Simulants and synthetics Violet sapphire does not appear to have been imitated; but from the time synthetic corundum was first produced, various shades of violet have been manufactured, along with the other varieties. Large quantities of violet synthetic corundum are still produced, faceted into every imaginable shape, from oval or round mixed cuts to true brilliants and square and rectangular step cuts. The curious thing is that these stones, which are often of considerable size and weight (even 10 to 20 carats) are sold throughout the world under the name of alexandrite, an extremely rare form of green chrysoberyl that changes color to red, and is therefore not even vaguely like synthetic corundum.

Liquid and solid inclusions in a violet sapphire (photomicrograph).

2.5 **Yellow sapphire**

This is the name given to the more-or-less yellow variety of corundum, in accordance with modern terminology for colors other than blue and red. It was also formerly known as "oriental topaz."

Appearance   Yellow sapphire may occur in quite a wide range of colors, from pale to canary yellow, gold, honey, and brownish yellow. The lighter, brighter colors are the most common. Medium-sized or large stones are often seen, generally with a mixed oval cut having a rather large pavilion (to increase the depth of color). Because of their transparency, veillike or lacelike liquid inclusions and even foreign crystals are often visible inside these stones. Like all corundum, they have considerable luster. Honey-colored stones, which are less common and often smaller, are equally lustrous and are given both oval and rectangular step cuts. The color can be quite similar to that of certain topazes.

Distinctive features   Like all corundum, the yellow type can often be distinguished from other gems by its luster, but not from yellow chrysoberyl, which is very similar in this respect. The canary yellow color is not often found in other stones, except citrine, which is, however, a bit less lustrous. Yellow zircon has luster similar to that of yellow sapphire but is usually distinguishable through a lens by its much stronger birefringence, the facet edges appearing much more clearly duplicated and both facets and edges giving an impression of less hardness and greater brittleness. The inclusions in yellow sapphires are also fairly characteristic, at least when viewed through a lens. All in all, however, many yellow gems show some resemblance to yellow sapphire and must, therefore, be distinguished by their physical properties.

Occurrence   Most light or canary yellow sapphire comes from Sri Lanka, and only a small proportion from Australia, which, however, supplies most of the less common honey, golden yellow or yellow-brown stones. Limited quantities are obtained from Burma.

Value   Somewhat surprisingly, even very attractive yellow sapphires with fine luster are of relatively low value compared with other secondary gems; they are, for example, worth a lot less than the pink variety.

Simulants and synthetics   Yellow sapphire was never really imitated by other substances until synthetic corundum was first produced. Since then canary and honey-yellow varieties have been widely manufactured. Like pink and colorless synthetic corundum, the yellow variety produced by the Verneuil flame fusion method is highly convincing and harder to distinguish from its natural counterparts than are rubies and sapphires produced in this way.

Above: Violet sapphire set in a ring. Below: Yellow sapphire.

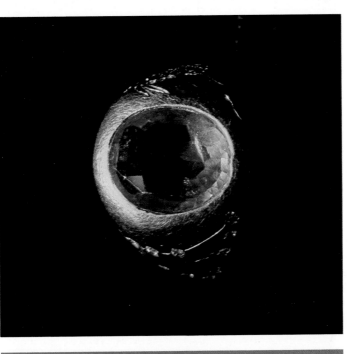

2.6 **Green sapphire**

This is the name given to the relatively uncommon, green variety of corundum. In the nineteenth century it was also known as "oriental emerald," just as violet and yellow corundum were called "oriental amethyst" and "oriental topaz." These names stemmed from a scant knowledge of mineralogy among gem merchants and have now been abandoned.

Appearance Due to its iron content, green sapphire is generally quite a strong, bright green color, sometimes with green to bluish green or yellowish green pleochroism. Individual stones are sometimes cut at different angles from the rough crystal, to bring out the best color. The luster is very good, as with all corundum. The mixed, oval cut is the most common, but square or rectangular step cuts are also used. These gems are usually small to medium-sized and rarely exceed a few carats.

Distinctive features The color is quite distinctive, especially combined with the particular luster of corundum. While green tourmaline can, at first glance, look fairly similar in color, it has more pronounced pleochroism, the direction corresponding to the bluer green often seeming rather opaque, and it is always, or nearly always, given a rectangular, step cut strictly aligned to the elongated shape of the prism. Green zircon can be quite similar to green sapphire in both color and luster, but it has far less obvious pleochroism and sometimes much stronger birefringence, easily detectable with a lens. Many green zircons, however, have weak or virtually nonexistent birefringence. In such cases, their density is also very similar to that of corundum, so the physical characteristics will need careful checking to establish a distinction.

Occurrence Green sapphire comes mainly from Australia, but it is also found in the United States (Montana) and Thailand.

Value As for all forms of corundum except ruby and sapphire, its value is quite low. It is perhaps worth a bit more than yellow sapphire, due to its greater rarity and the difficulty of finding stones of any size.

Simulants and synthetics Not being widely known or appreciated, this stone is not often imitated. But green synthetic corundum has occasionally been produced; it is of a brighter color than the natural mineral. Bluish green synthetic spinel has also been produced, whether to imitate green sapphire or zircon it is hard to say, as it bears little resemblance to either.

Above: Ring with yellow sapphire and small emeralds. Below: Green sapphire, 1.40 ct.

2.7 **Colorless sapphire**

When the crystal structure of corundum does not contain trace elements that act as colorants, it is completely clear, although this form is the least known and appreciated on the gem market. The name of leucosapphire, coined fairly recently, is derived from the Greek *leykòs,* meaning "white."

Appearance It is perfectly colorless or occasionally has a slight yellow tinge and has the typical luster of corundum. It can have fine veillike and lacelike liquid inclusions and even areas that look cloudy in bright light, due to the presence of fine, crossed needles or minute straws of rutile; it may also have small crystalline inclusions with minute cracks radiating from them, like much corundum from Sri Lanka. It is given a round (or almost round) mixed cut, or a slightly modified brilliant cut, having mainly been used as a substitute for diamond.

Distinctive features Despite its luster, it is very easily distinguished from diamond, which it was once meant to simulate. It has less dispersion and fire, plus weak birefringence, where visible. Diamond, of course, is singly refractive. The faint yellow coloration of some colorless sapphires can, however, make them more plausible as imitations. Colorless corundum is distinguished from colorless zircon by the pronounced birefringence of the latter.

Occurrence Colorless sapphire comes mainly from Sri Lanka, where quantities of light-colored corundum are found, but is apparently also found in Burma and elsewhere. It is of little interest as a gemstone and is chiefly used for industrial purposes as an abrasive.

Value Very low, but hard to quantify, as it now has scarcity value for collectors and amateurs.

Stimulants and synthetics Colorless corundum has not been imitated, but was formerly used to imitate diamond. It has been produced synthetically and as with the other pale varieties, the internal features characteristic of Verneuil synthetic corundum are very well disguised. Synthetic leucosapphire is used mainly as a diamond simulant, particularly for small stones, in which the differences are less apparent.

Above: Ring with green sapphire, 1.83 ct. Below: Colorless sapphire, 1.50 ct.

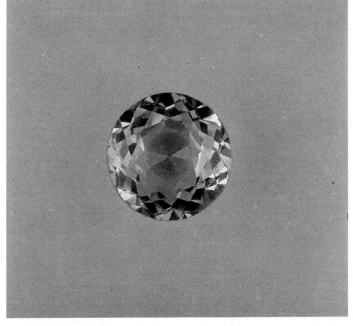

2.8 Star rubies and sapphires. Different-colored asteriae

Corundum often contains very fine needles of rutile (TiO_2) arranged in intersecting lines in accordance with the symmetry of the crystal. These apparently develop when the stone is formed: as the temperature falls, the TiO_2 is no longer soluble in the Al_2O_3 and forms separate crystals. When the needles inside the corundum are particularly numerous, and the stone is cut *en cabochon,* with its base (or widest diameter) parallel to the base of the prism, a silk-type reflection is visible in bright light; it is fairly mobile and has the appearance of a six-rayed star, the closer and thicker the rutile needles inside, the more clearly this stands out. When reasonably pronounced, this effect is considered attractive, contributing in the past to the aura of mystery surrounding some gemstones.

Appearance The most striking phenomenon of rubies and sapphires is the development of the six-ray star, arranged in perfect symmetry, which shifts its center as the stone is moved. It is clearly visible under a single light source such as the sun or a lamp; much less so in diffuse light. If two or more powerful light sources are set close together, as many stars (their centers not far apart) can be seen in the stone. Each light produces its own star, which is basically a reflection. The effect is usually less pronounced in more transparent stones. The ground color can be ruby red (or an almost grayish, dull red), in which case it is known as a star ruby, or sapphire blue, in which case it is known as a star sapphire, but it can also be blue-gray, smoke gray, or blackish, all of which come under the name of asteria, a generic term also applied to ruby and sapphire. Such stones are invariably given a round or oval cabochon cut. The most highly prized are the ruby-colored (provided they are not the opaque, grayish red of some Indian rubies) and sapphire blue varieties. The others are less valuable, but still sought after, provided the star is clearly visible and they are not too small (3 or 4 carats, at least). Some star stones may weigh 10 carats or more.

Distinctive features The star with its distinctive mobility is characteristic, having six rays, unlike star diopside, for example, which has four. But to be certain of distinguishing star corundum from the widely divergent (but very few) other gems which can display the phenomenon of asterism, one normally has to measure the physical properties.

Occurrence Rare but magnificent star rubies and sapphires are found in Burma, although most star corundums come from Sri Lanka, usually being light blue or gray. Dark asteriae are found in Australia, and dull red, opaque specimens are found in India. Despite being rubies and displaying the phenomenon of asterism, these stones are not very attractive.

Value Star rubies and sapphires of good or even above-average color are distinctly valuable, as much so as faceted stones of similar color. The value of the grayish or dark asteriae is lower, though not much, for unusually fine specimens. On the other hand, comparatively small stones of insipid color or with a poorly defined star are worth a

Above: Photomicrograph of the star in a star sapphire.
Below: The "Star of Asia" star sapphire, 330 ct.

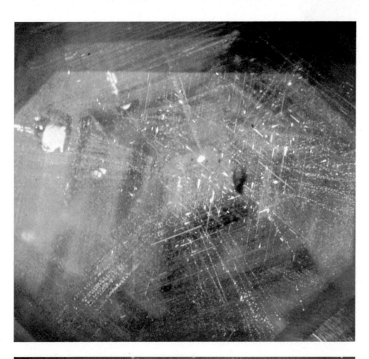

great deal less, and the same applies to dull-colored rubies, which often have a broad, smudgy star.

Simulants and synthetics Because of their undoubted attraction, star stones have been imitated in various ways. Efforts have been made to produce a star by engraving it on the base of a cabochon, or lining the base with a sheet of metal engraved with a six-rayed star. Milky quartz, which exhibits a weak form of the same type of asterism, has also been used, the base of the cabochon being covered with blue lacquer to give color to the stone and increase the contrast with the star; but the effect is somewhat different from that of natural star stones. In the last few decades, however, some manufacturers of synthetic corundum (using the Verneuil method) have found a way of producing both red and blue star stones with very pronounced stars (more pronounced than the natural versions), which are not as a rule too transparent and have an attractive, lively color; and these have been a great success in the United States.

Above: "Rosser Reeves" star ruby, 138 ct.
Below: Blue-gray asteria, 1.50 ct. Sri Lanka.

114

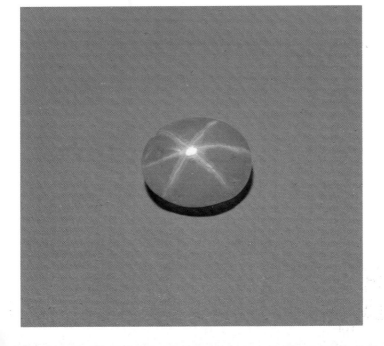

3 CHRYSOBERYL

$BeAl_2O_4$

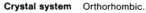

Crystal system Orthorhombic.

Appearance Single crystals are rare. Chrysoberyl is usually found as V-shaped twins or sometimes repeated twinning of flattened crystals, giving an appearance of hexagonal symmetry. It is normally cloudy, but when transparent, has considerable luster. The most common color is yellow, but it can also be grayish, greenish yellow, or even more or less green.

Physical properties It is quite hard: 8.5 on Mohs' scale, with a density of around $3.7 \ g/cm^3$. The refractive indices are roughly $n\alpha$ 1.74, and $n\gamma$ 1.75. It has weak prismatic cleavage.

Genesis Chrysoberyl occurs in granite-pegmatites and is an uncommon mineral.

Occurrence It is found in some pegmatites in the United States, in the Ural mountains in the Soviet Union, and in Sri Lanka, Rhodesia, Brazil, Madagascar, and Italy.

3.1 Alexandrite

This extremely rare gemstone of fairly recent history owes its name to the fact that it was first discovered in the Urals in 1830, on the day of Prince Alexander of Russia's coming of age.

Appearance Green: it can be almost emerald-colored, but is more often yellowish or brownish green. Its main characteristic is the ability to change color if exposed to a light source rich in red rays; by candlelight or tungsten light, it turns red or reddish. This unusual phenomenon is what distinguishes it from other green chrysoberyl. This pronounced color change from green to red is highly prized and, as always, the exact tone of the color, or colors, is important, the ideal being brilliant green turning to fiery red, although dull green turning reddish or slightly turbid blood red is more common, and given alexandrite's extreme rarity, even stones with a number of inclusions are cut. It is given an oval or round, mixed cut, or a rectangular, step cut. Alexandrite is so rare that few people have ever seen one; and perhaps for this reason, the name is applied to other, mainly synthetic stones, not remotely like it (usually violet-colored synthetic corundums).

Distinctive features The changing color is an unmistakable characteristic. However, in the last few years, small quantities of green or bluish-colored grossular garnet that turn red like alexandrite have been found in East Africa. To distinguish between the two, it is useful to look for signs of birefringence, as garnet, unlike alexandrite, is singly refractive. The refractive indices of the two stones, on the other hand, are very similar, as are their densities.

Occurrence Found in limited quantities in the Soviet Union, Brazil, Sri Lanka, and some East African countries (Zimbabwe and Tanzania).

Value Fine stones are extremely valuable and on a par with emeralds, rubies, and sapphires. When the colors are

Above: Rough tabular ''trilling'' (three intergrown crystals) of alexandrite chrysoberyl from the Urals.
Below: Alexandrite, 0.15 ct. Zimbabwe.

dullish, the value falls appreciably, but because of its rarity, all alexandrite is expensive. It is a collector's item.

Simulants and synthetics Attempts have been made in the past to imitate alexandrite's change in color using synthetic spinel and corundum, but the results have been modest. More recently, a violet-colored synthetic corundum has been widely marketed under the name of alexandrite, despite its lack of any real similarity to the natural stone. However, many who have never seen true alexandrite apply the name to this synthetic corundum and possibly for this reason, some manufacturers of synthetic corundum call their violet stones ''alexandrite type.'' Synthetic alexandrite has also recently been produced, but mainly for industrial purposes. For the time being, therefore, synthetic alexandrite is even rarer than the natural variety.

3.2 **Chrysoberyl**

This is the true chrysoberyl, also known as golden chrysoberyl, a synonym, the prefix ''chryso'' being Greek for ''golden.'' It is the most common variety of chrysoberyl.

Appearance The color varies from yellow to greenish yellow or green, brownish yellow, or pale yellow. It has basically the same color range as cat's eye (cymophane) with a bit more green or brown.

Mixed oval or round cuts or even triangular, marquise, or pear-shaped cuts are all used—any cut, in fact, which can set off the excellent luster of the stone, and allow it to be used even in jewelry of complex design.

Distinctive features The color can frequently be fairly similar to that of certain beryls, or to some particularly yellow olivines; but it has greater luster than these two stones. It also has quite different refractive indices and a different density from that of beryl. When the color is pale yellow, it can closely resemble what is known as yellow sapphire, but the density is different.

Occurrence Chrysoberyl is mainly found in Brazil, Sri Lanka, and Madagascar.

Value Although of some importance in the past, it is comparatively little known and appreciated today, probably on account of its rather weak color. Its value is accordingly quite low, about the same as that of beryls, tourmalines, and spinels of unexceptional color.

Simulants and synthetics Very occasionally, a few greenish yellow synthetic spinels, which could be regarded as imitations of chrysoberyl, appear on the gem market. Synthetic yellow chrysoberyl, on the other hand, does not appear to exist on the market, which is hardly surprising, given the modest value of the genuine article and the complexity and high cost of synthesis.

Above: Twinned crystal of true chrysoberyl from Brazil. Below: Chrysoberyl.

3.3 Cat's-eye or Cymophane

This is the name given to the yellow, yellow-green or gray-green variety of chrysoberyl, which displays the phenomenon of chatoyancy because of the inclusion of numerous fine, parallel crystal needles.

Appearance   The color is greenish yellow or yellowish, sometimes with a rather cold, almost grayish tone. Some fine stones are a honey brown. In the proper light, the near side will appear yellowish white while the brown of the far side will be intensified, creating a milk-and-honey effect. Cat's-eye is always cut *en cabochon*, round or oval, to emphasize the cat's eye effect, and can be fairly transparent. Due to its hardness, it takes and maintains good luster, and the more pronounced and pleasing the cat's-eye effect, the greater is its value.

Distinctive features   The most common cat's-eye stones are the quartzes, which, however, usually have a rather different color from chrysoberyl and are less transparent with brighter, but more superficial, chatoyancy. If there is any doubt, they can immediately be distinguished by their different density, because refractive indices are always hard to establish for curved stones.

Occurrence   Cymophanes are mainly found in Sri Lanka and Brazil, although they are not common.

Value   Cat's-eye is highly prized by collectors and connoisseurs. Its value is accordingly quite high. Very fine examples are less valuable than the principal gemstones, including alexandrite, but more so, for example, than a fine topaz or spinel. Due to its value and hardness, it is also known as "noble cat's-eye."

Simulants and synthetics   Various natural stones have been used as substitutes, including fluorite, which, however, is much softer, and kornerupine, a gem still rarer than cymophane, with lower hardness and density. Quartz has also been used, although its color rarely resembles that of cymophane and its density is also much lower. To our knowledge, no attempts have been made to produce this gem synthetically.

Two cabochons of cymophane, the cat's-eye par excellence.

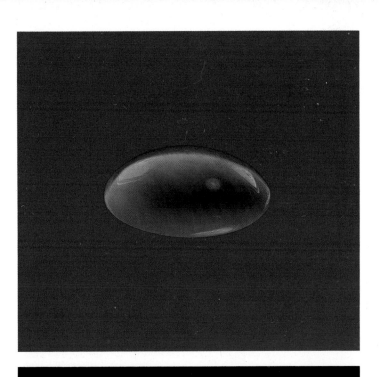

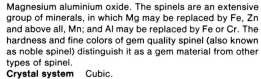

4 SPINEL
$MgAl_2O_4$

Magnesium aluminium oxide. The spinels are an extensive group of minerals, in which Mg may be replaced by Fe, Zn and above all, Mn; and Al may be replaced by Fe or Cr. The hardness and fine colors of gem quality spinel (also known as noble spinel) distinguish it as a gem material from other types of spinel.

Crystal system Cubic.

Appearance It normally occurs as distinct octahedra, as clusters also of octahedral habit, or as characteristic twins. The crystals are often isolated, sometimes aggregated, fairly complete, lustrous, and with a color varying from red to pink, violet red, pale lilac, violet blue, blue, or black. The possible color range is almost as extensive as that of corundum. It can be found as rolled pebbles in alluvium.

Physical properties Spinel has a hardness of 8. It is singly refractive, with an index of 1.71 or a little more. The density is 3.58–3.61 g/cm^3.

Genesis Spinel is formed by regional metamorphism or contact metamorphism in limestones, and also schists. It is also found in pegmatitic, pneumatolytic environments, together with corundum, and in alluvial deposits.

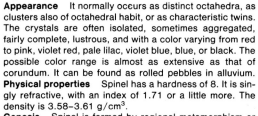

1.71

Occurrence It mainly occurs in Afghanistan, India, Burma, or the gem gravels of Sri Lanka, Madagascar, and Brazil.

4.1 Red spinel

The name spinel may come from the Latin *spina* or "thorn," referring to the triangular shape of the crystal faces, or from the Greek root *spinter,* meaning "spark," presumably referring just to the red variety. Like ruby and garnet, it has also been called "carbuncle," from the Latin *carbunculus,* or "small coal." However, recognition that the various types of carbuncle differed in hardness, led to their being valued accordingly. Undesirable confusion has been created by the alternative name of ruby spinel; and in fact, some of the largest and most famous "rubies" in the world, such as the "Black Prince's Ruby" in the English crown jewels, are really spinels, not corundums.

Appearance Spinel may be an intense, bright redlike ruby, but more often tends to be brick red, almost orange. It can have a violet tinge, and such stones were formerly referred to as Balas ruby, after the Badakshan (Balascia) region of Afghanistan where they were found. The color is often soft: pink, rather than red. Spinel has good luster and transparency. It is generally given a mixed, oval or round cut; alternatively, a square or rectangular, step or trap cut.

In earlier times, perfectly octahedral crystals were used in jewelry as they were, uncut, like diamonds. Stones found as worn pebbles or irregular pieces were summarily rounded and then polished, like some large spinels now seen in museums.

Distinctive features Red spinel is fairly similar to ruby; the red color fluoresces slightly in bright light, but much

Above: Crystal of noble spinel. Below: Red spinel.

less than ruby. Being singly refractive, it is not pleochroic. This feature is in contrast to ruby but in common with garnet, although the latter is nearly always a rather dull color, which is not heightened even by strong light. It can be hard to distinguish spinel from either of these gemstones, in which case the physical properties will need to be measured. However, spinel may contain several parallel rows of minute octahedral crystals of hercynite (iron spinel), which are highly distinctive and sometimes recognizable with an ordinary lens. Soft pink varieties can be hard to distinguish from some tourmalines, although the latter display varying degrees of birefringence, and have different physical properties.

Occurrence Red and pink spinels come from the Mogok region of Burma and Afghanistan. Spinels may also come from Sri Lanka and Thailand, where they are found together with corundum.

Value As secondary gems go, brilliant red spinels comparable in color to rubies are quite valuable, though they are only one-tenth or so the price of rubies themselves.
Pale pink or violet spinels, except for particularly fine or large specimens, are of much lower value.

Simulants and synthetics Synthetic spinel in many colors has been widely produced by the flame fusion method, but owing to difficulties in obtaining the red variety, the only examples found are extremely rare and of small size—a maximum of one carat or little more. These are distinguished from the natural variety by the typical internal structure and inclusions of gems produced by the Verneuil method. Recently, synthetic red spinel has also been produced by the more costly flux melt process, but it has not proved economical.

4.2 Blue spinel

The blue variety of noble spinel was in the past much less widely known and appreciated than the red variety.

Appearance The finest specimens, though rare, have a bright blue color comparable to that of some sapphires and are very attractive, lustrous, and transparent. Almost as pleasing are equally lustrous light violet-blue stones, resembling some sapphires of the same color. Most blue spinels, however, are a deep, dull color tending to sooty gray, albeit with a violet tinge; and their luster and transparency are marred by a touch of cloudiness. These are often cut quite shallow, in an attempt to lighten the color, usually with modest results. Like sapphires, they are normally given a mixed, oval cut.

Distinctive features Fine blue spinels are hard to distinguish at first sight from sapphires of a similar color. The latter may display clear pleochroism, but this is not always the case, particularly with medium to light blue specimens. Hence lack of pleochroism is not a sure distinction. But there is a marked variation in density, which is easy to establish, and the refractive indices are also different. Cloudy, deep-blue spinels, on the other hand, are quite distinctive.

Occurrence   Blue spinel is mainly found in the gem gravels of Sri Lanka and, rarely, in Burma.

Value   Attractively colored blue stones, which are rare
and not very large, are worth much the same as the red variety, whereas the fairly common, cloudy, less attractive
stones are very modestly priced.

Simulants and synthetics   Like synthetic ruby, dark-blue
synthetic spinel was one of the first synthetic gems to be
manufactured, at the beginning of the twentieth century.
Synthetic stones were not intended to imitate natural
spinel, but the much more precious sapphire, after early
unsuccessful attempts to synthesize the latter.

Synthetic spinel was colored by adding cobalt (in natural
sapphire, the coloring agent is iron). As a result, if one of
these stones is exposed to strong, tungsten light, it emits
strange gleams of red fluorescence of a type not seen in
any other stone, and this can be a valuable aid to recognition. Light-blue synthetic spinel is also produced in considerable quantities, to simulate another gem: aquamarine.

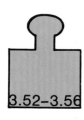

3.52–3.56

| 1.64 | 1.63 |
| 1.62 | 1.61 |

5 TOPAZ

$Al_2(SiO_4)(OH,F)_2$

Silicate of aluminium containing fluorine and hydroxyl. In earlier times, the name topaz mainly referred to a gemstone, olivine, extracted on an island then known as Topazos or St. John, and now called Zebirget in the Red Sea. It was probably also given to other, yellowish or yellow stones which were indistinguishable from one another without an adequate knowledge of chemistry and mineralogy. The name began to be applied to the mineral and gemstone now known as topaz in the first half of the eighteenth century.

Crystal system Orthorhombic.

Appearance Often found in short to long prismatic crystals, sometimes with characteristic terminal faces. It is often white, semiopaque, milky, or tinged a dirty yellow, but may be transparent, colorless, honey colored, golden brown, brown, or blue; much more rarely, pink or reddish. The transparent, colored crystals, which also have good luster, are widely used as gems.

Physical properties It has a hardness of 8 and a density of $3.52–3.56$ g/cm^3. The refractive indices are roughly $n\alpha$ 1.610, $n\gamma$ 1.618 or $n\alpha$ 1.630, $n\gamma$ 1.638. The density and refractive indices are interrelated and depend on the composition of the specimen: topazes richest in hydroxyl (OH) have a low density and high refractive indices, whereas those richest in fluorine have a higher density and low refractive indices. The stone has easy perfect basal cleavage.

Genesis Topaz is characteristic of pegmatitic and pneumatolytic deposits and is therefore found in dykes and contact aureoles around granitic intrusions. It is also found in alluvial deposits, but is, perhaps, the most vulnerable of the harder gemstones to attack by the elements, at least in tropical or equatorial regions.

Occurrence The mineral first classified scientifically as topaz came from Saxony. The topazes of Brazil are famous, some being of gigantic proportions. Topazes are also found in Mexico, the United States, Sri Lanka, Japan, the Soviet Union (both in Siberia and in the Urals), Nigeria, and Zaire, to mention just the main sources.

5.1 Topaz

True topaz or yellow topaz is the most typical variety, and no adjectives are needed to describe its color, although different shades are sometimes referred to as "golden topaz" or "sherry topaz."

Appearance The color can range from golden to honey yellow or can be golden brown or honey with a pink or reddish tinge. The crystals are usually cut into oval gems but pear and other mainly elongated shapes are also produced, usually with a crown and pavilion consisting of very many small lozenge-shaped facets, which bring out the luster of the stone. The longer stones often look darker at the ends. Easy basal cleavage makes these gems rather brittle, so they should be treated with care and protected

Above: Topaz crystal.
Below: Yellow topaz.

from the type of sharp blows to which ring stones are susceptible. Medium-large stones are relatively common, and even very large ones are not rare.

Distinctive features   A great deal of citrine quartz, which looks fairly similar, is sold under the name of topaz or topaz citrine, creating some confusion on the market. The color of topaz is, however, generally much warmer and more likely to have an orange or pinkish tone. The stone will also have a much greater luster. In any event, a quick check of the density, perhaps using one of the heavy liquids, would immediately distinguish between the two, and measurement of the refractive indices would remove all trace of doubt.

Occurrence   Topaz comes mainly from Brazil, and in smaller quantities, from the Soviet Union, Japan, Sri Lanka, Burma, and the United States. It is occasionally found in Germany.

Value   Well colored, medium-large specimens of true topaz are quite valuable, but perhaps less so today than in the past. Roughly on a par with secondary gemstones, such as the better tourmalines, it has probably suffered from the ready availability of citrine quartz, an inferior stone, which, by usurping the name, has made topaz seem more abundant than it really is.

Simulants and synthetics   The main problem is the practice of passing citrine quartz off as topaz. Synthetic corundum of a color similar to topaz has also been produced by way of imitation, whereas topaz itself has only been synthesized on a limited scale for scientific purposes and is not found on the market.

5.2 Pink topaz

As already mentioned, true or yellow topaz may be pinkish orange or yellow with a pink tinge. There is in fact a whole range of color gradations from yellow to pink, and it is hard to establish a dividing line between the two varieties.

Appearance   In some cases the color is pink with a distinctive yellowish or orange shade, but it is more often a definite light to medium pink, tending to red or violet in deeper colored stones. The color is not always evenly distributed and can show slight crystallographic zoning. The stones usually have few inclusions and are strongly transparent and lustrous.

The most common cut is the oval or pear shape, but many other old or antique faceted cuts are seen, as is the step cut. While it has always been comparatively rare, pink topaz was much appreciated in antique jewelry and stones weighing up to 10 carats are often found.

Distinctive features   At first sight, there is not a lot of difference between pink topaz, kunzite, morganite, and some pink tourmalines. But a density test with a heavy liquid such as methylene iodide, in which topaz sinks but the others float, will distinguish topaz from the others. It is harder to tell pink topaz apart from pink spinel and pink corundum, the former having about the same density as topaz, and the latter having a higher density. In case of

*Above: Yellow topaz,
1.50 ct. Brazil.
Below: Violet pink
topaz.*

confusion with these stones, other properties, such as the refractive indices, need to be examined.

Occurrence Pink topaz comes mainly from Brazil, but has also been mined recently in the Ural mountains of the Soviet Union. In both places, intensely colored reddish or purplish specimens have very occasionally been found.

Value When the color is fairly intense, it is one of the most valuable of the second level of gemstones (e.g. aquamarine). Specimens that are too pale have a low value. Like yellow topaz, it was perhaps more highly prized in the past than today.

Simulants and synthetics At one time glass imitations were occasionally produced. In antique jewelry, very pale stones were sometimes given a closed setting with a painted base to heighten their color.

The pink color of many topazes is due to heat treatment of pinkish-yellow stones from Brazil. This method goes back at least several centuries, so even antique stones may have been colored in this way. This procedure, however, has always been regarded as admissible in the gem trade, so the question of whether the color of pink topaz is natural or due to heat treatment does not arise.

5.3 Blue topaz

This is the variety of topaz most readily available on the market today.

Appearance It has a definite, uniform sky-blue color, usually without any overtones. Often pale, it can be bright or very rarely an intense blue. It sometimes has a slight gray or even greenish tinge, giving it a lifeless appearance. Gemstones of several carats or even several tens of carats in weight are relatively common. Furthermore, they are usually wholly or almost free of inclusions. This is often the case where large amounts of material of no great value are available; the less clear pieces are discarded. The most common cut is the oval, with the crown and pavilion consisting of very many lozenge-shaped facets, but all the mixed cuts, plus the step cut, are used. As with all light-colored gemstones, the value of blue topaz increases with intensity of color, provided this is attractive and not somber. Like other types of topaz, it cleaves readily and this can affect its durability.

Distinctive features There is, at first sight, some resemblance to aquamarine; but close observation will distinguish the two, as aquamarine always displays a very attractive pleochroism from blue to greenish blue or even bluish green. Topaz is usually a more definite blue, if anything with a grayish tone, which certainly distinguishes it from aquamarine. Measurement of the density alone is not enough to distinguish topaz from synthetic blue spinel, which can be very similar in color. Before measuring other physical properties, such as the refractive indices, the stone can be examined under a lens for signs of birefringence. Although faint, a doubling of the facet edges will be visible in topaz. If this is present, one can immediately rule out the possibility of its being synthetic spinel or glass, both of which are singly refractive.

Above: Pink topaz.
Below: Blue topaz.

Occurrence   Blue topaz is found in various parts of Brazil, Mexico, and the United States. It is mined in Burma (in
the Mogok region famous for rubies) and the Soviet Union
(chiefly in the Urals and the Kamchatka peninsula). It is
also found in Namibia and Nigeria.

Value   Quite low, several times less than that of aquamarine. The ready availability of blue topaz on the market,
even in pieces of considerable size, is probably responsible for this.

Simulants and synthetics   Because blue topaz is a relatively minor gemstone compared with aquamarine, it is the
latter that is imitated by glass or synthetic blue spinel. Although blue topaz has not been manufactured synthetically
on a commercial scale, a completely natural-looking blue
coloration has been produced during recent years in colorless topaz by means of irradiation. This practice, regarded
as legitimate in the trade, unless performed in such a way
as to cause appreciable residual radiation (fortunately,
very uncommon), is becoming increasingly widespread
and is one of the reasons for the present abundance of
blue topaz.

5.4 Colorless topaz

As a mineral, this is far and away the most common variety
of transparent topaz, although it is of limited importance as
a gemstone. All colorless gemstones compare most unfa-
vorably with diamond, their lower refractive indices and
lesser dispersion making them far less attractive. Topaz
has the advantage over the others of being found in large
stones and great quantities, and of having good hardness
and luster. Therefore it is of some interest to hobbyists.

Appearance   Gemstones are generally free, or almost so,
of inclusions because they can be culled from the large
quantities available; but they may show signs of extensive
internal cleavage. In large stones (of a few centimeters) the
mineral's weak birefringence can be detected with the aid
of a lens, the facet edges appearing double when seen
through a flat facet of the stone. The stones easily acquire
good luster and are only disappointing on the rare occasions when they are given the brilliant cut, prompting comparison with diamonds, which have a very different luster
and "fire."

Distinctive features   Colorless topaz differs little from the
colorless varieties of other minor gems, which, with the exception of quartz, are all much rarer. Incipient cleavage,
where present, may be a distinguishing feature. If the
edges appear double, denoting birefringence, this can distinguish it from synthetic colorless spinel, which has a similar density; but it cannot differentiate it from other minor
gemstones such as colorless beryl, tourmaline, and corundum. To distinguish it with any certainty from these, the refractive indices must be determined.

Occurrence   It is found in various parts of Brazil, the Soviet Union, the United States, Germany (Saxony), and
Japan. Africa, too, has a plentiful supply of colorless topaz
in the tin-mining areas of both Nigeria and Zaire. It is also
found in Namibia.

Ring with yellow topaz.

Value One of the lowest for transparent gemstones, even though it is greatly appreciated by amateur cutters as a raw material. Apparently, it is being used increasingly for the production of blue topaz by means of irradiation.

Simulants and synthetics It is neither imitated nor produced synthetically.

6 BERYL

$Be_3Al_2Si_6O_{18}$

7.5–8

2.7

| 1.56 | 1.57 |
| 1.60 | 1.60 |

Silicate of beryllium and aluminium.

Crystal system Hexagonal.

Appearance Beryl crystallizes as fairly complete hexagonal prisms, sometimes with basal faces or small bipyramidal facets. The crystals can be very large—from a few centimeters, up to some tens of centimeters—with occasional specimens over a meter in length. Beryl is often cloudy and, when transparent, has a vitreous luster. It is usually an opaque, milky white, or a faint yellow, very pale gray or green color. Stronger, more attractive colors, however, also occur: mainly blue, green, yellow or pink. Although rare, red and colorless specimens do exist. Crystals that combine brilliant color with transparency are highly prized as gems.

Physical properties It has a hardness of 7.5 to 8, but is fairly brittle, and may show ill-defined cleavage parallel to the basal plane. The density is normally 2.67–2.72 g/cm^3, but can be as much as 2.90 g/cm^3. The refractive indices, like the density, are somewhat variable, from n_ϵ 1.560, n_ω 1.570 to n_ϵ 1.595, n_ω 1.602.

Genesis Beryl occurs as an accessory mineral in granite rocks, and crystallizes mainly in pegmatites, where the largest individual crystals are found. It is also formed by metasomatism in the country rock surrounding pegmatites, and is associated with hydrothermal processes.

Occurrence Beryl is very widespread; it occurs in pegmatites in many areas from northern Europe to North America, South America, East Africa, South Africa, and Himalayan Asia. It occurs also in calcite veins, as a process of hydrothermal activity in the bituminous limestones of Bogotá, Colombia.

6.1 Emerald

$Be_3(Al,Cr)_2Si_6O_{18}$

The name is of ancient origin. The Latin *smaragdus* appears, in fact, to have referred to the stone we call emerald, which is now considered as a distinct species. It is basically the green variety of beryl, although not all gem-quality green beryls are called emeralds: yellow-green stones are called heliodors; soft blue-green or even pale green specimens (their color due to iron, not chromium, as in emerald) are called aquamarines.

Appearance The typical color is a beautiful, distinctive hue known, in fact, as emerald green and is due to traces of chromium in the crystal structure. But emeralds can be light or dark green, bright green or leaf green. The vitreous luster is not outstanding, and is strongest in medium-light stones with few inclusions. All emerald contains inclusions, although in the best quality stones, these are very faint and not visible to the naked eye. They show up under a 10x, 20x, or 40x lens. The most common shape for gems is the step or trap cut, which is also known as the emerald cut. They are occasionally given a mixed, oval cut, while antique stones are found with hexagonal, step cuts, cabo-

Above: Crystal of emerald beryl. Below: Emerald.

138

chon cuts, or pear shapes with a hole in them, often used as pendants.

Distinctive features   The typical emerald color is virtually unmistakable. It is only equalled by some very rare specimens of jadeite jade, which, however, is less transparent and has different physical properties. To the initiated, the inclusions in emerald can be highly distinctive: a bubble of gas in a liquid (like a spirit level), within spindle-shaped or, more rarely, truncated prismatic cavities; birefringent, circular plates of mica; multifaceted pyrite crystals or calcite rhombohedra. However, a microscope is almost always needed to recognize them. Although not the typical emerald color, some green tourmalines may look similar, but they can be distinguished either by their marked pleochroism, or by the fact that tourmalines which are given an emerald cut display alternating, longitudinal lines of lighter or darker color, when viewed through the table facet. Olivine may also be a verdant green color vaguely similar to that of some atypical emeralds; but the powerful birefringence of olivine is detectable with a simple lens, a double image of the opposite facet edges being clearly visible in certain directions through the table facet. In any case, the density of either tourmaline or olivine immediately distinguishes the stone from emerald.

Occurrence   The biggest and most beautiful emeralds come from the famous Chivor and Muzo mines of Colombia. Much smaller quantities of emeralds, mostly of medium-light color, come from Brazil, and small, very intensely colored stones, characterized by numerous minute inclusions of molybdenite with a metallic appearance, are found in the Transvaal.

In the last few decades, increasing quantities of emeralds have been found in a series of small deposits in East Africa—principally in Zimbabwe, Zambia, and Tanzania. These are quite a strong color, sometimes with a bluish-green tinge; and they often contain mica plates and, sometimes, thin crystal needles. The most famous of these emeralds are the ones from Sandawana in Zimbabwe, which are valued for their color. Emeralds with similar characteristics also come from the mountains of India and Pakistan, as well as the Soviet Union (Urals), and formerly Austria.

Value   Stones of fine color, weighing more than 2 carats, are among the most highly valued gemstones, and their price may equal or exceed that of diamonds. Less ideally colored varieties—too dark or too pale—are worth quite a lot less; and if they are slightly turbid as well, the value is reduced even further.

Simulants and synthetics   The Romans are known to have imitated emerald with skilfully worked green glass. Glass was also used in later centuries, extraneous particles sometimes being incorporated to simulate inclusions.

Doublets have also been used as imitations, with a lower portion of green glass and a top portion of garnet, or triplets, with a layer of colored cement sandwiched between two layers of colorless beryl, synthetic spinel, or quartz. Synthetic emeralds have likewise been widely produced over the last few decades. Generally of good color, these are mainly distinguished from the natural variety by their

Above: Inclusions in an emerald (photomicrograph).
Below: Jewelry with emerald and diamonds.

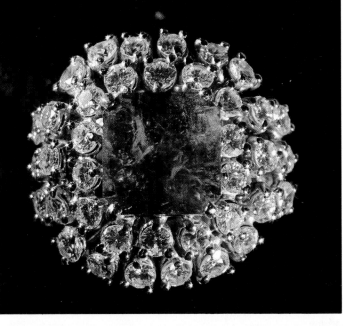

inclusions and other growth features. There are a lot of these synthetic stones about, but their cost is quite high, so that the market for them is saturated.

6.2 Aquamarine

The name refers to the palish blue, light blue-green or even light green variety of beryl. The green of aquamarine is a watery green without any trace of yellow and is due to iron, not chromium, as can be seen from examination with a gemological spectroscope.

Appearance   The most valuable color is a rich, sky blue; but because the stone is pleochroic, even the blue stones have a green or greenish-blue tinge in one direction. Quite large stones, ranging from several carats to more than ten or a few tens of carats, are relatively common. Many are virtually free of inclusions. (Again, where there is plenty of material available, poor quality specimens do not usually come to market.) The luster is vitreous and not exceptional. The most common cut is the emerald type, although mixed oval or pear-shaped cuts are not infrequent.

Distinctive features   The color of this stone, combined with its particular type of pleochroism and vitreous luster, distinguishes it fairly easily from blue topaz and light-blue synthetic spinel, the first being a definite blue color, the second having a gray or violet tinge, much stronger luster and no pleochroism.

Occurrence   Most aquamarine comes from the pegmatites of Brazil, where crystals weighing several kilos have been found. Other deposits are in the Soviet Union (Transbaikalia, Urals, and Siberia), Madagascar, the United States, and, recently, Afghanistan.

Value   Rich blue stones several carats in weight are among the most valuable of secondary gems. They are worth a lot more, for instance, than blue topaz of similar characteristics. Pale or green stones are much less valuable.

Simulants and synthetics   Aquamarine is imitated by blue glass, which faithfully reproduces the color, if not the pleochroism, but it is most often imitated by blue synthetic spinel, of a slightly different color, with superior luster and no pleochroism. Because of the general similarity, this is sometimes called synthetic aquamarine, although the latter, as such, is not produced. Light green or yellow-green beryl can be turned blue by heating it to a certain temperature for a certain length of time. This practice has been in use for several decades and is considered acceptable, as with zircon and sapphire.

Aquamarine crystal.

6.3 **Morganite**

The pink variety of beryl is named after the famous American banker and gem enthusiast John Pierpont Morgan.

Appearance   The color is usually quite a soft pink without any overtones. The pleochroism is not noticeable. It has glassy luster, like other beryls. The stones are usually fairly free of inclusions. Sometimes, however, irregular liquid and gaseous inclusions, of very uneven shape, are just visible. The step cut is most frequently used. Morganite is not a common gem, but specimens are often medium to large. As always with light-colored stones, the more richly colored specimens are in greater demand.

Distinctive features   Morganite is not easily distinguished from kunzite, pink topaz, and the more attractively colored pink tourmalines, except, of course, by its physical characteristics; but it is quite readily distinguished from dull pink tourmalines. It is less lustrous than pink sapphire and often a different color. In general, pink stones, unless of a distinctive shade, are not easy to identify visually. On the other hand, establishment of the stone's density will narrow the field and will usually be sufficient for positive identification.

Occurrence   Morganite is mainly found in pegmatites in the United States (California), Brazil, and Madagascar.

Value   Richly colored stones of at least a few carats are among the more valuable secondary gems. The price falls a lot for more weakly colored specimens.

Simulants and synthetics   Not being widely known, Morganite is not as a rule imitated, nor is it produced synthetically.

6.4 **Golden Beryl**

Yellow-colored beryl does not have a special name. As with the vast majority of stones of this color, however, the adjective *golden* is applied, at least where the color is particularly strong and lively.

Appearance   As the name implies, the color is yellow, ranging from almost canary to gold, in the best examples; other stones are a dull yellow, sometimes with a hint of green. The stones are usually given a mixed, oval, or sometimes round cut. Gems even 10 or more carats in weight are not uncommon. Inclusions in the form of roughly parallel bundles of narrow tubules may be clearly visible with a lens and can reduce the stone's transparency and luster. The perfectly transparent stones with the richest color are of course the most valuable.

Distinctive features   Golden beryl can sometimes look very similar to yellow chrysoberyl, from which it is distinguished only by its physical characteristics. Establishment of the density by an appropriate choice of heavy liquid would suffice. It is usually much less lustrous than yellow sapphire, which often has distinctive inclusions. It is normally a different shade from citrine quartz, and a different color from topaz, with inferior luster. Pale specimens are distinguished only by their physical characteristics from the rare gem-quality orthoclase of the same color.

Occurrence   Golden beryl is mainly found in Brazil, but also in the United States (chiefly Virginia and Massachusetts), and Madagascar.

Value   Brightly colored specimens are in demand with collectors and connoisseurs but among the lesser varieties of beryl, it is not one of the most valuable.

Simulants and synthetics   Not being widely known, it is neither imitated nor produced synthetically.

6.5 **Heliodor**

This name, meaning "gift of the sun," has been coined fairly recently for the yellow-green variety of beryl.

Appearance   Its main characteristic is its color, which is the yellow-green of olive oil. The shade, however, may vary considerably, and it is hard to establish a dividing line between heliodor and golden beryl. The normally medium or largish stones are generally given an oval or, more rarely, a step cut. They may have the liquid inclusions typical of beryl, but are usually quite clear.

Distinctive features   Yellower versions can look very much like olivine. But the strong birefringence of the latter, visible merely by observing the facet edges with a lens, readily distinguishes it. Heliodor may also be very similar to chrysoberyl; the latter, however, is usually more lustrous, and, of course, has different physical characteristics. Finally, heliodor can bear a resemblance to some yellow-green tourmalines, though the color of these is slightly duller. Here, too, the surest way to establish a distinction is by measuring the physical characteristics.

Occurrence   The best specimens come from Namibia, but heliodor is also found in Madagascar and Brazil.

Value   Collectors value heliodor at least as highly as aquamarine. It is not common on the market.

Simulants and synthetics   A yellow-green variety of synthetic spinel is used to imitate heliodor. Synthetic heliodor, however, does not exist.

6.6 Red beryl or bixbite

This is the extremely rare, ruby-red variety of beryl. The name bixbite is, however, controversial, due to the fact that it is easily confused with bixbyite, an opaque manganese-iron oxide of no gemological value, occurring, likewise, in rhyolite in the United States (Utah). Bixbite has a different origin from that of both emerald and pegmatite beryls, being found in effusive magmatic rocks, and is seen as small crystals, yielding gems usually no more than a carat in weight, although some may be 2 or 3 carats.

Appearance   Bixbite is a strong, almost ruby-red, or violet red, always with numerous inclusions and often, internal flaws. Its pleochroism is comparable to that of ruby.

Distinctive features   Too few examples have been seen to permit generalization. The refractive indices are high for beryl, ca. $n\epsilon$ 1.585, $n\omega$ 1.594.

Occurrence   Bixbite has only been found in rhyolite in the United States (Utah and New Mexico).

Value   Given its extreme rarity, attractive color and the publicity that surrounded its discovery, it is of high value, but extremely hard to come by, hence, an exclusive collector's item.

Simulants and synthetics   Being very little known, it has not been imitated, nor produced synthetically, at any rate not commercially.

Above: Bixbite crystal. United States (Utah).
Below: Bixbite, 0.85 ct. United States (Utah).

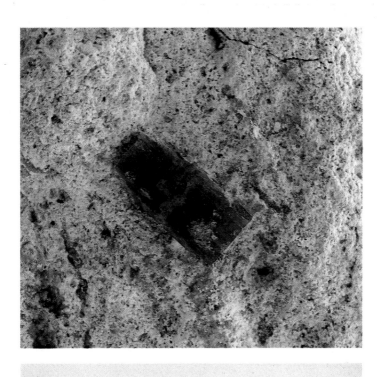

7 PYROPE-ALMANDINE GARNET

$(Fe,Mg)_3Al_2Si_3O_{12}$

7–7.5

3.6–4.2

1.73–1.83

Silicate of magnesium, iron, and aluminium, belonging to the garnet family. It is more correctly a group of minerals consisting of mixtures in variable proportions of the two end-members (the theoretical extremes are rarely if ever found in nature). Mixtures in which magnesium clearly predominates over iron are called pyrope; those in which iron predominates are called almandine.

The name garnet, now applied to the entire family, was originally given to the garnets of the pyrope-almandine series, due to their resemblance to red pomegranate seeds (Latin name, *malum granatum*).

Crystal system Cubic.

Appearance Usually in isolated, granular crystals, often in the form of a perfect rhombic dodecahedron. The color is often reddish brown, but can be a definite red, light red, violet red, or deep blackish red. The crystals, which are often semiopaque, can be transparent and limpid, with highly lustrous faces. They have no cleavage.

Physical properties The hardness is 7 or 7.5 (the higher figure refers to almandine). The density ranges from 3.65–3.87 g/cm³ for pyrope, to 3.95–4.20 g/cm³ for almandine. Likewise, the refractive index of about 1.730–1.751 for pyrope gradually increases, parallel to the density, to 1.76–1.83 for almandine.

Genesis Pyrope is normally found in peridotitic and eclogitic rocks and also in diamond-bearing kimberlite. Almandine is a characteristic mineral of metamorphic rocks. Due to their resistance to weathering, pyrope and almandine are often found in alluvial, secondary deposits or arenaceous rocks.

Occurrence This mineral is very widespread. Countries famous for garnets usable as gems include Czechoslovakia (Bohemia), South Africa, Madagascar, the United States, Mexico, Brazil, Australia, Burma, Sri Lanka, and India.

7.1 Pyrope

Magnesium-rich member of the pyrope-almandine series. The name comes from the Green *pyropós*, meaning "fiery," and is therefore similar to the Latin name *carbunculus* (small coal or ember), attributed to all red transparent stones. Its red color, sometimes very bright, is due to small quantities of chrome in the crystal structure.

Appearance Usually bright red, pyrope can be a much less attractive brick or dark red. It can be perfectly transparent, but this feature is less visible in dark specimens. It is either made into fairly convex cabochons, like almandine garnet, or faceted, with an oval or round mixed cut or, more rarely, a step cut. The faceted gems have good luster, rather less obvious in cabochons. The most valuable types are, of course, the transparent ones with the brightest red color. Pyrope is relatively common, although less so than almandine. Very large stones, up to several hundred

Above: Crystals of almandine garnet. Norway.
Below: Pyrope.

150

carats, have been found; but these are rare and are found in museums and famous collections.

Distinctive features Pyrope is singly refractive, but sometimes displays anomalous patches of birefringence and has a luster comparable to that of ruby and spinel. It is distinguished from the former by a lack of pleochroism and the fact that it does not turn bright red in strong light; but it can only be distinguished from the latter by measuring its physical characteristics. These are, however, somewhat variable, as iron is inevitably present, due to its isomorphic relationship with almandine. It is called pyrope when the density is between 3.65 and 3.87 g/cm^3 and the refractive index is between 1.730 and 1.751. (Stones with higher densities and refractive indices are called pyrope-almandine and then almandine.) The hardness is 7 or a little more.

Occurrence In the latter half of the nineteenth century, most pyrope came from Bohemia, where it is still found today. The main sources nowadays, however, are South Africa, Zimbabwe, Tanzania, the United States, Mexico, Brazil, Argentina, and Australia.

Value It is of quite low value as secondary gems go, probably due to its abundance. The darkest specimens, which are the most common, are worth very little. While even in early times pyrope could be distinguished from ruby because of its relative softness, it was more highly valued then than it is today, probably because of its color.

Simulants and synthetics Formerly, when it was more highly prized, pyrope was imitated by glass, which can look very similar, but does not have the same hardness. It is not produced synthetically.

7.2 Rhodolite

There is an intermediate group of garnets in the pyrope-almandine series. It is a deep pink or pinkish-red color (known as rhododendron pink) and is called rhodolite, from the Greek *rhódon*, "rose," and *líthos*, "stone." Rhodolite is a subvariety of pyrope-almandine characterized by its particular color.

Appearance The pinkish-red color is its main characteristic. The gems have good transparency and are almost always faceted, generally receiving a mixed, roughly oval or round cut. As always with transparent garnets, the luster is strong.

Distinctive features The color, luster and single refraction typical of garnets paint quite a clear picture. The stone is not, of course, pleochroic. The refractive index varies from 1.755 to 1.765 and the density from 3.74 to 3.94 g/cm^3—a very limited range. Rhodolite is distinguished from corundum of a similar color by its lack of pleochroism and the fact that it does not fluoresce in bright light, and from rubellite by its lack of pleochroism, greater luster, and absence of the marked birefringence of tourmaline, which is even visible with a lens. Its physical properties have to be measured, however, to distinguish it from spinel.

Occurrence Rhodolite is found in the United States, Zimbabwe, Tanzania, and Sri Lanka. It is not common.

Photomicrograph of inclusions in garnet.

152

Value Of the reddish garnets, it is in greater demand and therefore more valuable than pyrope and almandine.

Simulants and synthetics It is neither imitated, nor produced synthetically.

7.3 **Almandine**

Most remaining red garnets (usually a deep, violet-red) come under the name of almandine, even when their composition is midway between that of pyrope and almandine and similar, in many cases, too that of rhodolite. The reason for this is the similarity in their color and absorption spectrum characteristics. The name almandine comes from *carbunculus alabandicus,* after the city of Alabanda in Asia Minor, where gems were traded at the time of Pliny the Elder (*carbunculus,* as already explained, means ''small coal'' and has been used to refer to red stones in general).

Appearance The color is red, but often a deep, violet-red. It has brilliant luster, but its transparency is frequently marred, even in very clear stones, by excessive depth of color. The cabochon cut is widely used, often being given a strongly convex shape and sometimes a concave base, in an effort to lighten the color by reducing the thickness. Rose cuts have also been used, particularly in the past. Nowadays, when the material is quite transparent, faceted cuts are used as well, and sometimes square or rectangular step cuts. Gems of several carats are not uncommon. Faceted or even barely rounded pieces of almandine, pierced as necklace beads, were very common in the recent past, but are now considered old-fashioned.

Distinctive features The deep, almost violet-red is fairly typical, and has given rise to the expression ''garnet red.'' It is not enlivened, as are dark rubies, even by strong light, and its single refraction and lack of visible pleochroism should normally distinguish it from similarly colored rubellite. If fairly transparent faceted stones are viewed from above, some of the facets often look black on the inside (this is known as the ''garnet effect''). Almandine has a luster comparable to that of corundum. It is not easily distinguished from spinel, except by examining the physical properties, which can vary quite considerably, according to the composition: the density is between 3.95 and 4.20 g/cm^3, or thereabouts; the refractive index varies from 1.76 to 1.83 (the density increases parallel to the index). It has a hardness of about 6–7.5.

Above: Rhodolite.
Below: Almandine.
Namibia.

Above: Almandine cabochon.
Below: Crystals of spessartine garnet. Italy (Island of Elba).

Occurrence Almandine is obtained in large quantities from Sri Lanka and India, where it is also cut; other sources are Burma, Brazil, the United States, Madagascar, Tanzania, and Australia.

Value This depends on brightness of color and freedom from cracks and inclusions, but is always quite low. Almandine was extremely popular in the nineteenth century, but the name "garnet" is now automatically associated with cheap stones.

Simulants and synthetics Almandine has been imitated by glass, which can look very similar. It has apparently been produced synthetically, but not on a commercial basis.

8 SPESSARTITE GARNET (Spessartine)
$Mn_3Al_2Si_3O_{12}$

Silicate of manganese and aluminium, belonging to the garnet family. It is named after the Spessart region of Bavaria (West Germany), although only minor deposits are found there.

Crystal system Cubic.

Appearance Spessartine has the typical crystal form of garnets, usually occurring as isolated, well formed, rhombic dodecahedral crystals. The color is orange-pink, orange-red, or brownish yellow. It may be semiopaque or transparent. Transparent crystals are highly lustrous. It has no cleavage. The transparent specimens are used as gems.

Physical properties It has a hardness of 6.5–7.5. The density of gem-quality stones varies from 4.12 to 4.20 g/cm^3. The refractive index can vary from about 1.79 to 1.81.

Genesis Spessartine occurs in low-grade metamorphic rocks, but is uncommon.

Occurrence It is mainly found in the United States (Virginia and California), Mexico, and Madagascar, but also in West Germany and Italy (Piedmont and Val d'Aosta).

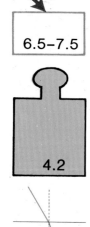

6.5–7.5

4.2

1.80

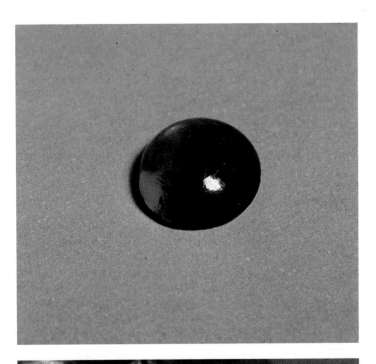

8.1 Spessartine

The gem variety of spessartine garnet is uncommon. It tends to be midway between spessartine and almandine in composition.

Appearance The "aurora red," orange-red or orange-pink color is typical. It has good transparency and considerable luster. It is normally given a mixed, round, or oval cut. The weight does not normally exceed a few carats. Gems of about 10 carats are extremely rare and usually of an atypical, rather dark, unattractive color.

Distinctive features The color, single refraction, and luster are useful means of identification, but the physical properties have to be measured to distinguish it, for instance, from some hessonite garnets. Examination of the absorption spectrum can be very useful; where clearly visible, which is not always the case, it is distinctive.

Occurrence Spessartine is extracted from the gem gravels of Sri Lanka and Burma. It is also found in the United States (Virginia and California), Brazil, and Madagascar.

Value Its value is a bit higher than pyrope and almandine, about the same as rhodolite. It is not often found on the market.

Simulants and synthetics It is neither imitated nor produced synthetically.

Above: Spessartine. Below: Crystals of grossular garnet. France.

---

9 GROSSULAR GARNET
$Ca_3Al_2Si_3O_{12}$

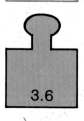

Silicate of calcium and aluminium, belonging to the garnet group. The name grossular is due to the fact that some of these crystals resemble gooseberries, the Latin name for which is *grossularia*.

Crystal system Cubic.

Appearance Grossular also has the typical crystal form of garnets, occurring in isolated crystals which are often complete, in the shape of a rhombic dodecahedron, sometimes combined with a trapezohedron. They vary from transparent to semiopaque. The typical color is light (gooseberry) yellowish green; but they can be a strong to bluish green, honey yellow or pinkish yellow, or even perfectly colorless. When transparent, the crystals have good luster. Like other garnets, they have no cleavage. The greenish to yellowish varieties are used as gems.

Physical properties The hardness is 6.5–7.5 or a little more. The density is somewhat variable: from 3.58 to 3.69 g/cm^3. The refractive index is about 1.74.

Occurrence Grossular is not a rare mineral. The types used as gems mainly come from the gem gravels of Sri Lanka (honey yellow variety); and the United States, Canada, Mexico, Madagascar, Kenya, and Tanzania (green variety).

6.5–7.5

3.6

1.74

9.1 **Hessonite**

The yellow-brown variety of grossular is called hessonite (or essonite). Its name comes from the Greek *ésson*, meaning "inferior," gems of this color being regarded as the least valuable.

Appearance   It is a honey-yellow or yellow-brown color, sometimes tending to a pinkish orange similar to that of spessartine. It has good luster and seemingly good transparency, but when viewed with a lens or other form of magnification, the interior always looks "treacly," with undulating, contorted areas of lesser transparency, like a highly concentrated sugar solution with frequent, rounded, transparent crystalline inclusions. The gems are normally given a mixed, oval, or round cut.

Distinctive features   Seen through a lens, the "treacly" appearance combined with the color are a sure means of identification. Nothing comparable is found in other gems of similar color, such as citrine quartz, topaz, and yellow sapphire. Its luster, in any case, is superior to that of citrine quartz. It is distinguished from zircon of a similar color by its lack of obvious birefringence.

Occurrence   It mainly comes from Sri Lanka, but is also found in the United States, Canada, and Brazil.

Value   The value of hessonite is rather low, like that of almandine and pyrope, despite its very attractive appearance.

Simulants and synthetics   It has neither been imitated nor produced synthetically.

9.2 **Green Grossular**

The green variety of grossular garnet, discovered a few decades ago and found mainly in Kenya, near the Tsavo National Park, is also known as Tsavorite (or Tsavolite).

Appearance   It is a light, verdant, or dark green, similar to the color of the better green tourmalines and sometimes, it is said, even comparable to African emerald. It has good luster. These gems, which are usually given a round or pear-shaped mixed cut, or occasionally a brilliant cut, are generally small, rarely exceeding one carat and never more than a few carats.

Distinctive features   Being singly refractive, green grossular is distinguished from green tourmaline, by the latter's strong birefringence and pleochroism, and from many green zircons, which are obviously birefringent, whereas measurement of the physical properties is necessary to distinguish it from green sapphire when the latter does not display clear pleochroism. It is very similar in all respects to a recent artificial product of comparable structure, namely green YAG (Yttrium Aluminium Garnet), from which it is distinguished by its physical properties.

Occurrence   It is very rare; being found mainly in Kenya and Tanzania, but also in Pakistan.

Value   If a good color (a lively, strong green), it can be in the top price bracket for secondary gems; this is especially true of the very rare examples weighing a few carats. Little

Above: Hessonite. Below: Tsavolite, 0.72 ct. Tanzania.

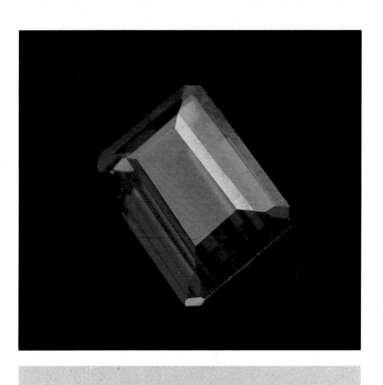

Above: Green grossular.
Below: Andradite garnet. Norway.

known by the general public, it is in demand by collectors and connoisseurs.

Simulants and synthetics   Green grossular has only been known for a few decades. Green YAG (an artificial product with the structure of garnet, but not containing silicon) closely resembles it and can be a good imitation. It is not produced synthetically.

---

10   ANDRADITE

$Ca_3Fe_2Si_3O_{12}$

6.5 – 7.5

3.8

1.88

Silicate of calcium and iron, belonging to the garnet group. It is named after a Portuguese mineralogist, J. B. D'Andrada.

Crystal system   Cubic.

Appearance   Andradite occurs in crystals in the form of a rhombic dodecahedron, like all garnets, or in convex aggregates of crystals, whose color varies with slight variations in the stone's composition, and which therefore have different names: the black variety is called melanite; the honey yellow variety topazolite; the green one, demantoid. It can also be blackish brown or blackish red. The crystals may be transparent, semiopaque, or opaque, and often have good luster.

Physical properties   These vary slightly according to the composition: the density ranges from 3.81 to 3.86 g/cm^3; the refractive index, from 1.882 to 1.889. The hardness is 6.5–7.5, similar to that of other garnets.

Genesis   It is found in metamorphosed limestone and, rarely, in certain intrusive and extrusive igneous rocks. The topazolite and demantoid varieties are found in serpentines, often together with asbestos.

Occurrence   Andradite is mainly found in alluvium in the Soviet Union (Urals) and the United States, but also in Norway and Germany.

10.1 **Demantoid**

This is a pale to clear green variety of andradite garnet, regarded as being comparable in luster to diamond; hence the name, attributed to it in the latter half of the nineteenth century.

Appearance   The color varies from a cold, very pale green (almost colorless with a green wash), to a mid or strong green, not as a rule a very lively color and similar to certain shades of green in tourmaline, zircon, or olivine. It often has good transparency and exceptional luster. Inclusions in the form of fine, curved fibers of asbestos are frequent and characteristic. These stones are usually given round, mixed, and brilliant cuts; more rarely, square or rectangular, step cuts. They are normally small. Specimens of more than one carat are uncommon, and those of several carats are extremely rare. Due to weakening inclusions the facets and edges are easily damaged with use.

Distinctive features   The greenish color combined with strong luster, single refraction, and possibly asbestos fiber inclusions, are quite characteristic. However, the physical properties have to be measured to distinguish it from green grossular, green YAG, and occasionally from certain green zircons with weak birefringence.

Occurrence   It is found mainly in the Soviet Union.

Value   Because of its attractive appearance, color (particularly when a lively, mid-green), and exceptional luster, plus its rarity, it is one of the most valuable secondary gems.

Simulants and synthetics   Green YAG, an artificial substance with the structure of garnet, is very similar and has been used to imitate both demantoid and green grossular. For the time being, at any rate, synthetic demantoid is not produced.

Above: Demantoid. Below: Inclusions consisting of thin fibers of amianthus in a demantoid garnet (photomicrograph).

11 ZIRCON
ZrSiO$_4$

6–7.5

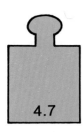

4.7

2.01 1.96

Silicate of zirconium, also containing thorium and uranium. The name may be derived from the Arabic *zarkùn*, meaning "red," or, more probably, from the Persian *zargùn*, golden yellow (hence the English *jargon*, a variety of zircon).

The presence of radioactive uranium and thorium in the structure sometimes causes a partial disruption of the crystal lattice of zircon (metamict), with a gradual change in physical properties which, in extreme cases, can be quite pronounced. The varieties used as gems are usually those least affected by this process. They have the highest density and refractive indices and strong birefringence and are referred to, in fact, as "high zircon." Zircons, however, are found with much lower densities and refractive indices, and very weak birefringence. These specimens in which the crystal structure is badly damaged are pseudomorphs, i.e., they retain their original external shape. Most of them are opaque and cloudy, but some, nearly always green ones, are sufficiently lustrous and transparent to be used as gems. These are known as "low zircon" or metamict zircon. There is a whole series of intermediate forms between the two extremes, transparent specimens almost always being greenish.

Crystal system Tetragonal.

Appearance Zircon is found in isolated crystals or as twins, in the form of squat prisms with bipyramidal terminations, sometimes cloudy, opaque, but often transparent with considerable luster. They are usually small. They can be light brown or gray, but also brown, yellow, reddish, green, blue, greenish blue, or colorless.

Physical properties The density of high zircon is usually about 4.70 g/cm^3. Its refractive indices are usually $n\omega$ 1.96, $n\epsilon$ 2.01 (with marked birefringence, obviously); and it has a hardness of 7.5. Medium to low zircons have a density of between 3.95 and 4.55 g/cm^3, refractive indices between $n\omega$ 1.880, $n\epsilon$ 1.890 and $n\omega$ 1.792, $n\epsilon$ 1.796 (with weak birefringence, therefore) and a hardness of about 6–6.5.

Genesis Zircon is generally formed in intrusive magmatic rocks and is also found in the pegmatites derived from them, except in metamorphic schists. Being fairly resistant to the elements, it is also found in the form of small, round pebbles in alluvial deposits.

Occurrence Zircon is found in Norway, Sweden, the Soviet Union (Urals), Australia, Brazil, and the United States, but the most famous sources of gem quality zircon are Sri Lanka, Cambodia, Vietnam, and Thailand.

Above: Brown zircon crystal. Soviet Union (Ural mountains). Below: Variously colored zircon crystals.

11.1 **Colorless zircon**

This is the variety best known to the general public, which for years regarded it as a substitute for diamond capable of deceiving anyone by its appearance. The name zircon has thus become synonymous with cheap imitation, hopelessly discrediting even the beautiful, colored specimens. Colorless zircon can, apparently, also be obtained by heat-treatment of brown or reddish stones. Variations in color achieved purely by heating are regarded as normal, not fraudulent, practice.

Appearance   Colorless, or with a faint grayish tinge, zircon has outstanding luster, although less than that of the diamond it has normally been required to imitate. It is mainly given a brilliant cut, but often of a slightly different type, with eight extra facets added to the pavilion, starting from the tip, to improve its luster (this is, in fact, known as a zircon cut). Antique stones are often not round, but squarish, with rounded corners, as was once the case with diamonds. Because zircon is somewhat brittle and not very hard, the edges are often slightly damaged. Therefore it is not very suitable for rings, as the stones can easily lose their polish.

Distinctive features   Marked birefringence, immediately detectable with a lens from doubling of the facet edges, was and still is the main feature used to distinguish zircon from diamond. Examination of the edges which, as mentioned, in the case of zircon always show signs of brittleness, is another clue to identification. With regard to the physical properties of high zircon, the refractive indices are not easily measured, being above the range of most refractometers, but density and hardness can identify it. Furthermore, most zircons, whatever the color, usually have a highly characteristic absorption spectrum.

Occurrence   Sri Lanka is so renowned for colorless zircons that, in the past, they were known as Matara diamonds (after the city at the southern tip of the island). But Thailand and South Vietnam also have important deposits.

Value   Distinctly low. No longer in demand as a substitute for diamond, it is of interest mainly to collectors.

Simulants and synthetics   It may seem odd that a gem that has chiefly been used to imitate another (diamond) should in turn be imitated. Yet every now and then colorless synthetic spinel, YAG, and cubic zirconia appear on the market under the name of zircon. They are obviously imitations, although there can be some confusion over the last because of the similarity of its name. Zircon is not at present produced synthetically.

Above: Colorless zircon (zircon cut).
Below: Colorless zircon (brilliant cut).

11.2 **Blue zircon** (also known as starlite)

This does not appear to have been known for long, partly because it is often (but not always) obtained by heat treatment of other colored zircons, which is standard practice commercially. The name starlite is not universally accepted.

Appearance The best color (not often seen) is a light, electric blue not found in any other gem, with pleochroism making it look greenish in one direction. It can also be sky-blue with less obvious pleochroism, a very soft, pale blue, or a distinctly greenish light blue. It is usually given a zircon-type brilliant cut, which is not always round; also used are rectangular or square, step cuts. Mixed cuts are less frequent. The strong luster is shown to best advantage by the zircon cut and is less obvious in the step cut. Unfortunately, the brittleness of zircon often results in the edges being slightly damaged and not clear-cut.

Distinctive features The marked birefringence——characteristic of most zircons——is easily seen with a lens and will distinguish blue zircon from other stones of a similar color. With a little experience (which is not easy to come by, as this is not a common gem), the color can be seen to be quite distinctive, particularly the electric blue. Blue zircon has the physical properties of high zircon, hence the refractive indices are not easily measured, but it nearly always has a highly characteristic absorption spectrum.

Above: Blue zircon. Below: Light greenish blue zircon.

Occurrence Blue zircons come from Cambodia, Vietnam, and Thailand, where they are cut (and, perhaps, treated). All stones are therefore sold as if coming from Thailand.

Value The best quality, electric-blue stones, which are relatively uncommon, but not in great demand because not widely known, are worth slightly less than the top secondary gems. Weak blue or blue-green stones are worth a lot less.

Simulants and synthetics The greenish-blue variety has been imitated by synthetic spinel, which is not, however, birefringent. This gem is not manufactured synthetically.

11.3 **Red zircon**

At one time this variety was known as hyacinth, although it did not match the description of hyacinth left us by Pliny the Elder. Indeed, a number of orange-red or brownish red stones were called by this name until the knowledge of mineralogy, which began to be acquired in the eighteenth century, caused these names based purely on color to be abandoned.

Appearance Red—often brick or orange red, but sometimes even a violet red. Like all zircons, it has considerable luster, shown to advantage by the zircon cut (a modified form of brilliant cut) sometimes used for these stones. Round or oval, mixed cuts with a brilliant-cut crown and step-cut pavilion are, however, more common, as they are with most other colored stones.

Distinctive features As always with zircons, the marked birefringence is a useful means of recognition. The color

(with faint pleochroism) and luster can make red zircon look like some spinels and possibly garnets, but these gems are singly refractive. Marked birefringence also easily distinguishes it from corundum, in which the effect is much weaker. It has the physical properties of high zircon, with refractive indices above the range of normal refractometers. As with other zircons, however, it almost always has a highly distinctive absorption spectrum.

Occurrence   Red or reddish zircon comes mainly from Sri Lanka, Cambodia, and Thailand.

Value   It is more or less equal in cost to the best blue zircons, and is therefore not one of the highest priced secondary gems.

Simulants and synthetics   These zircons are not sufficiently well known to be imitated. Red zircon is not produced synthetically.

11.4 **Yellow zircon**

This mineral was also known in the past as *jargon* (from the Persian *zargùn*); the name evolved into the word zircon, now applied to the entire mineral species.

Appearance   The color may vary from a rather pale yellow to canary yellow, gold, or greenish yellow. It has the typical, striking luster of zircon. It is most often given a round or oval, mixed cut. Like most zircons, it has delicate, brittle edges.

Distinctive features   Strong birefringence, easily seen with a lens, will readily distinguish it from yellow sapphire, which it can resemble, and from recent artificial products, such as YAG and cubic zirconia, which may also be yellow, but are singly refractive.

The brittleness of the facet edges is also characteristic. It has the physical properties of high zircon and the absorption spectrum is normally distinctive.

Occurrence   Yellow zircons come mainly from Sri Lanka and Cambodia, although those from the latter country are said to be obtained by heat treatment of brown or red-brown stones.

Value   Somewhat modest, lower than that of the blue and red varieties.

Simulants and synthetics   Yellow-colored artificial products like YAG and cubic zirconia have been marketed very recently as zircon and, hence, can be spoken of as imitations. It is not at present manufactured synthetically.

11.5 **Brown zircon**

This variety is very plentiful, but probably the least appreciated of all the zircons.

Appearance It is a brown color, which can vary from ''black tea'' to reddish brown, tobacco, or yellowish brown, all of which are uncommon in other gems. The luster is as fine as that of other types of zircon. Oval or round mixed cuts are the most common and the edges are often a bit chipped, as frequently happens with zircons.

Distinctive features The luster and marked birefringence are highly characteristic and easily established. The color is also distinctive as a rule. Only a few tourmalines or quartzes can resemble it, but they are quite different in other respects. Brown zircon has the brittle edges and physical properties of high zircon, with a distinctive absorption spectrum.

Occurrence Various shades of brown zircon come from Burma, Vietnam, Cambodia, and Sri Lanka.

Value Brown zircon is quite plentiful and not highly prized, even compared with other zircons, the color not being compatible with modern tastes in jewelry. Its value, therefore, is distinctly low, even for a secondary gem.

Simulants and synthetics Because of its own low market value, it is not imitated, nor is it produced synthetically.

11.6 **Green zircon**

This is a relatively common stone, but may vary a great deal in its characteristics, the green color generally being associated with the metamict state.

Appearance The color varies from a slightly brownish green to brilliant rather cold green, or yellow green. Some examples are perfectly transparent; others can look cloudy and display close, parallel striations, which are the main signs of the breakdown of the crystal lattice. The luster is affected by this turbidity and is often much less strong than in other zircons. The same is true of the birefringence, which is obvious in the clearer, more lustrous green zircons, but hard to see in the others. The oval or round, mixed cut is the most common. The edges are easily damaged, especially those of the cloudier stones, which are not so hard.

Distinctive features Clear, lustrous stones still display some birefringence. In cloudy specimens, this is not visible, but the appearance and presence of striations are equally characteristic. In either case, it is fairly easy to distinguish green zircon from green sapphire, but rather harder to tell it from olivine and some green tourmalines. Green zircons with good luster and clearly visible birefringence (thus with high density and refractive indices) may display the physical properties of high zircon, but the density, refractive indices and birefringence are often lower, considerable variation being possible. Despite the metamict process, the absorption spectrum is usually quite distinctive.

Occurrence Most green zircons come from Sri Lanka. Greenish to brownish-green specimens are also found in

Burma.

Value   Comparatively low, about the same as that of yellow zircon. Stones with inferior luster are even less valuable.

Simulants and synthetics   Being of low value, it has neither been imitated nor produced synthetically.

12   ANDALUSITE
Al_2SiO_5

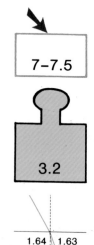

7–7.5

3.2

1.64 1.63

Silicate of aluminium.

Crystal system   Orthorhombic.

Appearance   It occurs as squat prismatic crystals with poor luster, or aggregates of elongated crystals arranged in "sheaves." The color varies from light yellowish brown to green-brown, light brownish pink, grayish green, or definite green with pronounced pleochroism making it hard to identify the main color. Some crystals have dense, darker inclusions in the center which in cross section, exhibit a cruciform pattern. These stones are known as chiastolite.

Physical properties   It has a hardness of 7–7.5 and a density of about 3.13–3.20 g/cm^3. The refractive indices are about $n\alpha$ 1.632, $n\gamma$ 1.643. It has distinct prismatic cleavage.

Genesis   Andalusite is a characteristic mineral of areas of contact metamorphism between granites and argillaceous rocks.

Occurrence   It is not a rare mineral. Fine crystals are found in Spain (Andalusia), whence the name. Other sources are Brazil, the United States (California, Maine, Massachusetts), Australia, Sri Lanka, Burma, Austria, and occasionally Italy.

12.1 Andalusite

This gem is named after Andalusia, where fine crystals occur.

Appearance It is a dull yellowish green with faint pink or brown reflections, or it may be yellowish brown-green or even violet brown-green or, rarely, a definite green. The difficulty in describing the color of this gem is because of its strong pleochroism, which is heightened by the facets of cut stones, to the point of being almost iridescent; but the colors are never very lively. It has unexceptional, vitreous luster. It is regularly given a faceted, mixed oval cut; square or rectangular step cuts are also used, but these are less suited to its modest luster and cannot do justice to its exceptional pleochroism.

Distinctive features Its peculiar color range, unusual pleochroism, and modest luster make it quite easy to distinguish from all other gems. Some say it can be confused with alexandrite, but the pleochroism of andalusite is very different from the true color change of the other. It is true that when alexandrite is a yellowish green with a faint color change, it may look vaguely similar; but checking the density would immediately distinguish between the two stones. The chiastolite variety with its black cross-shape is unmistakable.

Occurrence The gem variety comes mainly from Brazil (state of Minas Gerais), but also Sri Lanka, Burma, the Soviet Union, the United States and, of course, Andalusia.

Value Quite low, probably because of the rather drab color and poor luster. It is anything but a rare stone, yet it is not plentiful on the market and is mainly in demand with collectors. The most valuable stones are those with the most pronounced greenish to reddish pleochroism. The chiastolite variety has a longer history of gem use than the transparent type, having been worn as an amulet, but its value is equally low and similar to that of opaque ornamental materials.

Simulants and synthetics Not being valuable or well known, it is not imitated. Nor has it been produced synthetically, at any rate on a commercial scale.

Above: Andalusite.
Below: Chiastolite.

178

13 TOURMALINE

(Na,Ca) (Li, Al, Mg, Fe, Mn)$_3$ (Al,Fe)$_6$
B$_3$Si$_6$O$_{27}$(O,OH,F)$_4$

1.64 \ 1.62

Top: Crystals of watermelon tourmaline. In the other photos, variously colored tourmalines: left, dual-colored tourmaline, 4 ct., Brazil; right, colorless tourmaline, 0.79 ct., Afghanistan; bottom, yellow tourmaline, 1 ct., Mozambique.

A complex borosilicate of aluminium and alkali, with iron, magnesium, and other cations. The name is apparently derived from the Sinhalese *turamali*, referring to gems of unknown identity—probably zircons.

Crystal system Trigonal.

Appearance It usually occurs as long, three-sided prisms, which are often well terminated; but sometimes it is found as parallel or radiating groups of long, thin striated prisms. It has one of the widest color ranges in the mineral world. The most common color is black, but tourmaline may be pink, violet-red, brownish yellow, blackish brown, various shades of green, light blue, blue-green, dark blue, and (rarely) colorless. Fine crystals with concentric zoning are found; typically they are red on the inside and green on the outside, and are known as "watermelon" tourmalines. Also found are crystals with transverse zoning, the color of the crystal gradually changing from one end to the other, as in the "Moor's head" crystals found on the island of Elba. Tourmaline has good resistance to weathering and is therefore often found in alluvium.

Physical properties It has a hardness of 7 and a density of approximately 3.02 to 3.20 g/cm^3, with some variation between types; from 3.03–3.06 g/cm^3 for the pink, red, brown, and light green varieties; 3.08 g/cm^3 for the dark green; 3.10 g/cm^3 for the dark blue to yellow; and 3.15–3.20 g/cm^3 for the black. The refractive indices are about n_ϵ 1.62, n_ω 1.64, thus with quite marked birefringence, and strong pleochroism.

Genesis Tourmaline is found in differentiated dikes of silica-rich intrusive rocks and is quite common around granite, where pegmatitic, pneumatolytic mineralizations are abundant.

Occurrence It is widely distributed, the most common variety being black tourmaline, which is of no value as a gem. The most famous deposits are in Sri Lanka, the Soviet Union (Urals), Afghanistan, Burma, the United States (California, Maine, Connecticut), Brazil, Tanzania, Zimbabwe, and Namibia.

13.1 RUBELLITE

Pink to red tourmaline is called rubellite.

Appearance The color varies from pink of varying degrees of intensity to a red which is quite attractive, although usually a bit less lively than that of ruby; it may also be violet pink or red, and pink or red with a brownish tinge. Like all tourmalines, it has strong pleochroism, sometimes visible as a deeper color or lesser transparency along the axis of the prism. It is cut into all shapes; cabochons when the stone is too full of inclusions, but more often faceted oval, round, pear-shaped or other creative styles. Quite large stones are often seen.

Distinctive features In many cases, the color is fairly

distinctive: it is a bit subdued, and not enlivened by bright light like ruby. When the stone is cut with the table facet perpendicular to the axis of the prism, to achieve a deeper, redder color, it shows a strange loss of transparency. Pink tourmalines are, as a rule, also rather duller than other, similar gems, but may be a beautiful, brilliant violet-pink.

Occurrence   It is found in Siberia (to the extent that some call the violet-red variety siberite), Burma, Sri Lanka, Brazil, the United States (California), and Madagascar.

Value   The liveliest, bright red or very attractive pink gems with few inclusions are not common and are quite valuable secondary gems. Stones of more subdued color are readily available and quite modestly priced.

Simulants and synthetics   It is neither imitated nor produced synthetically.

13.2 **Indicolite**

This is basically the blue variety of tourmaline, but it may also be greenish blue or otherwise vary from the indigo color suggested by its name.

Appearance   Generally indicolite is quite a deep blue, even the color of dark blue ink, perhaps appearing green in one direction because of its strong pleochroism. Sometimes indicolite is an overall greenish blue, which, unlike the color of greenish blue sapphire, is very attractive. Stones are often clear and free of inclusions, but intense pleochroism may make them so dark in one direction as to appear lacking in transparency. This gem is given mixed, faceted and also rectangular, step cuts. It generally has good luster.

Distinctive features   The greenish blue color is unmistakable and particularly attractive. Loss of transparency in one direction is another distinctive characteristic and is best seen in rectangular gems. Because of its appreciable birefringence, if the stone is examined with a standard jeweler's 10x lens, the opposite facet edges look double in certain directions. Mid-blue zircon, with three times the birefringence, also shows this effect, but to a far greater extent, and is a very different, lighter color, with greater luster.

Occurrence   Indicolite is mainly found in Brazil (state of Minas Gerais), but also in the United States (Colorado, Massachusetts, California), Namibia, Madagascar, and the Soviet Union (Urals).

Value   Attractive, definite blue, bright blue or blue-green stones are priced similarly to fine rubellites, and are less common. But when the color is too deep, and inky blue, the value falls considerably, as it does with the less attractive rubellites.

Simulants and synthetics   It is neither imitated nor produced synthetically.

Above: Rubellite.
Below: Indicolite.

13.3 **Green tourmaline**

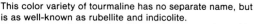

This color variety of tourmaline has no separate name, but is as well-known as rubellite and indicolite.

Appearance   Green-colored tourmaline comes in a wide range of different shades, so, at first sight, many green tourmalines may look very similar to other gems. Shades may include the yellowish-green of some olivines, or the stronger, deeper green of others; a lightish paintbox green, like some zircons, is also possible as is a stronger version of this color, like some African emeralds. Tourmaline can be a brilliant green, a touch colder than the color of emerald (this is typical of tourmaline); or leaf green, tending to deep olive green (also very typical and known, in fact, as tourmaline green). If they are large, green tourmalines are given either a step cut (not always with truncated corners) or a pear-shaped or oval mixed cut. If the stones are small, they are most often given a round or roundish oval cut. Mid- to light-colored specimens have good luster. Darker stones often look a bit opaque. Many are virtually free of inclusions.

Distinctive features   The more definite or darker shades are characteristic. Loss of transparency along the stone, particularly in gems that are cut rectangularly, is peculiar to tourmaline. Mid-green stones that are given a rectangular cut often show alternate longitudinal lines of lighter and darker color because of the way in which light is reflected from the pavilion facets. This optical effect is unique and therefore distinctive. But when the color is similar to that of other gems, the identity of the stones can only be distinguished by measurement of physical characteristics such as density and refractive indices.

Occurrence   Green tourmaline is found in Brazil, the United States (Maine), Tanzania, Mozambique, and Namibia. It is also extracted in the Soviet Union and from the gem gravels of Sri Lanka, where the lighter stones, somewhat like olivine, are the most common. It is quite plentiful and widespread.

Value   As with rubellite and indicolite, only the lively, mid-colored stones are valuable. When the color is an uncharacteristic pale green, or the most typical dark or olive green, they are worth much less.

Simulants and synthetics   It is neither imitated nor produced synthetically.

Above and below:
Green tourmaline cut
in two different
shapes.

CORDIERITE
$(Mg,Fe)_2Al_4Si_5O_{18}$

7–7.5

2.53–2.65

1.54 1.53

Silicate of aluminium and magnesium. Cordierite is named after French geologist P. Cordier. It is also known as dichroite, from the Greek, meaning "two-colored," or io-lite, from another Greek root, meaning "violet." The Vikings apparently knew how to use this mineral for navigational purposes. Because of its strong pleochroism, its behavior to the incident light indicated the direction of the sun on overcast days. For this reason, it has also been dubbed "Vikings' compass."

Crystal system Orthorhombic.

Appearance Cordierite occurs as short, multifaceted prismatic crystals. It is normally gray, light or dark blue, or violet, but can also be yellowish gray. It is not very lustrous, but when transparent has vitreous luster. Transparent crystals display very strong pleochroism from blue-gray to almost colorless or from violet to very pale grayish yellow.

Physical properties It has a hardness of 7–7.5. The density varies between 2.53 and 2.65 g/cm³ (but for gem quality stones is usually between 2.57 and 2.61 g/cm³). The refractive indices are ca. $n\alpha$ 1.532, $n\gamma$ 1.540, or sometimes $n\alpha$ 1.540, $n\gamma$ 1.549.

Genesis It is found scattered in silica and alumina-rich igneous rocks but mainly in larger crystals, in schists, and areas of contact metamorphism.

Occurrence It is found mainly in Germany (Bavaria), Norway, Finland, Brazil, and Madagascar.

14.1 Cordierite (or water sapphire)

Gem quality cordierite has the same name (or rather names) as the mineral itself, but was in the past also known as water sapphire, particularly when the color was not very intense. This is perhaps its most familiar name in the trade.

Appearance The color may vary from quite a deep blue to violet blue, light blue, or grayish blue; but it always has very strong pleochroism, being a much lighter gray or wan yellow in one direction. For obvious, aesthetic reasons, gems are cut so that this color is only visible from the side. The most common type of cut is the rectangular, step type, not always with truncated corners. One also comes across cordierites with a cabochon cut or minutely engraved, particularly in the case of less transparent specimens with numerous inclusions. Most stones are a few carats in weight; not too small, therefore, but never very large.

Distinctive features An essential characteristic of cordierite is its exceptional pleochroism, which may, however, resemble certain tanzanites. Many cordierites have a decidedly cold, grayish coloration, whereas tanzanite is a warmer color, always with a hint of violet. Testing the density, which is very different, would remove any uncertainty.

Occurrence Cordierite comes mainly from the gem gravels of Sri Lanka, but also from the United States and Namibia.

Value Rather low, that of minor gemstones.

Simulants and synthetics It is neither imitated nor produced synthetically.

Above: Cleavage masses of cordierite. Below: Cordierite, 1.37 ct. Tanzania.

15 QUARTZ

SiO_2

7

2.65

1.55 | 1.54

Silicon dioxide. The name may be derived from *querkluftertz* (through *querertz, quarts, quarz*) an old German word apparently referring to whitish, vein quartz. It is one of the most widely distributed minerals in the earth's crust, sometimes found as elegant crystals whose luster, hardness, and watery transparency or, conversely, pleasing colors have long been a source of fascination, causing it to be widely employed as a gem or ornamental material.

Crystal system   Trigonal.

Appearance   The most typical form consists of hexagonal, prismatic crystals with pyramidal or bipyramidal terminations, which are transparent, colorless, lustrous, and have no cleavage; but quartz may have a smoky appearance or even be black, yellow, brownish yellow, violet, or pink. Massive, white, milky vein quartz is very common. A microcrystalline variety of quartz, found as compact, massive concretions, is called chalcedony; this has separate colors, sometimes with distinct color banding, in which case it is known as agate, sard, cornelian, plasma, etc., depending on the color, a whole series of names having been evolved during its long history as a decorative material. Certain varieties of chatoyant quartz are also used as gems and ornaments (cat's-eye, tiger's-eye, hawk's-eye, bull's-eye). Of the semiopaque, massive varieties, the pink is also used in this way. A granular, metamorphic rock consisting mainly of quartz (but often containing green mica), known as aventurine, is used as an ornamental material.

Physical properties   It has a hardness of 7. The density (2.65 g/cm^3) and refractive indices ($n\omega$ 1.544, $n\epsilon$ 1.553) are very constant because of the invariability of quartz's chemical composition.

Genesis   The largest crystals originate from the fluids associated with intrusive magmatic phenomena and are found in pegmatitic, pneumatolytic and hydrothermal deposits. Quartz also occurs in sedimentary and metamorphic environments, but as very small crystals. The microcrystalline varieties are often associated with hydrothermal processes, even under the sea.

Occurrence   Quartz is extremely widespread, the most famous localities for magnificent, large crystals being the French Alps, the St. Gotthard massif in the Swiss Alps, the United States, Brazil, and Madagascar.

Above: Crystals of colorless quartz, or rock crystal.
Below: Crystals of amethystine quartz.

15.1 Amethyst

The violet, purple to almost pink variety of quartz is called amethyst, an ancient name derived from the Greek *a-méthystos*, meaning "not drunken," as it was believed to protect those who wore it from drunkenness. It is the most highly prized variety of quartz.

Appearance   The typical color is a rich, violet-purple, often distributed in patches or bands. It can also be quite pale, but is generally the same basic color, without any overtones. It is given both oval and drop mixed cuts, step

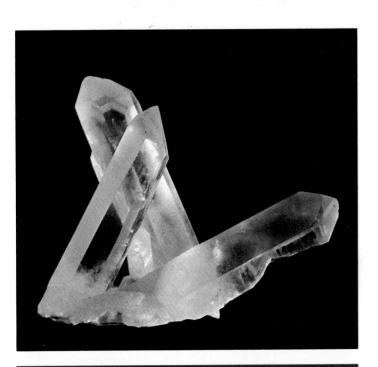

cuts, and other types of cuts used for colored stones. Specimens of good color but with too many inclusions are cut *en cabochon*. Stones of 10 or so carats in weight are often found and even larger ones are not rare. Amethyst normally has good luster and transparency. Well-formed, characteristically colored groups of crystals (geodes and druses) are even used in their natural state as ornaments.

Distinctive features The distribution of the color, in striking patches and bands, is characteristic. When the stones contain inclusions, a series of discontinuous, wavy parallel lines, visible with a lens, indicates that they are certainly amethyst.

As with nearly all quartzes, the interference figure has a distinctive profile, which usually makes identification immediate. Quartz may resemble some violet synthetic corundum, but the latter turns reddish in strong artificial light or full sunlight. Amethyst can also look vaguely similar to violet cordierite, which also has a strong, distinctive pleochroism. The much rarer violet scapolite may look quite similar, and its physical characteristics are almost the same as those of quartz. Therefore they can only be distinguished by an expert.

Occurrence The finest amethysts come (in great quantities) from Brazil and neighboring Uruguay, from the United States, Madagascar, and the Soviet Union, India, Australia, South Africa, and many other countries.

Value A few centuries ago, deep-colored amethyst was highly prized. Its value fell greatly with the discovery of the large Brazilian and Uruguayan deposits at the end of the nineteenth century. Now relegated to the status of a secondary gem, its value is quite low.

Simulants and synthetics Amethyst was much imitated by colored glass in the past, when it was more costly. Nowadays, despite the limited value of the natural stone, fair quantities of synthetic amethyst are produced, using the knowledge acquired in the production of synthetic quartz for technological purposes. The cost of the synthetic product is not much less than that of the natural gemstone.

15.2 **Citrine quartz**

Oddly enough, the basically yellow variety of quartz is known as citrine quartz, or simply citrine, despite the fact that generally the color is nothing like lemon yellow. It was and still is called topaz or topaz quartz as well, because of a similarity in color, much to the detriment of true topaz, which is thus considered more plentiful, and less valuable, than by rights it should be.

Appearance The color varies from pure yellow to dull yellow, honey, or brownish yellow, sometimes even with a russet tint. As with amethyst, the color is often broken up into patches or bands, although due to its depth of hue, the zoning is less obvious. It has good luster (like amethyst) and is generally very clear and virtually free of inclusions because the amount of raw material available allows for considerable selectivity. It is fashioned into all the styles normal for transparent stones, except the brilliant cut.

Large stones of 10 carats or even more are often seen.
Distinctive features   Color zoning, where present, may
be an aid to recognition. The density of citrine (together
with that of orthoclase) is the lowest for stones of this color
and is much less than that of topaz, in particular. Although
normally good, its luster is slightly inferior to that of topaz,
and the latter can show signs of incipient cleavage, never
seen in citrine.

As with the majority of quartzes, the interference figure is
characteristic, where this can be established. Citrine is far
less lustrous than yellow sapphire, which also normally has
highly characteristic inclusions. As a rule, however, citrine
can only be distinguished from the numerous other yellow
stones by an examination of the physical properties.

Occurrence   Large quantities of citrine are obtained from
Brazil. It is also found in the United States (North Carolina,
California), Spain, and the Soviet Union.

Value   Quite low, for a secondary gem; less than that of
amethyst. Like amethyst, it was much more highly valued in
the past than it is today.

Simulants and synthetics   It is not imitated; but despite
its low value, it is synthesized, like amethyst, on a large
scale. The cost of the synthetic version is equal to or only
slightly lower than that of the natural gemstone. Amethyst,
when heated, assumes the yellow color of citrine.

15.3 **Rose quartz**

This is the pink variety of quartz found in anhedral masses
rather than distinct crystals.

Appearance   Due to minute inclusions of foreign substances, sometimes roughly oriented by the crystal, rose
quartz is always somewhat milky rather than perfectly
transparent. The color is generally a very delicate soft pink,
which is probably brought out by the stone's relative lack
of transparency. Stones may exhibit cloudier patches or
streaks and may have a discontinuous look. The internal
cloudiness is often due to cracks or discontinuities, which
make this the one type of quartz that is somewhat brittle. It
is pierced and made into necklace beads, engraved and
fashioned into pendants, or made into small sculpted ornaments.

Occurrence   Rose quartz is not very plentiful and mainly
comes from Brazil, the United States, and Madagascar.

Value   It is valued as an ornamental material for its very
attractive color and comparative rarity, but this is offset by
its tendency to be brittle.

Simulants and synthetics   It is imitated by glass designed to simulate not only the color, but the internal
streaks. This process, however, often produces air bubbles, clearly visible under a lens.

15.4 **Colorless quartz or rock crystal**

This is much the most common and most widely distributed variety of quartz. It must have been known since prehistoric times, and the Greeks named it "crystal," or ice, believing it to be a form of the latter, irreversibly frozen by some process of extreme cold.

Appearance   Although quite common, it has been used as a gemstone (albeit an inexpensive one) because of its beauty. It was and still is cut into all shapes, except, perhaps, the brilliant, which would mercilessly display its inferiority to diamond. It has been used much more frequently for the fashioning of elaborate, finely engraved cups, jugs, and vases. Veritable masterpieces were produced in the past and there are still places where the tradition is continued. Simpler pieces make use of quartz that has striking inclusions in the form of long, thin yellow-brown rutile needles or black tourmaline prisms, sometimes crossed in various ways. Such quartz specimens make attractive ornaments, despite being harder to work.

Distinctive features   It is distinguished from glass, particularly of the type sold under the name of lead crystal, by its birefringence. Glass also frequently contains minute air bubbles. Some difference in hardness (7 for quartz, no more than 5 for lead glass) may also help distinguish it.

Occurrence   Large quantities of quartz come from Brazil and Madagascar, but the colorless variety is found almost everywhere. In the nineteenth century, magnificent objects were made from quartz discovered in the French and Austrian Alps.

Value   As a gem, its value is extremely low. It is now cut almost exclusively for collectors and amateurs. As an ornamental material, its value largely depends on the way in which it is fashioned. Fine examples may be quite valuable and more costly than similar pieces made from more opaque materials. Finely worked antique pieces are, of course, still more valuable.

Simulants and synthetics   The confusion of lead crystal glass with rock crystal is generally due to misunderstanding rather than imitation. Large amounts of synthetic quartz are produced nowadays, but only the amethyst and citrine varieties are of interest to the gem trade. The colorless variety is made only for technological purposes.

COLORLESS

Above: Plate in rock crystal, by G. Bernardi (sixteenth century). Museo degli Argenti, Florence. Below: Faceted imitation in colorless quartz of the "Regent" diamond.

15.5 Cat's-eye, tiger's-eye, hawk's-eye, and bull's-eye quartz

When quartz contains similarly oriented fibrous inclusions, appropriately cut, curved stones display what is known as chatoyancy. The result is a series of minor gemstones differing only in their ground color and that of the mobile reflection. The variety crocidolite is quartz pseudomorphous after riebeckite.

Appearance When the ground color is greenish gray or green, the gem is known as cat's-eye quartz; if the ground is blue-gray or bluish, the variety is called hawk's-eye; a golden yellow reflection on a brown ground is called a tiger's-eye; and a stone with a mahogany-colored ground is called bull's-eye or ox-eye. It is normally cut *en cabochon*, to bring out the chatoyancy, which is, after all, its main characteristic; but it can be cut into more or less round, polished pieces, for necklaces and pendants. The tiger's eye variety, in particular, is also used for carvings, boxes, ashtrays, and other ornamental items, although in these, the fibers are seen as stripes of color, not chatoyancy as such.

Distinctive features The colors and clearly fibrous appearance are normally distinctive, although other stones, as, for instance, some nephrites or chatoyant feldspars, may look quite similar. Cymophane chrysoberyl, on the other hand, is usually much more translucent and greenish yellow, with much greater hardness and density.

Occurrence Cat's-eye quartz comes mainly from Sri Lanka and West Germany (Bavaria), but also from Burma. Hawk's-eye, bull's-eye, and the much more plentiful tiger's-eye, in particular, come principally from South Africa.

Value Despite its attractiveness, this material is not very valuable. The less common hawk's-eye variety is worth somewhat more.

Simulants and synthetics Chatoyant quartz has sometimes been imitated by glass, but is not produced synthetically.

Above: Crystal of cat's-eye quartz (crocidolite).
Center: Cat's-eye, left; tiger's-eye, right.
Below: Hawk's-eye, left; bull's-eye, right.

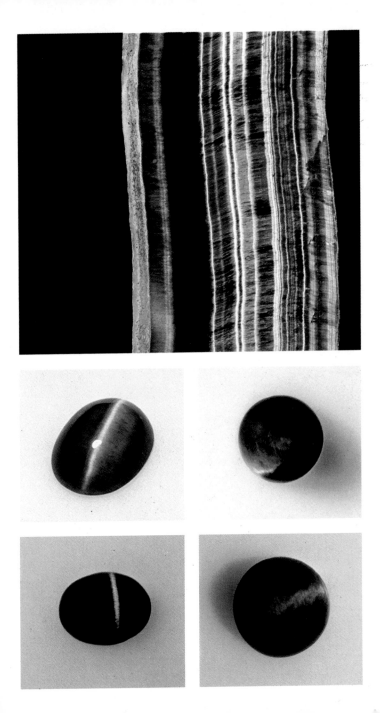

15.6 Chalcedony

This is the name given to the microcrystalline varieties of quartz that form concretionary deposits (partially of organic origin in the case of jasper). They have been used since time immemorial both as gems, because of their color, hardness, and ability to take a good polish, and as precious materials for the production of ornaments or small sculptures.

The different combinations of colors and patterns have given rise to a specialized nomenclature that was once of great importance. The name chalcedony probably comes from Calcedon or Calchedon, an ancient port on the Sea of Marmara, in Asia Minor. Ornamental materials were mined in that area, and it was an active trading center for precious stones of various types and origins. The Greek *khalkedón* and Latin *charchedonia* do not appear, at least from the description of Pliny the Elder, to be the same mineral as the modern chalcedony.

Appearance The typical color is blue whitish-gray, but for ornamental purposes, the types that have been variously colored by small quantities of other elements are usually used. These colors can cover the entire mass, as with jasper, or just a few thin, successive layers, as with agate and onyx. The most highly prized colors for the concretionary varieties, which are translucent to semiopaque, are brownish yellow (sard), red (cornelian), black, green (chrysoprase), black-and-white or gray-and-white (onyx); and yellow, red, brownish red or black for jaspers, which are semiopaque to opaque. All varieties are cut into cabochons, engraved, or made into seal stones or rounded, polished, and pierced for necklaces and other items of jewelry. Various forms of chalcedony were used extensively in the past for bases and handles of gold items (statuettes, goblets, cruets) and for stone inlay work. Agate and onyx, with their consecutive layers of different colors, make excellent material for cameos; the contrast between the different layers is used to heighten the relief.

Some variegated pieces are used for the carving of multicolored figurines similar to those made from jadeite. The most highly prized variety nowadays is chrysoprase, which is a bright green color (commonly known as leek green).

Distinctive features The characteristic colors arranged in zones and the mid-level hardness and exceptional luster of the stones generally make identification of chalcedony quite easy. It is worth remembering, however, that it has a slightly lower density ($2.61 \ g/cm^3$) and hardness (about 6.5) than other quartzes. As with all microcrystalline gems, it has only one refractive index (about 1.53), which is also slightly lower than that of most quartz.

Occurrence Large amounts of chalcedony come from Uruguay and the bordering regions of Brazil, but it is found in many other countries.

In Germany, Idar-Oberstein is famous for agate, although the term agate apparently comes from *Akhátes*, the Greek name for a river in Sicily where these stones were found several centuries BC. Chrysoprase comes mainly from Germany, the Soviet Union, the United States, Canada, and Brazil.

Top to bottom and left to right: Chrysoprase, agate, cornelian, plasma, sard, onyx, green jasper, red jasper.

Value Its value was quite high in antiquity, when chalcedony was one of the main gems used. Nowadays, it is fairly low, except for chrysoprase, attractively colored specimens of which are quite valuable. Objects in chalcedony of considerable artistic merit tend to fetch high prices.

Simulants and synthetics In the past chalcedony was imitated by glass, moulded pieces even being used to simulate carved stones. It is not produced synthetically. Because chalcedony is porous, it has long been the practice to impregnate it with artificial dyestuffs, making it look like onyx, even where the original color is almost uniform. This process is facilitated because the porosity of chalcedony often varies from one layer to another, so that one layer can absorb color well, whereas the adjoining one absorbs it little or not at all. Agate has been artificially colored for so long and the procedure is so widespread that it is regarded as normal, not fraudulent, practice. Chalcedony is also colored green to simulate chrysoprase. This practice is considered fraudulent as the value of chrysoprase depends almost exclusively on color. Equally fraudulent is intensification of the color of chrysoprase by the same means.

15.7 **Aventurine**

The name aventurine is applied to an ornamental material consisting mainly of quartz. It is therefore described here under this heading, although it is actually a metamorphic rock, a quartzite, containing platelike crystals of other minerals, usually green mica. It is also, improperly, called Indian jade. It should not be confused with aventurine feldspar, a red variety of albite.

Appearance Consisting as it does of minute, juxtaposed grains, it is normally not transparent, but somewhat turbid. Sometimes the green mica plates are obvious and greatly influence the color, which may be an attractive, bright green. More often, it is merely greenish off-white or grayish white. The overall appearance can be quite similar to that of some jadeite.

It is generally cut into curved pieces for necklaces or other jewels, or for use as pendants, but is also much used for carving and figurines. Because of its heterogeneous structure, it does not easily acquire a good polish.

Distinctive features The granular appearance, the possible presence of distinct green fibers, and its particular translucence are the most distinctive characteristics. Specimens similar to jadeite jade are immediately distinguished by their density. It is also much more brittle than jade.

Occurrence Aventurine comes mainly from India, the Soviet Union, Brazil and Australia, but also from Germany. It is also fashioned in all these countries.

Value Very modest, when, as is usually the case, the material is whitish to grayish or dull green and the workmanship is of a low level. But expertly fashioned, bright green pieces are almost as valuable as true jades.

Simulants and synthetics Aventurine feldspar is imitated by glass, usually in the form of a brown paste con-

Above: Cameo in agate (21 mm). Below: Aventurine.

taining golden metallic fibers, hence somewhat dissimilar. Some people, in fact, claim that the name aventurine was originally given to a type of Murano glass containing metallic fibers and only subsequently applied to the ornamental mineral which looks as (very vaguely) like it. It is not manufactured synthetically. Because of its granular structure, minute discontinuities and porosity, aventurine absorbs artificial colorants quite easily, and consequently it is sometimes given a bright green color, with a view to greatly increasing its value.

16 JADEITE

$NaAlSi_2O_6$

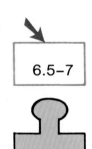

Silicate of sodium and aluminium. Jadeite is a member of the alkaline pyroxene group of minerals, and is so called because it is the source of one of the ornamental materials commonly known as jade, a word possibly derived from the Spanish *ijada*, or "flank," due to its alleged therapeutic action on diseases of the kidneys. (People believed that if a piece of jade was worn close to the diseased organ, it had the power to cure it.)

Crystal system Monoclinic.

Appearance It occurs as granular aggregates of small crystals, but has occasionally been found in crystals of a few centimeters. The color varies a great deal because of minimal differences in composition. As a rule it is off-white or grayish white, but it may be brown, yellowish brown, orange-yellow, reddish orange, lilac, blue-gray, or various shades of gray and green.

Physical properties It has a hardness of 6.5–7, with extraordinary tenacity (the opposite of brittleness) for a mineral, especially one in which the tiny individual crystals sometimes display obvious cleavage traces. The density varies from approximately 3.30 to 3.36 g/cm^3 but is usually 3.34 g/cm^3. The very dark green variety can be as much as 3.40 g/cm^3. The refractive indices are $n\alpha$ 1.655, $n\gamma$ 1.667, but the massive material used for ornamental purposes normally only gives one index, of about 1.66.

Genesis It is formed by regional metamorphism and occurs in lenticular masses or veins. It is also found as alluvial pebbles and even boulders.

6.5–7

3.3

...1.66...

Above: Carved disc of jadeite jade depicting silk weaving (seventeenth century Chinese).
Below: Jadeite jade cabochon.

Occurrence Jadeite comes mainly from northern Burma, where it is recovered from rock rather than alluvium. Very small quantities of jadeite are also found in Japan, Tibet, the United States (California), and Guatemala, where many items were made from it in antiquity. It is also found as small crystals in the Swiss Alps, even in crystals of a few centimeters.

16.1 Jadeite jade

The variety of jadeite pyroxene used as a gem or ornamental material consists of microcrystalline aggregates which, together with similar aggregates of tremolite-actinolite amphibole (nephrite), come under the general name of jade. For reasons of clarity, we shall therefore be using the term *jadeite jade*, rather than either *jadeite* or *jade* alone.

Appearance Jadeite jade is a semiopaque to highly translucent aggregate of juxtaposed, very firmly interconnected granular crystals. Only in rare instances are there visibly elongated crystals, in fibrous radiating or parallel groups. The general impression is not so much of individual crystals as of a mass with a fairly finely interwoven network of numerous, minute discontinuities. These are the boundaries between one crystal and another or the cleavage surfaces inside some of the crystals. Despite this minutely fractured appearance, the principal characteristic of jadeite jade is, in fact, extreme tenacity and toughness. On the surfaces of antique pieces in particular, one can see a similar network of small discontinuities which keep the pieces from having a perfect polish. On modern pieces polished with diamond powder, this network is much less visible. Many different shades of green are possible, the most valuable being emerald green. Jadeite jade of this color is quite translucent and is called imperial jade. Other shades of light and bright green are also very lively and attractive. Dark green is less common. The most frequent color is semitransparent to nearly opaque white, or off-white to very pale hazel; others are red (generally of an orange or brown hue), yellow, light and often grayish blue, gray, pink, and pale lilac. The brightest colors generally occur only in zones or in blurred, fringed streaks within the block. Pebbles recovered from alluvium often have an outer layer of a brown color because of oxidation, that fades away on the inside. It is used as a gem, cut into cabochons or engraved stones for settings, beads, or other ornaments, especially when the background color or limited patches of color are an attractive shade. Last but by no means least, jadeite jade, like nephrite jade, is made into exclusive types of decorative ware or small sculptures. Because of its tenacity, which is almost equal to that of metals, generations of craftsmen in the Far East have used it to produce staggering *tours de force*, such as chains with unjointed, individual links made from a single piece of stone, thin-walled vases generally with loose links on the handles and lids, cutting weapons (daggers and parade swords), cups with engraved decorations, buckles, and other finely pierced objects. Its other distinctive feature, the presence of patches and streaks of bright color inside and outside the uncut

stones, has been skilfully manipulated into wonderful multi-colored pieces. Typical examples are birds sculpted in such a position and such a manner that a splash of orange on the block of stone, for instance, serves to produce the beak, a streak of green simulates the flight feathers of the wings, an area of brown is used for the feet, and so on. Cups decorated with brown-stemmed vine shoots, green leaves and fruit, and colored flowers and butterflies are among the other prodigious works of art that have been made from jadeite jade.

Distinctive features Its almost alabastine translucence, the minute internal network of discontinuities and corresponding effect on the outer surface, its degree of hardness, the graduated streaks of color, and the incomparable shades of green, are frequently sufficient to distinguish jadeite jade from similar materials of lesser value, notably serpentine (which is highly translucent, greenish white to oil green, of uniform color, less hard, and less dense) and what is known as Transvaal or Pakistan jade (which is a mixture of microcrystalline hydrogrossular and vesuvianite, that ranges from highly translucent to almost opaque, lacks the internal appearance of jadeite jade, and has a rather different range of colors, fractionally higher density, and higher indices). But many natural materials are occasionally used as substitutes, and it may be hard to tell them apart.

Occurrence Most jadeite jade used in Chinese art since the latter half of the eighteenth century and most of that used today comes from northern Burma. Thus, nowadays, the name "Burmese jade" is synonymous with jadeite jade. It has also been found in Japan, the United States (California), and Guatemala, and only rarely in a few other places. It is, therefore, much less common and more localized than nephrite jade.

Value Jadeite jade has a very wide range of possible values. As a gem, the translucent emerald green variety known as imperial jade can fetch prices only just below those of the principal gemstones, particularly emerald, which it so much resembles. Yet pieces in other colors are worth no more than other fine, hard opaque stones.

Where the material is used for carving and engraving, the value depends very much on the quality of the workmanship, the skill with which any patches of color have been exploited, and the standard of finish. It is, nevertheless, the most valuable of materials used for this purpose, worth more than nephrite jade, except for very finely worked or antique pieces, where no distinction is made between the two.

Simulants and synthetics Some whitish pale-green or green aventurine, also of granular structure, is occasionally used as a substitute for jadeite jade and known as Indian jade, though it lacks the exceptional mechanical and chromatic properties of true jade. Synthetic jadeite does not exist.

A problem which has arisen recently over jadeite is that of coloration. Because of the minute discontinuities present in the mass, it is easily impregnated with artificial dyes, to pleasing effect. In this way, for example, whitish jadeite can be made to look like the much more highly prized impe-

rial jade; and the other colors are also often imitated in this way. One can usually distinguish cases in which the color, rather than being contained in individual crystals, is distributed in the minute fractures and cleavages of the mass, but a microscope is needed for this.

17 SPODUMENE

$LiAl\,Si_2O_6$

Silicate of lithium and aluminium. This is a lithium-rich member of the monoclinic pyroxene group, similar to jadeite. Its name basically means "ashen," because this mineral is often grayish white or ash gray. In the past, it was also called triphane, a word of Greek derivation meaning "three aspects," due to its clear trichoism.

Crystal system   Monoclinic.

Appearance   Spodumene frequently occurs as very long, large unevenly terminated, flat-sided crystals, often with longitudinal striations. Some are among the largest in the mineral world: crystals a few meters in length, weighing over a ton, have been found. The main color is a faintly green, nontransparent whitish gray; whence the name. Violet pink, bright green, yellow green or yellow specimens are much less common and transparent crystals of these are used as gems. Transparent crystals have vitreous luster and marked pleochroism. The semiopaque crystals look almost pearly.

Physical properties   Spodumene has a hardness of 6–7. The density is between 3.17 and 3.23 g/cm^3. The refractive indices vary from $n\alpha$ 1.654, $n\gamma$ 1.669 to $n\alpha$ 1.664, $n\gamma$ 1.679, with quite obvious birefringence. It has very easy prismatic cleavage.

Genesis   Spodumene is a typical mineral of pegmatites, particularly those rich in lithium.

Occurrence   Pegmatites containing spodumene are found in Great Britain, Sweden, some parts of the United States (South Dakota, Connecticut, New Mexico, Massachusetts), Brazil, and Madagascar.

17.1 Kunzite

This is the violet pink, transparent variety of spodumene, named after the American mineralogist G.F. Kunz, a noted gem expert active at the turn of the century.

Appearance   The characteristic color is a violet pink, which can be quite intense. It has marked pleochroism, seen as a clear difference in depth of color in different crystallographic directions, rather than a color change as such. The crystals used as gems generally have few inclusions and good transparency. Plane surfaces, looking both specular and transparent at the same time, can sometimes be seen on the inside and are the warning signs of cleavage. In fact, its easy cleavage makes this gem quite brittle, sensitive to knocks, and therefore unsuitable as a ring stone. It is usually given a (sometimes quite elongated) oval mixed cut, a pear-shaped or triangular mixed cut, or even a step cut. Although it is often found as large crystals, the smaller section of the crystal is used for cutting, the strongest, most valued color being perpendicular to this surface. Gems several carats in weight are not uncommon and some of 200–300 carats have even been cut as museum pieces.

Distinctive features   Some pink stones look very much alike: e.g. kunzite; pink topaz, and morganite. Kunzite, however, has the strongest pleochroism, best seen, of course, in larger, richer-colored stones. It has much clearer birefringence than the other two minerals, a factor easily established in larger stones, with the aid of a lens, by the presence of a double image of the back facet edges. Kunzite is also somewhat less hard than the others. This can be established by touch, the less acute facet edges feeling almost oily or soapy if rubbed between forefinger and thumb. Pink tourmaline can sometimes also look like kunzite. In this case, there is no appreciable difference in birefringence and the pleochroism can be vaguely similar. The physical properties are also quite close, but are nonetheless sufficiently different to establish the distinction.

Occurrence   Kunzite is found in the United States (in various parts of California, source of the largest crystals, Maine and Connecticut), Brazil, and Madagascar.

Above and below: Kunzite, showing different cuts and shades of color.

Value   Not very high; as secondary gems go, it is more or less on a par with good quality red garnets. Gems several carats in weight are common; small stones, especially pale ones, are of very limited value.

Simulants and synthetics   It is mainly imitated by pale pink corundum. It is not synthesized, at least not commercially.

17.2 **Hiddenite**

This is the green variety of spodumene, which has only been known for about a century and is named after A.E. Hidden, a mine-owner in the United States, where the mineral was first discovered. Some people nowadays maintain that the name hiddenite refers only to the emerald green or rich green variety of spodumene, whereas others apply this name to all gem-quality green spodumene, including pale and yellowish-green specimens; this seems the most practical definition.

Appearance   The best, and very rare, specimens are a bright, almost emerald green, with quite strong green to blue-green pleochroism; but hiddenite may be a rather dull, pale green or even green with a yellowish tinge. The step cut is the most common. Strongly colored stones are usually small to medium-sized; paler specimens are often a bit bigger, but never as large as kunzite.

Distinctive features   It is hard to generalize about a gem of such rarity and diverse appearance. Depending on the specimen, hiddenite may resemble both pale and strong-colored emeralds, bright green and yellowish tourmalines, chrysoberyl, and diopside. The physical characteristics always have to be measured in order to identify it.

Occurrence   The finest gems used to come from North Carolina. The less attractive, paler types, perhaps with a yellowish tinge, come from California, Brazil, and Madagascar.

Value   Its attractive color, rarity, and the difficulty of finding reasonable-sized stones make intensely colored hiddenite one of the most valuable secondary gems. Paler-colored specimens, which are easier to find in a good size, are of quite low value, similar to that of kunzite.

Simulants and synthetics   Being little known and of recent history, hiddenite is not imitated. Nor is it produced synthetically, at any rate not on a commercial scale. Yet large stones, in which the medium-light green color is due to some form of treatment (probably irradiation) of very pale or colorless stones, or even very pale kunzite, do appear on the market from time to time.

Above: Crystal of hiddenite. Afghanistan.
Below: Hiddenite.

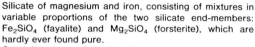

18   OLIVINE (PERIDOT)
(Mg, Fe)$_2$SiO$_4$

6.5–7

3.3

1.69 | 1.65

Silicate of magnesium and iron, consisting of mixtures in variable proportions of the two silicate end-members: Fe$_2$SiO$_4$ (fayalite) and Mg$_2$SiO$_4$ (forsterite), which are hardly ever found pure.

Crystal system   Orthorhombic.

Appearance   In iron- and magnesium-rich intrusive rocks it usually occurs as anhedral crystals; but in effusive rocks, such as basalts, it more often has a prismatic appearance. The color is a yellowish (olive) green, a stronger, almost bottle green, or pale yellow tinged with green. It has unexceptional, vitreous luster, increasing its resemblance to olive oil.

Physical properties   Olivine has a hardness of 6.5–7. The density varies a great deal according to the composition of the specimen: in gem quality stones it is about 3.32–3.35 g/cm^3, although the mineral itself ranges from 3.25 to 4.35 g/cm^3. It has strong birefringence with indices of about $n\alpha$ 1.654, $n\gamma$ 1.690. It has indistinct prismatic cleavage and, often, conchoidal fracture.

Genesis   Very widely distributed in iron- and magnesium-rich igneous rocks, it is found as large crystals on the island of Zebirget in the Red Sea, and in basalt in the United States and in certain lavas on the Hawaiian islands. It also occurs in Burma and is known in the volcanic bombs of Vesuvius, Italy and the Eifel region of Germany.

18.1 Peridot, olivine, or chrysolite

This stone has been known for a very long time. The ancients (including Pliny the Elder) spoke of a gem called *topazos* (corresponding to our word topaz) which, from the description, appears to be olivine. This gem was called *topazos* because it came from an island in the Red Sea named Topazos, now known as Zebirget, a fact which tends to confirm that it was indeed olivine. This is obviously one of those cases in which an old gem name has survived but has subsequently become attached to a different gem.

Appearance   Typically olive green, olivine can be a strong, almost bottle green, or yellowish green. In the gem trade, the greener type tends to be called peridot, and the yellower type chrysolite. It has vitreous luster. Stones are usually transparent, with few inclusions and are given all types of mixed cuts, oval, round and pear-shaped, plus rectangular and square, step cuts. Gems of several carats are often seen, but very large stones are hardly ever found. Small stones are also cut and arranged in intricate patterns in jewelry.

Distinctive features   The particular color and luster are highly characteristic, although some tourmalines, zircons, and chrysoberyls may look much the same. A quick way of distinguishing them is by testing the density. Chrysoberyl and olivine also have very different refractive indices and chrysoberyl is usually more lustrous.

Occurrence   The island of Zebirget still supplies excel-

Above: Crystal aggregate of olivine in volcanic ejectamenta.
Below: Olivine, 2.40 ct. United States (Arizona).

lent olivines, as it did in antiquity. Others come from the United States (Arizona), the Hawaiian islands, Burma, and Brazil.

Value   Much appreciated in the past, olivine is the victim of changing fashions and is far less highly prized today. Even exceptionally fine, large stones do not fetch very high prices and smaller ones are very low-priced.

Simulants and synthetics   Olivine has been imitated by appropriately colored glass, synthetic corundum and synthetic spinel. It has also been synthesized experimentally, but its low value has discouraged such attempts.

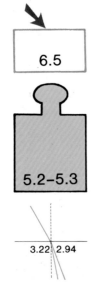

19   HEMATITE

Fe_2O_3

Iron oxide. This is a relatively common iron ore. The name comes from the Greek root *aima* or *ema*, meaning "blood," because of the red color of the powdered hematite (even the dust of the metallic-looking form) and the color of some larger examples.

Crystal system   Trigonal.

Appearance   It occurs as thin, relatively brittle, lamellar crystals, polyhedral crystals of lenticular habit or mamillated aggregates, all of which are black or dark iron-gray. The lamellae or individual crystals have strong, metallic luster. It may also be incoherent, almost earthy, and red in color.

Physical properties   It has a hardness of 6.5 and a density of 5.2–5.3 g/cm^3. The very high refractive indices of $n\epsilon$ 2.94, $n\omega$ 3.22 are extremely hard to measure and therefore not of use for identification.

Genesis   It is deposited in hydrothermal veins associated with magmatic rocks, although the largest deposits are of sedimentary origin.

Occurrence   It is found in large quantities in the United States, Canada, Venezuela, and Brazil, in smaller quantities in Italy (Elba), Great Britain, Germany, and Spain.

6.5

5.2–5.3

3.22 2.94

19.1 Hematite

Reasonably thick crystals (not, therefore, the lamellar ones) and compact, concretionary masses are suitable for cutting into gems and were particularly popular in the recent past.

Appearance Dark, blackish gray, nontransparent and with a metallic luster, hematite is faceted, cut into cabochons, or engraved; it lends itself well to the manufacture of signet rings. Other pieces are fashioned into necklace beads or pendants.

Distinctive features The metallic luster and color are highly characteristic; still more so is the red streak it leaves if drawn across a piece of unglazed porcelain.

Occurrence Now used comparatively rarely, the type from Great Britain, Switzerland, Germany, and the island of Elba is suitable for ornamental purposes.

Value Very low. Skillfully engraved items are worth more.

Simulants and synthetics Despite its modest value, it has been imitated by a ferromagnetic, sintered product, moulded to look like engraved stones. It does not appear to have been produced synthetically.

Above: Engraved hematite (16 mm). Below: Crystals of pyrite.

20 PYRITE
FeS$_2$

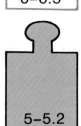

Iron sulphide. The name of the mineral comes from the Greek root *pyr*, meaning "fire," because it is one of the stones that produces sparks if struck by iron.

Crystal system Cubic.

Appearance It occurs as cubic crystals with striated faces, or in the form of pentagonal dodecahedra, usually well-crystallized, either isolated or in small, often well-formed groups. It is a characteristic, brassy yellow or pale-gold color, opaque and with a metallic luster. It sometimes occurs as nodules or concretions, consisting of aggregates of minute crystals.

Physical properties It has a hardness of 6–6.5 and a density of about 5.0–5.2 g/cm^3. It is brittle and will crumble beneath a hammer blow, unlike gold, with which it has even been confused (the popular name is fool's gold). The powder is (again, unlike gold) black or grayish.

Genesis Very common and widely distributed, it is deposited both by magmatic segregation from basic rocks and as a result of intrusive processes in general, especially during hydrothermal phases. It also occurs in certain sedimentary environments.

Occurrence Large deposits are found the world over, but those of Spain, Italy, Norway, Sweden, Germany, Japan, and the United States are famous. Very well formed crystals or nodules are also found away from major deposits.

20.1 **Pyrite**

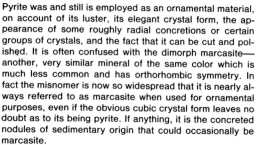

Pyrite was and still is employed as an ornamental material, on account of its luster, its elegant crystal form, the appearance of some roughly radial concretions or certain groups of crystals, and the fact that it can be cut and polished. It is often confused with the dimorph marcasite—another, very similar mineral of the same color which is much less common and has orthorhombic symmetry. In fact the misnomer is now so widespread that it is nearly always referred to as marcasite when used for ornamental purposes, even if the obvious cubic crystal form leaves no doubt as to its being pyrite. If anything, it is the concreted nodules of sedimentary origin that could occasionally be marcasite.

Appearance Isolated cubes with striated faces, pentagonal dodecahedra, or small groups of these two forms with their natural facets are normally used, although sometimes the nodules are used instead. These consist of minute crystals with a flattened, radial structure, a minutely granular surface and the characteristic, metallic yellow color. Small stones (2 to 3 millimeters in diameter) have sometimes been given a flattened circular, rose cut with only three polished facets on top. They are generally set in white metal, for obvious reasons of contrast, and are sometimes merely glued, rather than set, onto their supports. They are often found on necklace clasps and old-fashioned, inexpensive brooches.

Distinctive features In uncut stones, the shape of the crystal combined with the color, luster, and high density, or the form of the nodules, are unmistakable. Even when cut, its appearance is unique.

Occurrence It is very common and widely distributed throughout the world, even in the qualities suitable for ornamental purposes.

Value Extremely low.

Simulants and synthetics Because of its widespread occurrence, it is neither imitated nor produced synthetically.

Above: Radiating concretion of pyrite. France.
Below: Cut and polished nodule of marcasite.

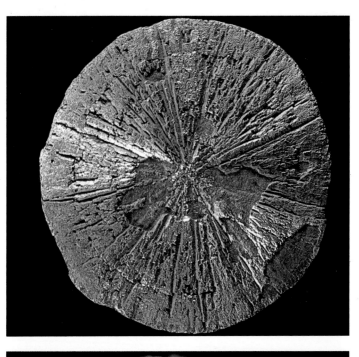

21 OPAL

SiO_2nH_2O

Noncrystalline hydrous silicon dioxide. Opal has the same chemical composition as quartz, but contains from 1 to 2 percent water, and is not crystallized. It has a certain type of regular structure, but not at the atomic level, being composed of alignments of tiny spheres (from 40 to 4000 Å in diameter) which form a compact, three-dimensional network. The name *opal* is apparently derived, through the Greek *opállios,* from the Sanskrit *upala,* meaning "precious stone."

Crystal system   Noncrystalline.

Appearance   It occurs as narrow veins of up to 10 centimeters or more, or as nodules, inside cavities or cracks in silica-rich rocks. It may also be found pseudomorphous after other minerals. It may have a whitish to light gray, pale green, sky-blue, smoke gray, black, yellowish to orange or reddish background color. It can be semiopaque, with a vaguely porcelainlike appearance, or similar to broken glass, with shiny, conchoidal fracture. It is more often translucent and milky, with an appearance that is so characteristic, it is described as opalescent. Opals can even be fully or largely transparent; such stones are usually orange-yellow to red in color. The most highly prized varieties display internal iridescence due to light diffraction by the network of tiny spheres of which they are composed. These types are collectively known as noble opal or precious opal. The range of colors apparently depends on the size of the spheres, or rather, the distance between the rows.

1.44–
1.46

In gem quality precious opal, three sets of distinctions are made. The first, according to the ground color of the material, distinguishes light or white opal from dark or black opal. The second, applied to each of these two varieties, is based on the range of colors in the iridescent patches; and the third is based on the size, shape, and distribution of the patches. The transparent or semitransparent, noniridescent variety (known as common opal) is also used as a gem if it is attractively colored. Because of its orange-yellow to reddish orange color, it is known as fire opal.

Physical properties   Opal has a hardness of 5.5 to 6.5 and very low density; from about 1.98 to 2.20 g/cm³, depending on the water content. The refractive index varies from 1.44 to 1.46 or a little more. It is singly refractive. It may be somewhat porous, in which case it is dangerous to immerse it in liquids other than water.

Genesis   Opal is normally found in assocation with effusive magmatic rocks, such as rhyolites, andesites, and trachytes, having been deposited in cracks and cavities by aqueous fluids at low temperature. In Australia, it is found both in connection with trachytes and basalts, and in siliceous sandstone where hydrous silica has been precipitated, perhaps through alteration of feldspars by percolating waters in an environment subjected to very long periods of stable water conditions.

Occurrence   One area of eastern Czechoslovakia formerly belonging to Hungary has been mining opal since Roman times and was the only source of noble opal for Eu-

Above: Rough opal. Australia.
Below: Rough precious opal.

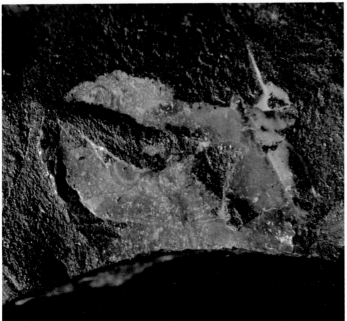

ropeans until the nineteenth century. Nowadays, most opal comes from Australia, where the finest quality opals are found. Other sources are Mexico and, to a lesser extent, Guatemala and Honduras. Low-value or subgem quality varieties of opal are found in many other places, especially the United States (xyloid opal or petrified wood) and Iceland (where it is deposited by hot springs).

21.1 **White precious opal**

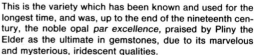

This is the variety which has been known and used for the longest time, and was, up to the end of the nineteenth century, the noble opal *par excellence*, praised by Pliny the Elder as the ultimate in gemstones, due to its marvelous and mysterious, iridescent qualities.

Appearance   It has a whitish (watered-down milk) to light grayish, dull yellow, light blue-gray, or pale-blue ground color. The range of colors of the patches, due to diffraction, depends on the size of the minute spheres of which the gem is composed: patches will be violet to blue for structures with very small spheres, gradually turning to green, yellow, orange, and red as the size of the spheres increases. The wavelengths diffracted depends on the distance between rows of spheres. When this becomes too great, diffraction no longer occurs. The patches of color can be more or less clearly defined, extensive, and homogeneous in size. Pieces with angular, polygonal, evenly distributed patches in a wide range of color with clear-cut edges are known as harlequin opals: this is the most valuable variety, for both black and white opal. Varieties with heterogeneous patches of color and poorly defined edges are less highly prized.

White opal is, whenever possible, cut into fairly convex cabochons. It is sometimes cut flat but here there is a risk of breakage, as the stone is brittle. The most valuable cabochons are the strongly curved, oval ones. Many others have a vaguely triangular shape with rounded corners or, at any rate, less symmetrical shapes, which permit a higher yield from irregular rough stones.

Distinctive features   White opal is unmistakable, more immediately recognizable than any other gem. There is, of course, the problem of distinguishing it from black opal, given the wide range of gradations from one to the other. It is called black when the background color is mid-gray, smoke gray, blue or black; otherwise it is called white.

Occurrence   As already mentioned, white opal has been mined for centuries in Czechoslovakia; but production there is nowadays extremely limited. Most white opal now comes from Australia, mainly from the Andemooka and Coober Pedy deposits in South Australia. Light-colored opal, including some fine opal, with the iridescence of noble opal, also comes from Mexico.

Smaller quantities are also extracted in the United States, Brazil, Japan, and Indonesia.

Value   The best quality gems fetch very high prices, exceeded only by the four principal gemstones (diamond, emerald, ruby, and sapphire), imperial jade, alexandrite, and black opal. The potential price range, however, is very extensive and hard to quantify without direct experience.

Above: Rough fire opal. Mexico.
Below: White opal.

Many specimens which are very pleasing in appearance are quite modestly priced, costing no more than other secondary gems. Specimens with weak, barely visible iridescence are fairly cheap.

Simulants and synthetics   It was long considered impossible to imitate opal. In recent years, however, an imitation, which, at first sight, looks deceptively similar to opal has appeared on the market. It is called "Slocum stone," after its inventor. A plastic imitation has also recently come onto the market. It is very similar indeed to the natural stone, being composed of microscopic spheres, like opal. Fortunately, its low melting point, hardness, and density can distinguish it, despite its appearance. White opal has been manufactured synthetically by a French company for nearly a decade; the appearance of its iridescent patches is fairly distinctive (each being in the form of a mosaic), but it can nonetheless only be distinguished by an expert.

21.2 Black precious opal

This variety has only been known and appreciated since the beginning of the twentieth century, after the discovery of the Australian deposits. Before that, it was only found occasionally, as a true rarity, and was regarded with some mistrust. In some cases it was known to be obtained by artificial coloration of the mass, using the same procedures used for agate, to highlight the patches of iridescence.

Appearance   It has a bluish gray, smoke gray to black color. This dark ground greatly enhances its appearance by emphasizing the patches of color caused by diffraction. The range of colors and shapes of the patches are roughly the same as for white opal, and the standards and terminology employed are identical. Here, too, when the patches are angular, polygonal, clear-cut, and of uniform size, it is called (black) harlequin opal, and this is the most valuable type of all.

Naturally, the cabochon cut is used and thicker gems are preferred, those of regular outline, better suited to jewelry, being the most highly prized.

Distinctive features   Like white opal, it is unmistakable. Only the dividing line between black and white opal is not clear-cut, one type merging into the other. Care needs to be exercised to ensure that what may appear to be a black opal is not really a thin layer of white opal on a piece of dark-colored rock. Examination of the stone from the side will reveal this combination.

Occurrence   Black or dark opal comes almost exclusively from Australia, the main deposit being at Lightning Ridge (New South Wales); less important sources are Tintenbar (New South Wales) and Mintable (South Australia). Very small quantities also come from Indonesia.

Value   Very high; the highest for opal, and therefore immediately after the principal gemstones (diamond, emerald, ruby, and sapphire). Naturally, the value is slightly lower when the contrast between the iridescent patches and background color is less pronounced, when the patches are less clearly defined, and when the range of colors is limited; or, finally, when the patches are arranged

Above: Harlequin variety of white precious opal, 2.50 ct. Below: Black precious opal, 1.30 ct. Australia.

haphazardly, are uneven, or at any rate less attractive. Nevertheless, all black opal is expensive.

Simulants and synthetics   Black opal is harder to imitate than white opal. The French company which produces synthetic white opal has succeeded in producing very attractive black opal, but at a very high cost, which few are willing to pay for a synthetic stone because, for the same price, one could obtain quite a fine, natural white opal. Because of the value of black opal, even very thin veins are used for ornamental purposes. By reason of opal's extreme brittleness, it is used either as the base of doublets with the top, convex part of colorless quartz, or as an intermediate layer of triplets, the base of which consists of common opal and the top part of quartz. These doublets and triplets are not regarded as false, but are obviously much less valuable than all-opal cabochons. But when, as sometimes happens, the triplet is made with white opal, the underside of which is cemented to the bottom layer with black glue, to make the entire gem look more valuable, this is a clear case of falsification. Recently, treatment of white opals has recommenced, taking advantage of their natural porosity to darken their color, and thereby increase their value. These processes are very hard to detect.

21.3 **Common and fire opal**

Apart from precious opal, there is another type of opal known as common opal. It is usually fairly translucent, cloudy, and without opal's characteristic iridescence, due to the fact that the spheres of silica composing it are too large. It is generally rather a dull, pale, unattractive color; however, the best known and appreciated variety, fire opal, is brightly colored.

Appearance   The color is yellow to orange, or brilliant scarlet. Fire opal may be a bit cloudy, or almost perfectly transparent. For this reason, it is both cut into cabochons and faceted, unlike precious opal. Transparent specimens may have good luster. Signs of iridescence are sometimes visible in bright light, the passage from common to noble opal being continuous, without a clear separation.

Distinctive features   Fire opal is strongly characterized by its color, combined with an "amorphous" look, unlike that of transparent crystalline gems.

It has a very low density, lower than that of glass, with which it could be confused. On the other hand, it is quite hard, like other opals. There is no other stone that resembles it.

Occurrence   It comes mainly from Mexico, but also from Guatemala, Honduras, and the United States. It is also found in some parts of Australia, which is, however, best known for the more precious varieties.

Value   There is no comparison between the value of noble opal and that of fire opal, which is quite inexpensive even compared with other minor gems. It is worth somewhat more when a few splashes of color are visible inside the stone. It is valued by collectors as a curiosity but is little used in jewelry.

*Above: Fire opal,
1.80 ct.
Below: Crystals of
microcline.*

Simulants and synthetics It is hard to say whether or not certain types of glass of a similar color have been made to imitate this modestly priced gem. It is not produced synthetically.

---

22 MICROCLINE
$KAlSi_3O_8$

Silicate of potassium and aluminium, belonging to the feldspar group; it is the phase of this compound that is stable at low temperature.

Crystal system Triclinic.

Appearance Individual crystals are squat, vaguely prismatic, with a fine network of striations consisting of whitish, slightly more opaque veins corresponding to twinning planes. The color can be milky, white, pink, or pale to blue-green; it has very poor transparency. Compact aggregates of crystals are also common.

Physical properties It has a hardness of 6. The density is 2.56–2.58 g/cm^3. The refractive indices are $n\alpha$ 1.522, $n\gamma$ 1.530. It has two directions of cleavage which are almost at right angles to each other: hence its name, which means "small angle."

Genesis It is found in metamorphic rocks, intrusive magmatic rocks, and pegmatites, which provide the largest crystals.

Occurrence It is widely distributed in the form of minute crystals in rocks. Fine crystals occur in Brazil, the United States (Colorado and Virginia), Madagascar, Norway, the Soviet Union (Urals), India, and Italy (in the granite of Maddalena island).

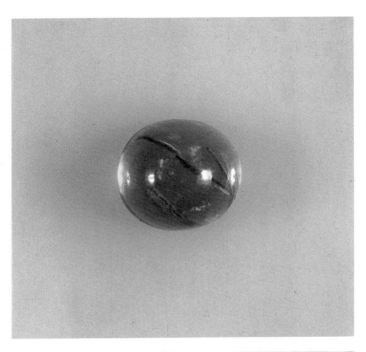

22.1 Amazonite

Pale green to blue-green semiopaque microcline has been used since time immemorial as an ornamental material. It was called amazonite in the belief that it came from the Amazon river.

Appearance It is usually light green, or sometimes blue-green or bluish with a mottled appearance and sometimes a fine crisscross network of light striations. It is semiopaque, with poor luster and easy cleavage.

It is cut into cabochons, or roundish pieces for necklaces and pendants, or carved into figurines and other items.

Distinctive features The network of striations, usually visible with a lens, distinguishes it from certain jades or opaque beryls, which it can resemble quite closely. Incipient cleavage cracks, where present, are also fairly characteristic.

Occurrence It is found in Brazil, but mainly in the United States, Madagascar, Namibia, Zimbabwe, Australia, and the Soviet Union.

Value The value of the stone itself is low, but expertly fashioned and/or antique pieces (it was used by the ancient Egyptians) can be quite valuable.

Simulants and synthetics Amazonite was occasionally imitated in the past by necklace beads made from special types of glass. It is not produced synthetically.

Above: Amazonite.
Below: Crystal of orthoclase.

---

23 ORTHOCLASE
$KAlSi_3O_8$

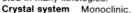

1.53 1.52

Silicate of potassium and aluminium, belonging to the feldspar group. The mineral got its name because it has two directions of cleavage, which are orthogonal (at right angles). It has the same composition as microcline, but is stable at slightly higher temperatures. It is widely distributed in many lithologies.

Crystal system Monoclinic.

Appearance It occurs as prismatic, sometimes flat-sided crystals, but in rocks it is usually anhedral. It may be perfectly transparent and yellow or almost colorless, but is more often semiopaque and white to grayish white, yellowish white, pink, or reddish.

Physical properties It has a hardness of 6. The density is about 2.56 g/cm^3. The refractive indices are approximately $n\alpha$ 1.520, $n\gamma$ 1.527. It has two directions of cleavage at right angles to one another.

Genesis It is common in intrusive, magmatic rocks, and metamorphic rocks, but the largest crystals are found in pegmatites.

Occurrence It is widely distributed. Important sources are Italy, Switzerland, Czechoslovakia, and Spain. The transparent variety comes from Madagascar.

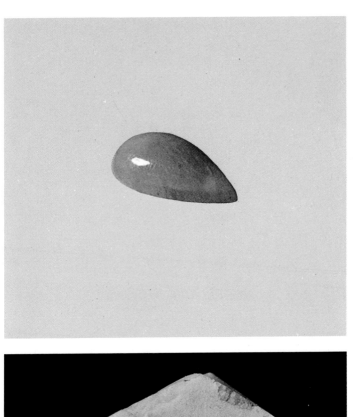

23.1 Noble orthoclase

This is the name given to the somewhat rare variety of transparent orthoclase which is basically yellow in color and usable as a gem.

Appearance The color varies from mid- to golden yellow. It is perfectly transparent with vitreous luster. The cut most commonly used with this gem is the step cut. Gems are usually free of inclusions.

Distinctive features Noble orthoclase principally resembles softly colored citrine and beryl, which can only be distinguished from it by their physical properties.

Occurrence It comes mainly from Madagascar, where it is found in pegmatites.

Value Low, even compared with other secondary gems. Being somewhat rare, however, fine specimens are sought by collectors and connoisseurs.

Simulants and synthetics It is neither imitated nor produced synthetically.

23.2 Adularia moonstone

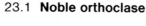

A microperthitic association of orthoclase and albite (with a predominance of orthoclase). Because of its slightly turbid transparency, gems cut *en cabochon* show a mobile reflection, which is softer and more diffuse than that of chatoyant stones.

Appearance Moonstone generally has an almost transparent ground, which is practically colorless, pale gray, or tinged with yellow, with a whitish to silvery white or blue shimmer. It is normally cut into cabochons or curved pieces for threading into necklaces, etc. Incipient cleavage cracks may be visible inside the stone.

Distinctive features Adularescence (a slight turbidity with a mobile reflection) is in itself distinctive. Another feldspar, albite, can look identical (for the same reason) and is also called moonstone. If necessary, the two may be distinguished by their density, which is lower in orthoclase. An imitation form consisting of synthetic spinel is much milkier in appearance, without a mobile reflection.

Occurrence Adularia moonstone is found mainly in Sri Lanka, Burma, India, Australia, Madagascar, Tanzania, the United States, and Brazil.

Value Fairly low, but the type with a blue reflection is quite highly prized.

Simulants and synthetics It has been imitated by milky synthetic spinel, which does not have a proper mobile reflection. It has not been manufactured synthetically.

Above: Noble orthoclase. Madagascar. Below: Cabochons of adularia moonstone. Sri Lanka.

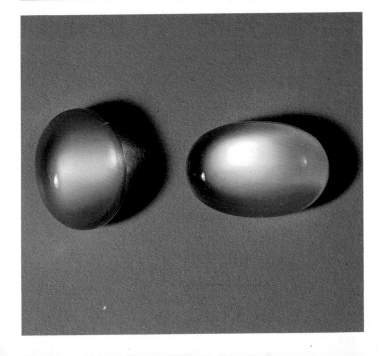

PLAGIOCLASE FELDSPARS

$NaAlSi_3O_8$-$CaAl_2Si_2O_8$ (albite-anorthite)

6–6.5

2.6–2.8

| 1.54 | 1.53 |
| 1.59 | 1.58 |

Silicate of sodium and aluminium to silicate of calcium and aluminium. This is an isomorphous series of minerals, of the feldspar group, consisting of solid solutions of one or other component in variable proportions. Depending on the amount of each component, the mineral may be called albite (the mainly sodium end-member), oligoclase, andesine, labradorite, bytownite, or anorthite (the mainly calcium end-member). They are very widely distributed in rocks.

Crystal system Triclinic.

Appearance Plagioclase feldspars occur as crystals of prismatic, often tabular habit, with fine striations (twinning planes or cleavage surfaces); also as crystalline masses. The crystal form is hardly ever developed in rocks. They can be transparent, or (rarely) almost fully opaque to semiopaque. The color is often whitish or grayish white, but can be yellowish, pale green, or even pink. It sometimes displays iridescence on a dark gray ground. The varieties used as gems are mainly albite, which is mostly or wholly transparent, and labradorite, which is iridescent.

Physical properties It has a hardness of about 6–6.5. The density steadily increases from about 2.62 g/cm^3 for albite to about 2.76 g/cm^3 for anorthite. The refractive indices also increase, from $n\alpha$ 1.525, $n\gamma$ 1.536 for albite to $n\alpha$ 1.576, $n\gamma$ 1.588 for anorthite.

Genesis These minerals crystallize in nearly all magmatic rocks, both intrusive and extrusive, in many metamorphic rocks, and in pegmatites.

Occurrence They are very common and distributed worldwide. Large crystals are found in pegmatites in Norway, the Soviet Union, and the United States.

24.1 Albite moonstone

The sodium-rich end-member of the plagioclase feldspar group, called albite, from the Latin *albus*, because of its whitish color, may look similar in appearance to adularia moonstone if cut *en cabochon*. Furthermore, in both cases, the composition is midway between that of orthoclase and that of albite: albite moonstone can, in fact, be defined as a microperthitic association of albite and orthoclase with a predominance of albite. For this reason, it is considered acceptable to use a similar name for the two gems.

Appearance It is typically misty, semitransparent or semiopaque with a pale, shimmering reflection, less well defined than in chatoyant stones. It may be milky white in color, or dull yellow, yellow-gray or greenish gray. It is almost always cut *en cabochon*. Curved pieces are also cut as necklace beads or pendants.

Distinctive features The adularescence is quite distinctive. This is also found in adularia moonstone, but the two are distinguishable by their density, which is higher (from about 2.62 to 2.65 g/cm^3) in albite moonstone. The refractive indices, which are always hard to establish in

Above: Crystals of albite, with quartz. Below: Cabochon of albite moonstone.

curved stones, are slightly higher ($n\alpha$ 1.525, $n\gamma$ 1.536) than those of orthoclase, with slightly stronger birefringence as well. The yellowish or light brown coloration of some specimens also distinguishes it from adularia moonstone.

Occurrence   It comes mainly from Canada and Kenya but occurs also in India and Sri Lanka. In the latter two countries, however, it is confused with the similar variety of orthoclase.

Value   Somewhat low, like adularia moonstone.

Simulants and synthetics   It is imitated by milky synthetic spinel, which, however, (virtually) lacks the mobile reflection. It is not manufactured synthetically.

24.2 **Labradorite**

This is a sodium-rich plagioclase feldspar which displays a particular type of iridescence on a dark ground. The name labradorite is derived from its main source: Labrador, in Canada. The effect is probably due to the presence of very fine platelets of different compositions and minute inclusions of ilmenite, rutile and, perhaps, magnetite, which cause diffraction.

Appearance   The ground color is a dark smoke gray, but when light strikes it in a particular direction, it displays striking rainbow-colored reflections (violet, blue, green, yellow, and even orange and reddish) known as labradorescence. It is cut into gems, or small, not too convex, polished plaques for setting. It is also used as an ornamental material for carving and engraving. The background color is uninteresting and it is the strength of the labradorescence that gives the stone its value. The particularly brightly colored variety found in Finland is sometimes known as spectrolite.

Distinctive features   It is highly distinctive at first sight; but there is an ornamental material, used in slabs and consisting of a rock containing large pieces of potassic feldspar, which looks similar to labradorite. This material, which is called larvikite after the place where it is found in Norway, is used for building purposes only.

If necessary, the two could be distinguished by their densities.

Occurrence   The labradorite used in gems comes mainly from Canada and Finland.

Value   Quite low, partly because it is hard to use. Few types of work can bring out its characteristic colors.

Simulants and synthetics   It does not appear to have been imitated or produced synthetically.

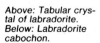

Above: Tabular crystal of labradorite.
Below: Labradorite cabochon.

238

25 ZOISITE

$Ca_2Al_3Si_3O_{12}OH$

6.5

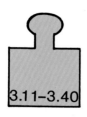

3.11–3.40

1.70 | 1.69

Silicate of calcium and aluminium.

Crystal system Orthorhombic.

Appearance It usually occurs as poorly defined crystals, aggregates of small, possibly rod-shaped crystals, or flattened crystals. Normally white, grayish or greenish, it may also display brilliant colors such as pink, blue and bright green. It has perfect prismatic cleavage.

Physical properties It has a hardness of about 6.5. The density is 3.11–3.40 g/cm^3 (lower in the massive varieties, higher in distinct crystals). The refractive indices are about $n\alpha$ 1.69, $n\gamma$ 1.70. Individual, colored crystals may have marked pleochroism.

Genesis The minute crystals distributed in rocks are produced by metamorphism of plagioclases. Larger crystals are sometimes found as well.

Occurrence It is widely distributed wherever metamorphic rocks and gabbro are found together. The varieties used for gems and ornaments are, however, confined to restricted areas of East Africa (tanzanite and massive green zoisite) and Norway (thulite).

25.1 Tanzanite (blue zoisite)

The basically blue variety of zoisite discovered in Tanzania in 1967 is commonly known as tanzanite.

Appearance This gem has a characteristic blue color, usually with a violet tinge. In lighter-colored specimens, it is almost lavender. This is the principal color, visible from the table facet in cut stones, because another characteristic of tanzanite is strong pleochroism from violet-blue to violet, grayish, or greenish. It has vitreous luster. The stones have few inclusions; where present, these sometimes look like thin, parallel tubules. It is normally given a round or oval, mixed cut, but the step cut is also used.

Distinctive features The particular color, combined with the type of pleochroism described and moderate luster, make it fairly easy to distinguish. It can sometimes resemble cordierite, but this has much lower refractive indices and lower density. It is sometimes confused with sapphire, but compared with this, it is visibly less lustrous and much less hard. It also has different pleochroism and different refractive indices. It is said to have very low resistance to ultrasound. Tanzanite jewelry should, therefore, never be cleaned with the ultrasonic cleaners commonly used by jewelers and watchmakers. On a number of occasions, stones thus treated have suffered irreparable damage.

Occurrence Very limited quantities are found, almost exclusively in Tanzania, where, moreover, the chief deposit is apparently nearly exhausted.

Value Given its attractive color, its rarity, and the publicity which greeted its discovery, the value of tanzanite is quite high, little less than that of the violet-blue sapphires it resembles. But it is rarely seen on the market and is very much a collector's item. Its modest hardness makes it un-

Above: Crystal of zoisite (variety tanzanite). Tanzania. Below: Tanzanite, 2.50 ct. Tanzania.

suitable for rings which are, of course, susceptible to knocks and abrasion.

Simulants and synthetics Being little known and of very recent history, this stone has neither been imitated nor produced synthetically.

25.2 **Massive green zoisite**

An ornamental material consisting of crystalline aggregates of green zoisite with ruby inclusions, also recently discovered in Tanzania.

Appearance The ground color is bright green, forming a striking contrast with the isolated crystals of ruby which are bright red (although nontransparent), some tens of millimeters in size, and evenly distributed throughout the mass. The overall effect is very pleasing and this material is sawn, turned, sculpted, and polished mainly into items such as ashtrays, boxes, and small carvings.

The use of diamond-tipped tools obviates the problem of the difference in hardness between zoisite and ruby.

Distinctive features The general appearance is unmistakable. There is nothing else like it in the mineral world.

Occurrence As already mentioned, this material is found in appreciable quantities in Tanzania, which supplies both the ornamental material and collectors' markets.

Value Given its strikingly beautiful appearance, even to the uninitiated, and its reasonable hardness, it is prized as an ornamental material. The price of items made of massive green zoisite depends, of course, on the quality of the workmanship.

Simulants and synthetics It has neither been imitated nor produced synthetically.

Above: Crystalline aggregate of massive green zoisite with ruby inclusions. Below: Detail of carving in massive green zoisite with ruby inclusions.

26 NEPHRITE

$Ca_2(Mg,Fe)_5Si_8O_{22}(OH)_2$

5–6

2.9–3.4

1.61

Silicate of calcium, magnesium, and iron, containing fluorine and hydroxyl. It is an amphibole, of the actinolite series.

Crystal system Monoclinic.

Appearance The amphiboles of the tremolite-actinolite series usually occur as elongated, parallel, radiating or even fibrous crystals; but the variety known as nephrite has a very compact, felted microcrystalline structure, which gives it the extreme tenacity characteristic of jade. The color varies from whitish—or, at any rate, very pale—for the magnesium end-member, to darkish green or gray for members with a high iron content.

Physical properties It has a hardness of 5–6. The relatively easy cleavage of the amphibole group is not found in this microcrystalline material. The density ranges from 2.90 to 3.40 g/cm^3. The refractive indices are about $n\alpha$ 1.606, $n\gamma$ 1.632, but only one index can normally be established in this compact, microcrystalline material; it is about 1.61.

Genesis Nephrite occurs in both contact and regionally metamorphosed iron and magnesium-rich rocks.

Occurrence The amphiboles of this series are relatively common minerals, widely distributed in metamorphic and basic magmatic rocks. Even the densely felted form typical of nephrite is found in large deposits in the Soviet Union (Siberia, Turkestan) and New Zealand, but in small quantities almost everywhere.

26.1 Nephrite jade

This stone is known as nephrite, because in early times it was used in amulets against kidney disorders. Both jadeite and nephrite are known as jade, so the term nephrite jade, rather than merely nephrite, will be used here to distinguish between the two. Although it is one of the two types of minerals which are fully entitled to be called jade, nephrite jade is less highly prized nowadays than jadeite jade, which more often has strong, attractive colors. But nephrite jade was very important in ancient Oriental art, especially in China, where fine objects were fashioned from it up until the mid-eighteenth century, the use of jadeite jade only being established after that period.

Appearance It is generally found in fairly homogeneous opaque to translucent masses, which are a fairly strong but not very lively green. However, the color can be dark green to blackish, gray or blue-gray. Grayish white is also very common. It may contain brown, yellow-brown or orange streaks of iron oxide. Because of its exceptional toughness, it is used for the carving of figurines, bas-reliefs, and elaborate, thin-walled vases. It is also made into necklace beads and pendants and, much more rarely, cabochons and engraved pieces for setting in jewelry. It takes a good polish. Pale, slightly translucent and not too lustrous specimens have a greasy or waxy appearance that is characteristic of much antique Chinese jade.

Above: Carving in nephrite jade.
Below: Nephrite jade cabochon, 15 mm. Taiwan.

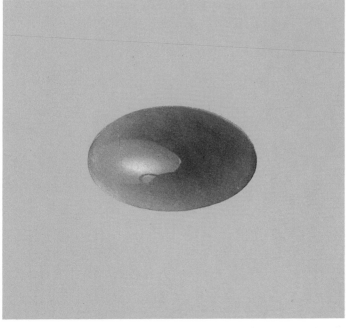

Vase in nephrite jade. New York. Rare Art, Inc.

Distinctive features It is distinguished from jadeite jade by its felted, rather than granular, structure, as well as its lower density and different refractive indices (although these are hard to establish). It is mainly distinguished by its density, but also by its greater hardness, from some varieties of serpentine, which look very similar to the more translucent type. It is also distinguished by its density from certain rocks containing hydrogrossular and vesuvianite, which are often translucent and very similar. These are known as Transvaal or Pakistan jade, depending on their place of origin.

Occurrence Nephrite jade is fairly widespread, so much so that it was used virtually everywhere by Neolithic man for polished stone weapons. The chief sources are the Soviet Union (Turkestan, Siberia) and New Zealand. It is also found in Canada, the United States, and Australia.

Value On the whole, it is of very modest value, being widely used for necklaces and other items of modern jewelry; but its extraordinary mechanical properties and particular appearance have been exploited (generally by Oriental craftsmen) to produce works of art of outstanding aesthetic value and complexity of detail, such as loose chains with unjointed links; small vases intricately entwined with fantastic dragons and often having handles with loose chains hanging from them; bells with moving clappers, which work as well as metal ones; and minutely engraved knife or weapon handles. Such items are valuable and where artistic merit is combined with antiquity, nephrite fetches extremely high prices.

Simulants and synthetics An imitation of nephrite jade consisting of a paste, recrystallized to form a translucent material with felted or fascicular zones of crystals, has been produced in Japan in recent years. This has a lower density (ca. 2.65 g/cm^3) than nephrite jade and a refractive index of about 1.53. It is known as imori stone or metajade. Natural materials such as aventurine, serpentine, and the polycrystalline mixtures of hydrogrossular and vesuvianite look very similar, at first glance, to nephrite jade, and are used as substitutes. These are called jade, preceded by their place of origin, i.e., Indian jade, Korean jade, Transvaal jade, respectively. Such names are considered an abuse of proper gemological terminology. These materials have interesting ornamental properties, but their value is lower than that of nephrite jade, and lower still than jadeite jade. Synthetic nephrite is not produced.

27 RHODONITE
MnSiO₃

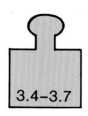

Silicate of manganese.

Crystal system   Triclinic.

Appearance   Rhodonite sometimes occurs as distinct, translucent to semiopaque crystals, but more often it is in compact, crystalline masses of a patchy, pink, flesh red or brownish red color, often with blackish veining due to oxidation of manganese.

Physical properties   It has a hardness of 5.5–6.5. The density ranges from 3.40 to 3.70 g/cm³. The refractive indices vary between $n\omega$ 1.733, $n\varepsilon$ 1.744 and $n\varepsilon$ 1.716, $n\omega$ 1.728 (the optic sign therefore changing from negative to positive), but the massive material normally gives one value, of about 1.73.

Genesis   It is formed by metamorphism (with addition of silica) of other manganese minerals, probably including rhodochrosite ($MnCO_3$).

Occurrence   It is fairly widespread, mainly found in Sweden, Great Britain, the Soviet Union, India, Australia, South Africa, the United States, and Mexico.

27.1 Rhodonite

Like rhodochrosite, its name is derived from the Greek root, *rhódon*, meaning "pink."

Appearance   The color is reddish pink, with thin veins or patches of gray to black. The translucent to semiopaque polycrystalline form is cut *en cabochon* or shaped into beads, which can take a good polish. Rare transparent crystals have also been faceted into gems for collectors and connoisseurs. The individual crystals have prismatic cleavage.

Distinctive features   It is distinguished from rhodochrosite by its greater hardness and the fact that it is not attacked by hydrochloric acid.

Occurrence   It comes mainly from the Soviet Union, India, Australia, and the United States.

Value   Somewhat low compared with other ornamental materials.

Simulants and synthetics   It has neither been imitated nor produced synthetically.

Above: Crystalline mass of rhodonite. Below: Rhodonite cabochon.

28 DIOPSIDE

$MgCaSi_2O_6$

5.5-6

3.3

1.72 | 1.69

Silicate of calcium and magnesium, of the monoclinic pyroxene group. The name is derived from the Greek *dis* and *ópsis*, meaning "double vision," because it is clearly birefringent. Some of the magnesium may be replaced by iron.

Crystal system Monoclinic.

Appearance Diopside occurs in somewhat stocky or elongated prismatic crystals, or as aggregates of rod-shaped crystals, the color often being bottle green to blackish green, but also bright green or dull yellowish green. In some cases it is semiopaque, with internal fibrosity. The fairly transparent types are used as gems, as are the semiopaque specimens that exhibit chatoyancy or asterism if appropriately cut.

Physical properties It has a hardness of 5.5–6, therefore not very high. The density varies from 3.27 to 3.31 g/cm³, increasing with the iron content. The refractive indices are about $n\alpha$ 1.671–1.702, $n\gamma$ 1.699–1.726, so there is a very marked birefringence of 0.028–0.024.

Genesis Diopside is common in contact metamorphosed limestones or serpentinous rocks and the kimberlites of South Africa.

Occurrence It is fairly widespread, found mainly in South Africa, Burma, Sri Lanka, Madagascar, and Brazil, but also Italy (Val d'Ala), Austria (Tyrol), Finland, and the United States. It is occasionally found in metamorphosed blocks of limestone ejected by Vesuvius.

28.1 Diopside

The transparent, greenish varieties are used as gems and have no separate name; however, the brilliant green variety, which also contains chrome (as can be seen, for example, from the absorption spectrum), is known as chrome diopside.

Appearance Gem diopside is generally a dark, bottle green, but may also be light, rather dull, yellowish green. However, when the color is due to chrome, it can be a livelier, almost emerald hue. It has unexceptional, vitreous luster, and is given both mixed, oval, and cabochon cuts. It is not very common, and gems weighing many carats are rare.

Distinctive features The bottle green color with quite strong birefringence is fairly characteristic, but as it can closely resemble certain tourmalines and olivines of a similar color, the physical properties normally have to be measured to confirm identification.

Occurrence Gem diopside comes mainly from Brazil, Sri Lanka, Burma, and Madagascar. New York, Italy, Austria, and Switzerland also produce fine quality gemstones. Chrome diopside is found in South Africa and Finland.

Value It is not a very well known gem, outside the areas where it is mined and cut, and is not highly prized. The brilliant green (chrome diopside) varieties are of low value,

Above: Cleavage mass of diopside. Below: Diopside.

even compared with other secondary gems. The dark or light green varieties are worth still less.

Simulants and synthetics It is neither imitated nor produced synthetically.

28.2 **Star diopside**

Recently, diopside displaying asterism when the stone is cut *en cabochon* has been seen quite often on the market for minor gemstones.

Appearance This is generally a blackish or blackish green color; rarely a definite green. It is, of course, cut into round or oval cabochons, which are generally biconvex with a roughly shaped, unpolished base. The star characteristically has four rays, two of which are straight, while the other two, not at right angles to the first pair, look slightly wavy (the crystal does not, in fact, have fourfold symmetry). Sometimes, oriented acicular (needlelike) surface crystalline inclusions are clearly visible, especially from below.

Stones weighing several tens of carats are also found, but they are not normally cut so large, as this makes them hard to use.

Distinctive features Star diopside has only binary symmetry, and the star has four rays, rather than six like other star stones.

When the gem contains conspicuous needlelike crystals (of magnetite) it is easily attracted by a magnet.

Occurrence Star diopside comes mainly from India.

Value Very low, one of the lowest for gems, even though asterism always has a certain appeal.

Simulants and synthetics It is neither imitated nor produced synthetically. It is sometimes passed off as star sapphire, although the resemblance is highly superficial, given the obvious difference in asterism.

$CuAl_6(PO_4)_4(OH)_8.5H_2O$

5-6

2.7

1.61

Hydrated phosphate of copper and aluminium.

Crystal system Triclinic.

Appearance It occurs as microcrystalline aggregates in the form of irregular, lobed or indented nodules or in thin strips (usually of no more than a few centimeters), which are more compact and strongly colored at the center, lighter and porous on the outside. It is blue-white to sky blue, light greenish blue to light green. It is generally opaque, only thin pieces being translucent.

Physical properties The hardness, which is apparently related to the grain size of the crystalline aggregate, has a surprisingly wide range, gradually descending from 5 to 6 to a consistency almost like that of blackboard chalk (this type is also whitish). The density, which also depends on the grain size and consequent porosity, varies between 2.65 and 2.90 g/cm³. Individual crystals have refractive indices of about $n\alpha$ 1.61, $n\gamma$ 1.65, but the compact, microcrystalline material only gives one index, of about 1.61.

Genesis It is a secondary or supergene mineral and is deposited by surface waters in cracks and cavities in alumina-rich extrusive rocks, together with other similar phosphates, chalcedony and limonite. It is present also in weathering copper deposits as in Arizona.

Occurrence It is found in Iran, where it has been mined since time immemorial, and the United States (Nevada, Arizona, California, New Mexico). Small quantities are also found in the Sinai peninsula.

29.1 Turquoise

The name of the gem is apparently related to the fact that it was brought to Europe from the Eastern Mediterranean by Levantine traders, generally known as Turks. It has served as an ornament for a very long time, having been used by the Egyptians some thousands of years BC. Nowadays, it is one of the most controversial gems, because much of the material sold has undergone so many different treatments that its original appearance has been completely transformed.

Appearance On the rare occasions when it has not been interfered with in any way, it has a uniform surface appearance almost like that of unglazed china or very fine-grained, homogeneous rock. It may be a strong blue color, but is more often pale sky blue, greenish blue or pale green. It can contain narrow veins of other material, either isolated or as a network; these are usually black or brown, though sometimes yellowish brown. It may also contain patches of whitish foreign minerals, with occasional, minute crystals of pyrite. It is used almost rough, in lightly polished nodules or, more often, in the form of spherical or summarily rounded, polished pierced stones (for necklaces and other items of jewelry). It is also made into cabochons, carved gems, or figurines. When, as very often happens, it has been impregnated with paraffin, the surface appearance under a lens is distinctive, with small,

Above: Turquoise. United States (California). Below: Turquoise cabochons. Left, of uniform color; right, with veining.

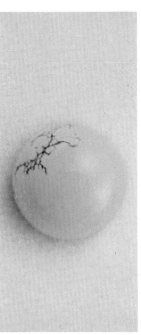

whitish, opaque patches juxtaposed with and interpenetrated by bluer, translucent areas, sometimes set against a faint pattern of larger, indented patches. Like all gems which are basically pastel in color, the richer-colored types are the most appreciated. The preferred color is strong sky blue, the pale greenish-blue being less highly prized, and the pale green even less so. Given the wide range in hardness for this gem, the hardest types with values at least in excess of 4–4.5 are obviously worth the most.

Distinctive features Because the most striking external feature of turquoise is its color, it is readily imitated by all types of similarly colored surrogates. Ceramic material, marble, and nodules of other minerals (howlite, magnesite) that have been externally stained, artificially colored compressed powders, and plastic are merely a few of the numerous substitutes currently encountered. As a rule, a few negative criteria make a rough, preliminary distinction possible:

- *It is not turquoise* if it appears under a lens to consist of numerous, minute grains of polygonal shape, juxtaposed in an artificial manner, with a homogeneous blue or heterogeneous light and dark blue or light blue and whitish color;
- *It is not turquoise* if it reacts in a matter of seconds, ten at the most, to a drop of hydrochloric acid, showing fairly strong effervescence, a change in color, or obvious surface damage (all this must be verified under a lens);
- *It is not turquoise* if it is warm to the touch, light like plastic, and burns with the characteristic odor of plastic when touched by a thin piece of red-hot iron wire.

Apart from these distinctions, not even establishment of the basic physical properties (the hardness is extremely variable, thus not characteristic) is sufficient to identify turquoise with any certainty and this must, therefore, be left to experts.

Occurrence In ancient times, turquoise was mined in the Sinai peninsula and Iran, while certain Central American peoples, the Aztecs in particular, extracted it in what is now known as New Mexico.

The best quality turquoise still comes from Iran, but in relatively small quantities. Recently, deposits in the United States (New Mexico, Arizona, California, Nevada) have been increasingly exploited. Much of the material extracted from these sources is of low quality, but it is used, nevertheless, after being treated to improve its hardness, consistency, and color.

Value Because it has been fashionable for a number of years, turquoise is quite highly prized in relation to comparable nontransparent gems, although it is fairly plentiful on the market. Its value is exceeded only by lapis lazuli and top quality jadeite jade.

Simulants and synthetics The ancient Egyptians apparently imitated turquoise with ceramic material. More recently, it has been so widely simulated by the most diverse materials that imitations are nowadays perhaps more plentiful on the market than turquoise itself.

Ceramic material, glass, plastic, agglomerates of artificial powders, and nodules of artificially colored rock are among the most common simulants. Attractive synthetic

Above: Turquoise necklace.
Below: Chinese carving in turquoise (250 mm high).

256

Above: Jewelry in gold, silver, and turquoise.
Below: Microcrystalline aggregate of lazurite.

turquoise has also been produced for about a decade. This has a highly characteristic honeycomb structure, which is recognizable under a lens. What complicates matters considerably is the fact that large quantities of turquoise are put on the market which are not of gem quality, but which, because of their extraordinary porosity, have been impregnated with various substances to improve their appearance, resistance, and ability to take polish. The most common cases are:

- *Impregnation with paraffin or wax* to enliven the color, eliminate porosity, and make material of low hardness easier to polish. When this treatment is carried out on good quality material, which absorbs very little and is only slightly improved, it is admissible.
- *Impregnation with colorless or colored plastic* to enliven the color, reduce brittleness, and allow the specimen to take an exceptional polish. This treatment, which is a partial falsification, is not acceptable.

30 LAZURITE (Lapis lazuli)

$(Na,Ca)_8(Al,Si)_{12}O_{24}(SO_{41}Sn)$

Silicate of sodium and aluminium, containing sulphur. It is a feldspathoid of the sodalite group.

Crystal system Cubic.

Appearance It occurs as aggregates of crystals, which are sometimes microscopic, sometimes about a millimeter, or even several millimeters in size. The aggregates are, however, thick, their color tending toward dull violet, due to the presence of sometimes numerous minerals of the same group such as sodalite, nosean, and haüyne. Calcite is also frequently encountered in the form of bright patches or light, even whitish veinings. It is frequently found associated with pyrite.

Physical properties It has a hardness of 5–5.5. The density is about 2.38–2.45 g/cm³, but may be higher in the aggregates used as an ornamental material, due to an abundance of foreign minerals. The refractive index is about 1.50.

Genesis It is a contact metamorphosed, metasomatically altered limestone.

Occurrence It is mainly found in Afghanistan and Chile. Other sources are the Soviet Union (Siberia), Burma, Angola, Canada (Labrador), and the United States (California). It is also found in Italy in limestone blocks ejected by Vesuvius.

5–5.5

2.4

1.50

30.1 Lapis lazuli

The name of the gem is derived, through the medieval Latin *lapis lazulus*, from the Arabic word *lazward*, from which the word *azure* comes; but according to the description of Pliny the Elder, the ancient Romans called it *sapphirus*. The name *sapphirus* was, of course, subsequently applied to the blue variety of corundum. Scientifically speaking, lapis lazuli is a "rock," because it consists of an association of minerals: lazurite and variable quantities of calcite, pyrite, and other feldspathoids of the sodalite group, such as haüyne and nosean.

Appearance It has a uniform, massive or sometimes granular appearance, with fairly distinct crystals. It is semi-opaque or opaque, with a surface that can take a good polish—like jades, for example. It is a strong but lively blue, sometimes with a hint of violet. It often contains grayish or off-white patches or veins, consisting of distinct, interwoven crystals which are minutely fringed at the edge of the patches, interpenetrated by and interwoven with the minute crystals of blue. The presence of white patches reduces the gem's value. The most highly prized varieties are those which are uniformly colored, preferably without a violet tinge. It often contains minute, scattered crystals of pyrite, which do not detract from its value. It is made into spherical or curved beads and even faceted, polyhedral ones, in which the flat facets can take a very good polish. It is also fashioned into carved gems, boxes, mosaics, small ornaments, vases, and figurines, the largest of which may be tens of centimeters in size. At one time, it was much used for sealstones. The Egyptians used it for their cylindrical seals.

Distinctive features The particular, very attractive color and speckling with minute crystals of pyrite give lapis lazuli an unmistakable appearance. As for the physical properties, the density of gem-quality material is very variable due to the presence of pyrite and other foreign minerals, but in any case, it is much higher than that of the mineral lazurite. It is normally between 2.7 and 2.9 g/cm^3, but can be as much as 3.0 g/cm^3. On contact with a minute drop of hydrochloric acid, lapis lazuli immediately gives off an odor of hydrogen sulphide (like the smell of rotten eggs).

Occurrence The best quality lapis lazuli comes from Afghanistan, where it has been mined since remote antiquity. The ancient Egyptians probably obtained their supplies from there. It is also found in Chile, but usually with numerous light patches and veins. Much smaller quantities come from the Soviet Union (Siberia), Burma, Pakistan, Angola, the United States, and Canada.

Value It is one of the most valuable semiopaque ornamental materials, worth about the same as good quality turquoise and the better jades (excluding imperial jade). When it contains light veins of other minerals, the value diminishes, but not excessively, as the effect is still very pleasing.

Simulants and synthetics It was and is much imitated, by glass, sometimes containing minute specks of metal to simulate pyrite, by stained chalcedony, and by a deep blue sintered aggregate of minute grains of synthetic spinel

Above: Lapis lazuli, 4 ct. Afghanistan. Below: Vase in lapis lazuli and gold (sixteenth century Florentine).

Above: Sculpture in lapis lazuli (Chinese).
Below: Microcrystalline veins of serpentine.

(plus the usual metal fragments to simulate pyrite). A product has recently appeared on the market which is extremely homogeneous, very deep blue with a violet tinge and scattered with minute fragments of pyrite. This is called synthetic lapis lazuli, although it does not correspond exactly with the natural stone in chemical composition. Furthermore, as the pyrite consists of ground fragments, it never displays the characteristic crystal form. The white patches in low quality lapis lazuli are sometimes colored blue and this practice is not always easy to detect. Natural stones are sometimes impregnated with paraffin to improve surface polish and heighten the color. This is the same procedure often used with poor quality turquoise, but the effects are not so far-reaching, perhaps because lapis lazuli is much less porous.

31 SERPENTINE GROUP
$Mg_3Si_2O_5(OH)_4$

Hydrated silicate of magnesium. Serpentine can contain three polymorphs: lizardite, chrysotile and antigorite. At least two of the three are usually present. Gemologists recognize serpentine as a species. Mineralogists recognize it as a group name, geologists as the rock type serpentinite. It is so named because of its resemblance to the reticulations of snakeskin.

Crystal system Orthorhombic for lizardite; monoclinic for antigorite and chrysotile.

Appearance Minerals of the serpentine group occur in microcrystalline veins (more rarely, masses) of translucent, waxy appearance, of a greenish gray to grayish white, or green color, in dark green or blackish colored rocks, i.e. serpentinites.

Physical properties The densities within the group vary from 2.3–2.6. The hardness also varies from 2–3, but serpentinite itself can be as hard as 5. As is often the case with microcrystalline materials, only one refractive index can normally be established; it is usually about 1.55–1.56.

Genesis It is a product of regional metamorphism, in a strongly aqueous environment, of magnesium-rich minerals, mainly olivine, but also pyroxenes and amphiboles.

Occurrence It is a very common mineral.

31.1 **Serpentine**

The massive varieties of serpentinite are particularly appreciated by gemologists when they have a definite, pleasing color, and are then called simply serpentine or maybe "serpentine jade." The term jade is a misnomer, but it is understandable because, as in the case of jadeite jade and nephrite jade, it relates to the uses made of these materials as a result of certain properties they possess, rather than to their mineralogical status.

Appearance   It is translucent, waxy, usually greenish white to soft pale green. Sometimes, groups or rows of small, striking, whitish cloud shapes are visible on the inside. The yellow-green to definite green varieties are less common. Multicolored pieces are also found, with light green to green, yellow-green, or brown patches. Serpentine is mainly used for the carved figurines or decorated vases up to eight to twelve inches high, typical of Chinese art. Being fairly tenacious (although less so than jade), it is suitable for the fashioning of the classic vases with hanging chains carved from a single piece of stone. Very elaborate compositions are often found as well, such as leafy branches, groups of birds, and flowering shrubs. Skillful use of different patches of color increases the value of such pieces. But serpentine is used still more often for the large-scale production of low quality items, because it is less costly than true jade and easier to work, being less hard. Typical of this type of work are small elephants or oriental divinities. The less common, green, yellow-green or yellow varieties are also rounded, polished, and made into beads for necklaces and bracelets.

Distinctive features   When the color is greenish white, with a waxy translucence and the characteristic white cloud formations just below the surface, it is easily recognizable at first sight. It differs from jadeite jade in having a lower density and hardness. It is mainly distinguished from nephrite jade, which is normally a bit less translucent and less waxy, by its density, while the difference in hardness is less clear (the serpentine used for ornamental purposes has a hardness range of 4.5 to 5.

Occurrence   Most serpentine used for ornamental purposes comes from England, New Zealand, Korea, China, and the United States.

Value   Its value is slightly lower than that of nephrite jade. It is therefore quite high for finely crafted objects, possibly fashioned from multicolored pieces, but distinctly low for mass-produced items.

Simulants and synthetics   Oriental-style figurines have been produced from a light green, translucent, waxy-looking plastic. These are highly deceptive at first sight, looking very much like serpentine. Their density is much lower, but it is not always easy to detect without proper measurement. Serpentine has not been produced synthetically.

Serpentine figurine.

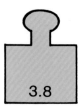

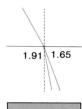

1.91 | 1.65

32 **MALACHITE**

$Cu_2CO_3(OH)_2$

Basic copper carbonate. It is an ore of copper.

Crystal system   Monoclinic.

Appearance   It occurs as rounded (mamillated) masses or encrustations, consisting of radiating or parallel aggregates of minute elongated crystals. It has striking color stratification from quite bright to dark green. The stratifications are curved according to the outer surface of the mass. It is opaque or semiopaque.

Physical properties   It has a low hardness of about 4, like other carbonates. The refractive indices are $n\alpha$ 1.655, $n\gamma$ 1.909, but are difficult to establish, both because the material is semiopaque, and because $n\gamma$ is very high, well above the range of ordinary refractometers. It has a density of about 3.8 g/cm^3.

Genesis   It is commonly formed by the action of atmospheric agents on copper mineral outcrops.

Occurrence   Large quantities of malachite are found wherever copper outcrops occur: in Chile, the United States, Zaire, Zimbabwe, Namibia, the Soviet Union, and Australia. But it is found almost everywhere in the form of small encrustations, together with azurite.

32.1 **Malachite**

The name is derived from the Greek *malákhe*, meaning "mallow," evidently because of the color.

Appearance   The color is always green, varying from a mid green which can be described as mallow green, to a very dark, even blackish green. These tones appear, as a rule, in alternate stripes (transverse to the length of the crystal), which are obviously successive layers of concretion and have an arrangement similar to that of the veins in other concretions, with broad curves, dome shapes, and undulations, generally following the direction of the outer surface of the stone. It has a fairly low hardness, but can acquire exceptional (though not very durable) polish. It is easily damaged by acids. Large blocks are used for slabs, balusters, and other sculpted objects. It is also employed for mosaics, boxes, figurines, cabochons, and beads.

Distinctive features   The green color, veining, shape of the veins, and polish make it unmistakable.

Occurrence   In the past, most malachite came from the Soviet Union (Urals), but nowadays large quantities are also obtained from Zaire, Zimbabwe, Namibia, Chile, the United States, and Australia.

Value   It is not often used as a gem and has a very low value. It is much admired, however, as an ornamental material and is quite highly priced for its category, especially when the attractiveness of the material is matched by fine workmanship.

Simulants and synthetics   It has not been imitated and is not produced synthetically.

Above: Microcrystalline aggregate of malachite.
Below: Malachite incense burner (Oriental). New York. Rare Art, Inc.

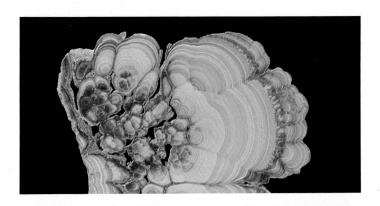

33 RHODOCHROSITE

MnCo$_3$

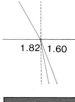

Manganese carbonate. Rhodochrosite is a mineral of the calcite series, its name being derived from the Greek *rhódon,* meaning "pink."

Crystal system Trigonal.

Appearance It occurs as semitransparent, rhombohedral crystals with poor luster, or as concretionary masses, sometimes with irregular, contorted veining. Normally a definite pink, it can be faded pink or slightly orange. Chemical alteration turns it blackish or dull brownish.

Physical properties It has a low hardness of about 4. The density is usually 3.4–3.7 g/cm^3. The refractive indices are $n\alpha$ 1.60, $n\omega$ 1.82. It has perfect rhombohedral cleavage.

Genesis Rhodochrosite is found in hydrothermal veins, but also in sedimentary deposits of chemical origin.

Occurrence It is quite a common mineral, especially in the United States, Argentina, Mexico, Namibia, Spain, Romania, and the Soviet Union.

33.1 Rhodochrosite

Despite its rather low hardness, this mineral is used as an ornamental material because of its pleasing color.

Appearance The massive material is characterized by a bright pink color, generally in distinct bands (as with agate and malachite), which may be curved or finely contorted, with narrow pale pink or whitish veining. Small slabs are used for mosaics, boxes, pots, and figurines, but the mineral is somewhat brittle. It is also made into necklace beads or other types of jewelry and recently, quite large, almost transparent crystals have yielded attractive, curved gems.

Distinctive features It has a color similar to that of rhodonite, but is distinguished from the latter by its concretionary structure and by the fact that it is visibly attacked by hydrochloric acid. It is also much less hard.

Occurrence The ornamental material mainly comes from Argentina, the United States (Colorado and Montana), Namibia, and the Soviet Union.

Value Somewhat low. Necklaces of transparent pieces are worth more, although the gem's relative lack of hardness can make it lose its polish easily.

Simulants and synthetics It is neither imitated nor produced synthetically.

Above: Concretionary mass of rhodochrosite.
Below: Box in rhodochrosite.

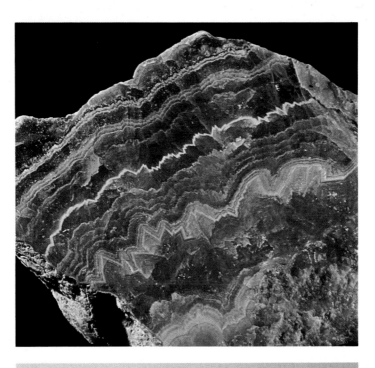

INTRODUCTION

Ornamental materials produced by biological processes, whether animal or vegetable, come under the heading of "organic" gems. There are four main organic materials normally regarded as distinct from precious stones, chiefly because of their low hardness, which is a fundamental property of gemstones. They deserve, nonetheless, to be considered alongside the more prestigious "precious stones," on account of their very pleasing appearance, which makes them invaluable for the preparation of items of personal adornment such as rings, bracelets, necklaces, cameos, and to an even greater extent, decorative objects such as vases and figurines.

The materials in question are pearl, coral, ivory, and amber, which are all of biological origin, but differ widely in their appearance and chemical composition. The only truly organic substance among them is amber, which is noncrystalline, fossilized resin from conifers. The other three materials consist mainly of inorganic compounds: oxyapatite, or calcium phosphate for ivory and calcium carbonate for the others. This appears in the form of aragonite for pearls and calcite for coral. But none of these chemical compounds is in the pure state, the exact chemical composition varying between specimens, according to their place of origin, color, and age.

This variability in chemical composition produces strong variations in physical properties as well, as may be seen from the following table. The table does not give refractive indices for nontransparent materials, such as pearls, coral, and ivory, but the values of their respective principal mineralogical components, aragonite, calcite, and oxyapatite, respectively, are shown for information.

	H	$d(g/cm^3)$	n
Amber	2½	1.06–1.08	1.54
Pearl	2½–4½	2.40–2.80	. . .
	(3½–4)	(2.94)	(1.53; 1.69)
Coral (calcareous)	(3½–4)	2.60–2.70	. . .
	(3)	(2.71)	(1.49; 1.66)
Ivory	2½–2¾	1.80	. . .
	(5)	(2.90)	(1.64; 1.65)

Note that ivory has much lower density and hardness than its mineralogical components in the pure state. This is because it has a relatively low proportion of the chief constituent: oxyapatite.

Pearl fishing, by Alessandro Allori (sixteenth century). Palazzo Vecchio, Florence.

34 PEARL

$CaCo_3$ (mainly aragonite)

2.5–4.5

2.7–2.8

Above: Variously colored pearls. Below: The different arrangement of the crystals of aragonite in pearl and mother-of-pearl. a) Cross section of a pearl with layers of aragonite arranged concentrically around the nucleus; b) cross section of mother-of-pearl nucleus with flat, parallel layers of aragonite. Cross sections of two cultured pearls: c) pearl with large nucleus and few concentric layers of nacre; d) pearl with small nucleus and numerous concentric layers of nacre.

Pearls consist of about 92 percent of calcium carbonate, or $CaCo_3$, in the form of aragonite crystals, held together by an organic substance, conchiolin (about 6 percent), which is identical to the horny outer layer of oyster shells, plus a small quantity of water (about 2 percent). Mother-of-pearl has a similar chemical composition, but with less calcium carbonate (about 66 percent) and more water (about 31 percent) and is used as the nucleus of cultured pearls. Pearls are undoubtedly the most costly and important of "organic" gems. They have been known since time immemorial in the Orient and were known to the Greeks and Romans, evidently following the conquests of Alexander the Great.

All manner of fantastic explanations for the origins of pearls were advanced in earlier times, some of them highly poetic. There is, for example, the old eastern legend quoted by Pliny, according to which oysters rose to the surface of the sea beneath the moon's rays, opened their shells and were fertilized by drops of dew. It was not until the mid-sixteenth century that a Dutch scholar by the name of Rondoletius recognized that pearls were pathological formations in pearl oysters.

Crystal system   Aragonite crystallizes in the orthorhombic system.

Appearance   Pearls are globular, usually almost spherical cysts, which form inside the tissues of the mollusk. Sometimes, they are pear-, egg-, or bean-shaped, or display more pronounced irregularities consisting of roundish apophyses or even sharp crests. The color is generally much the same as that of the inside of the oyster shell. Most pearls, therefore, are white with a touch of gray to yellowish gray-white, but they may be grayish, blackish, or iridescent from gray to green-blue-violet, and pink (the latter color applies to rare pearls produced by marine gastropod mollusks of the *Haliotis* and *Strombus* genera). Pearls are composed of numerous, thin, concentric layers, which are deposited successively by the mollusk ("onion" structure, Fig a). To some extent, the older the pearl, the bigger it is, and the more numerous are the constituent layers. But in cultured pearls, which nowadays far outnumber the others, the inside consists of a spherical nucleus of mother-of-pearl, often taken from the shell of another mollusk, artificially shaped into a bead, but composed of flat, parallel layers (Fig. b), surrounded by a number of concentric layers of nacre deposited around it by the pearl-producing mollusk (Fig. c,d).

Physical properties   Pearls have a hardness of 2.5–4.5; but they are fairly resilient, due to the organic substance they contain and their compact, concentrically layered structure. The density varies from 2.40 to 2.80 g/cm³, but most of those used as gems have a density of about 2.68–2.74 g/cm³ in the case of natural pearls and 2.73–2.78 g/cm³ in the case of cultured pearls. The refractive index can only be measured by complex procedures.

Genesis   Pearls form when a foreign body, such as a

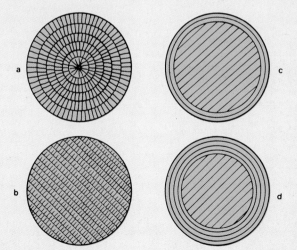

grain of sand, or more often a small parasite, finds its way into a pearl oyster which, in self-defense, surrounds the intruder with a cyst, and goes on depositing layer after layer of pearl over it, even when the intruder has been completely encapsulated and rendered incapable of doing any harm. Many mollusks produce pearls, but the most important ones belong to different species of the genus *Pinctada* (formerly known as *Meleagrina*), including *P. margaritifera*, *P. maxima*, *P. martensi*, *P. fucata*, and *P. vulgaris*. These are medium-large bivalve mollusks (about 25 cm) of the Pteriidae family (Filibranchia order). Less valuable pearls are produced by many other mollusks, including some freshwater bivalves and marine gastropods.

Ever since antiquity efforts have been made to speed up the natural processes of pearl formation and obtain more, bigger, and better-shaped pearls from oysters. The first serious attempts apparently date from the twelfth century, when the Chinese devised a method according to which variously shaped objects—typically images of Buddha—were placed between the mantle and shell of certain types of mollusk; after a couple of years it would be covered with a layer of mother-of-pearl. The production of cultured pearls, however, was pioneered in Japan around the turn of the twentieth century, by Mikimoto, who achieved the first positive results in 1893 with the production of blister pearls; by Mise, who set up production in 1907; and finally by Nishikawa and Mikimoto, to whom we owe the present method of cultivation, which dates from 1919. Briefly, the procedure consists of cutting a small piece of mantle out of a live oyster, wrapping it around a mother-of-pearl bead, and inserting it into the living tissue of another oyster. The oysters thus treated are placed in cages suspended from rafts in calm waters, at variable depths depending on the seasons, to ensure a temperature of not less than 50°F. The depths usually range from 2 to 3 meters in spring–summer and 5 to 6 meters in autumn–winter, thus achieving a balance, over the course of a year, between the effects of shallow water, conducive to rapid growth, and greater depth, which enables the pearls to acquire better color and luster.

The pearls can be harvested after five to seven years, but better results are achieved with longer periods of up to twelve years. Much shorter periods of growth—even less than half—are being used in another center of production which is developing alongside the famous Japanese industry, in areas of northern–western Australia, where the average temperatures are higher.

Occurrence The largest quantities of pearls are harvested from Sri Lanka, the Philippines, China, Japan, northern Australia, the Persian Gulf, and the Red Sea. Pearl production in the Americas is less important and is mainly confinéd to the Gulf of California and the Caribbean.

Top to bottom and left to right: Fishing for pearl oysters; insertion of foreign body in oyster; the oysters thus treated are placed in water in cages suspended from rafts; finally, the pearl which has formed over a number of years.

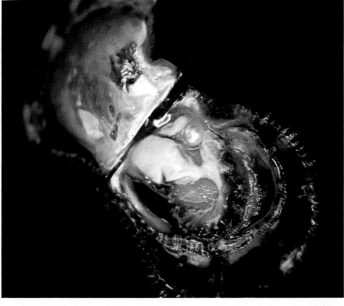

34.1 **Natural Pearls**

This is the type formed by accident, without human intervention, and was virtually the only one known before the beginning of the twentieth century.

Appearance Most natural pearls used in jewelry are roughly spherical, and this is the most suitable shape for ordinary necklaces. Pearls may, however, be somewhat irregular in shape. If they have rounded, not too obvious projections, they are known as baroque pearls. These are also pierced and threaded, especially if medium-sized or small, while larger specimens are used as parts of designs, for instance, as the head or body of an animal, a human face, or a fruit. Pearls may also be pear-shaped, in which case they are normally used as pendants, or they may be flattened at one pole, or both, in which case they are generally "rested" on a piece of jewelry, such as a ring, brooch, or earring.

When examined under a 10x or 20x lens, pearls often display small, superficial irregularities, roughly conical protuberances, barely visible furrows arranged in "parallel," or tiny flaws like miniature craters on the moon, sometimes with a cometlike tail on one side. At higher magnifications, the normally smooth and shining surface displays closeset, minute, sinuous lines, evenly distributed throughout. The color varies from white with a hint of gray to white with a yellow tinge, but can also be silvery gray or more noticeably yellow. In strong light, pearls have characteristic "pearly " or "nacreous" luster and may also be iridescent, with the emphasis on pink or other colors, which give a very pleasing effect. Alternatively, they can be slightly translucent, revealing faint speckles or marks on the inside, this generally being due to the presence of abnormally large quantities of the organic component, conchiolin, and water, which makes the pearl more liable to deteriorate.

Many antique pearls look badly damaged. Sometimes part of the outer surface of nacre has been worn away or there may be loss of luster, caused by dehydration of the organic component or by the dulling effect of acid perspiration on the mineral component (calcium carbonate). Therefore, one often finds that some of the pearls in an antique piece of jewelry have been replaced, usually by modern, cultured pearls.

Distinctive features Pearls can generally be distinguished by their surface appearance—which is lustrous but with microscopic, discontinuous wavy lines—from glass imitations with a very different surface or from other imitations covered by a special, minutely granular varnish made from ground fish scales. A much harder problem is distinguishing natural from cultured pearls. Individual pierced pearls can be distinguished by observing the inside of the hole with a strong lens or binocular microscope. A succession of concentric layers (possibly with a dark center, if the pearl is slightly grayish) is characteristic of natural pearls, while a compact, almost waxy-looking nucleus, with a single, clearly different layer around it is characteristic of cultured pearls. Although it is impossible to judge a single unpierced pearl by its outward appearance,

Brooch in the form of a bunch of grapes, in gold, silver, brilliants, and white and gray pearls. Van Cleef and Arpels, Paris.

278

in the case of a string of, say, a few dozen to a hundred or so pearls, simple observation of their outward appearance can be conclusive. In fact, although natural pearls are almost spherical, if one looks closely at a string of natural pearls, they nearly always appear to be bodies revolving about an axis (along which the hole is drilled), slightly flattened at one or both poles, perhaps even tending to a cylindrical shape. On the other hand, most, although not all, cultured pearls are more or less spherical, even when they have superficial irregularities and protuberances. This is because they consist of few layers of nacre on a strictly spherical support. Nonspherical cultured pearls, which are very similar in shape to most natural pearls, do occur, but are not common and, as a rule, there will be very few on a string. The physical properties of pearls are not easily measured (except for the density) and are not normally used for recognition; but, on average, natural pearls have a slightly lower density (2.71 g/cm^3) than cultured pearls (2.73–2.74 g/cm^3). Grayish natural pearls have a still lower density (2.61–2.69 g/cm^3) due to an excess of conchiolin. To distinguish natural from cultured pearls with any certainty, specialist laboratories use both radiography and the X-ray diffraction method, which give precise information on the arrangement of the internal layers of nacre and the prismatic crystals of aragonite of which they are composed.

Occurrence   Most of the few natural pearls harvested nowadays come from the Persian Gulf, Sri Lanka, the Red Sea, and the Philippines; still smaller quantities are collected from the sea off the coast of Venezuela and from the Gulf of California. In other places, such as the seas of Japan and along the northwest coast of Australia, the industry for cultured pearls has now developed to such an extent that the possibility of finding natural pearls as well is disregarded.

Value   One of the most valuable gems in antiquity, pearls are still highly valued today, although not to the same extent. They are evaluated according to size, color, luster, regularity of form, compactness (the more watery, translucent ones are less durable, therefore less valuable). In the case of a number of pearls in a piece of jewelry, much depends on their uniformity of color or, at any rate, how well matched they are. A string of pearls of equal diameter is worth much more than one consisting of pearls of graduated diameters (larger at the center, smaller at the ends), because numerous pearls of a uniform size are harder to find. Even a pair of matching pearls is worth more than double the price of a single pearl because of the quantities that have to be sorted to find two that are identical. But many natural pearls are old or antique and when they are in a poor state of repair, dehydrated or cracked, brittle or yellowed with age, their value is greatly reduced.

Simulants   Cultured pearls are not really imitations, but something much better. We shall, therefore, be discussing these fully below. Pearls have been imitated, at least since the mid-seventeenth century; hollow spheres of thin glass, coated on the inside with a special varnish made from fish scales, and usually filled with paraffin or wax, were used. For this reason, pearls were once tested between the

Above: Baroque pearls in a piece of jewelry from the sixteenth century. Victoria and Albert Museum, London. Below: Another piece, 1890, by Peter Carl Fabergé.

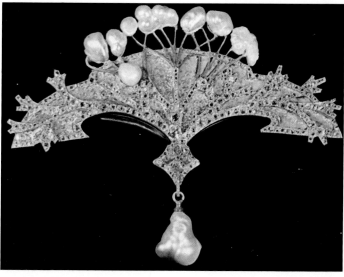

teeth: if they broke, they were clearly false. They were subsequently imitated by (solid or hollow) spheres of glass, or mother-of-pearl, varnished on the outside in the same way. All these imitations are very easily recognizable if observed under a magnifying glass, which shows the typical features of glass fusion around the hole, the paraffin wax filling, and the translucent outer layer in one case, and, in the other, the minutely granular appearance of the special varnish used. From a distance, however, they look very much like real pearls, and there is a thriving industry for them in both Japan and Majorca.

34.2 **Cultured Pearls**

The cultivation of pearls, which now accounts for the vast majority of pearls issued on the market each year, involves, as mentioned, introducing mother-of-pearl beads into the tissues of certain types of mollusks, which deposit concentric layers of nacre around the foreign body. These spheres are quite large in relation to the final volume of the pearl. In fact, depending on the size of the mollusks, beads from 1 to 3–4 millimeters in diameter are used (nuclei of 6–7 and even 8 millimeters are only used for Australian pearls).

Appearance Cultured pearls are generally more spherical in shape than natural ones. Less regular, baroque or pear-shaped pearls are also found, or specimens slightly flattened at one or both poles, which are inevitably of more limited use. The most common types of minor irregularities are either a small, almost conical protuberance or small, barely noticeable cavities with a white base, resembling lunar craters, which are also found, though much less often, in natural pearls. Protuberances are partially removed with a file, and the site is used for the hole in pierced pearls. When magnified twenty or more times, cultured pearls also display a close pattern of minute, sinuous lines. As with natural pearls, the normal color is gray-white to yellowish gray-white, but cultured pearls sometimes display a rather unattractive greenish tinge in strong light. Their luster and iridescence are not noticeably different from those of natural pearls. One does not normally see the faint gray, dark-centered coloration of natural pearls, but cultured pearls may be a definite gray color, even in the layers near the surface; this coloration is always artificial and due to treatment. Cultured pearls often have highly translucent outer layers because of an excess of water and conchiolin, which makes them more liable to deteriorate. Australian cultured pearls are a special case. Being produced by large mollusks, they are often 10–12 millimeters in diameter, and even over 15 millimeters, with striking luster, great compactness and a very white, almost silvery color, probably due to lack of bleaching, but no iridescence. They may be perfectly spherical, but sometimes have a series of small furrows arranged like the parallels of a globe, or are slightly flattened at the poles, or tend to a biconical shape.

Distinctive features In pierced cultured pearls, the junc-

Cultured pearls. Top to bottom: extracting the pearl from the mollusk; grading the pearls; composing strings of pearls.

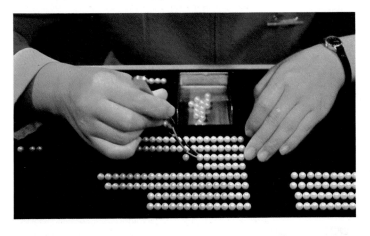

tion between the external layers of nacre and the uniform nucleus at the center may be quite clearly visible through the drill hole, not always easy to see with a lens, but certainly visible with a good binocular microscope of 15x or 20x magnification. It is most easily recognizable when the hole that has been drilled is at the site of a small protuberance, which has been filed down and which generally has a small cavity bounded on the inside by the convex surface of the spherical nucleus.

Sometimes, when a cultured pearl whose external layers are either too thin or translucent is viewed against a strong light, horizontal lines can be seen. These are the flat, parallel layers of the artificial nucleus and have nothing to do with the concentric layers—never visible, incidentally—characteristic of natural pearls. Even simple observation of the external shape can provide information useful for purposes of distinction, when one is dealing with whole strings of pearls rather than individual pearls. If the pearls are all perfectly spherical in shape or have only very faint protuberances, rather than slight but extensive spherical defects, it is very probable that there is a turned nucleus inside, forming a sizeable, rigid infrastructure onto which the oyster has been forced to deposit the nacre in a spherical shape. This factor, combined with the two preceding ones (viewing against the light and observation of the drill hole) should almost always make it possible to identify a string of mainly cultured pearls. Australian cultured pearls are unique. These, in fact, have a highly characteristic appearance (and size), which makes them quite easy to identify.

As already mentioned in the discussion of natural pearls, the physical characteristics of this gem are not easy to measure, except for the density. This is usually slightly higher in cultured pearls than natural pearls and is about 2.74 g/cm³. When cultured and natural pearls cannot be distinguished by the types of direct observation just described, radiography and X-ray diffraction techniques are used, as they are with natural pearls, and these will positively identify even unpierced specimens.

Occurrence The main center of production for cultured pearls is Japan. Other, less important centers are chiefly along the northwest coast of Australia. More recently, cultivation of pearls has begun along the coasts of India.

Value There is a big difference between the value of natural pearls and that of cultured pearls, which on average cost at least ten times less. The same criteria are used to evaluate them as to evaluate natural pearls, i.e., color, luster, regularity of form and compactness. When dealing with a string of many pearls, great importance is attached to their general homogeneity. Furthermore, a string of cultured pearls of uniform diameter is worth more than one of graduated diameters and a pair of identical pearls is worth more than two different ones. The thickness of the pearly layer surrounding the nucleus is especially important in evaluating cultured pearls. A thicker layer in relation to the diameter of the nucleus takes longer to produce (the average period of cultivation is four to five years, but sometimes it is extended to six to seven years) and therefore costs more. Furthermore, a very thin layer, sometimes seen in

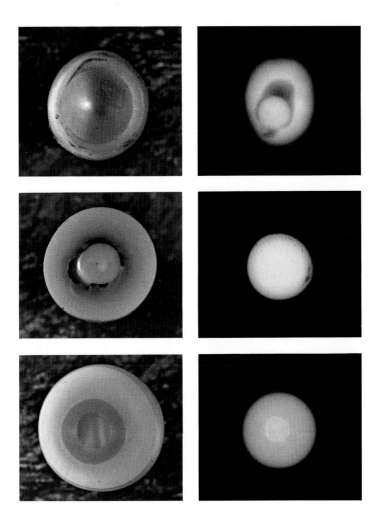

The relationship be-
tween the nucleus
and the nacreous
coating of cultured
pearls. The nucleus
has been removed
from the pearl in the
top photo, leaving
the layers of nacre
deposited around it.
The middle photo
shows a cross sec-
tion of a pearl; the
cavity between the
nucleus and nacre is
due to poor initial
adherence between
the epithelium and

nucleus. Such a flaw
is unimportant if the
layer of nacre is
thick, but can lead
to damage in time if
it is thin. The bottom
picture shows a
cross section of a
high-quality cultured
pearl.
A nondestructive
method of analyzing
pearls, which is
much used and
often gives excellent
results, is by use of
X rays. These can
reveal both the

thickness of the
nacre and any cavi-
ties between it and
the nucleus. Top to
bottom, radiographic
images of a pearl
with a large cavity
between the nacre
and nucleus; a cul-
tured pearl with a
thin layer of nacre
and a cavity
between this and the
nucleus; lastly, a
pearl of the type
shown in cross sec-
tion in the photo be-
side it.

poor quality pearls, is much less durable. Lastly, a thick layer of nacre usually, if not always, gives an appearance closer to that of natural pearls. Despite their rather cold color and lack of iridescence, Australian cultured pearls are worth much more than the others partly because of their size. Sometimes they have a thick layer of nacre, because one of the many qualities of the mollusks used to produce them is the ability to complete their task with considerable speed. Nowadays, however, the tendency is to restrict culture to only three years, more pearls in a shorter time being preferred to pearls with thicker layers.

Simulants These are the same as already mentioned for natural pearls. Majorca is now famous for the production of imitation pearls, which look very convincing at a distance.

34.3 **Nonnucleated Cultured Pearls**

Around 1935, during experiments to improve methods of pearl culture, it was discovered that pearls could be obtained simply by grafting a piece of soft tissue from another mollusk. In this case, the pearl produced has no artificial nucleus inside, but only the small cavity left after the fragment of foreign tissue has decomposed. Experiments showed that an elongated freshwater mollusk, *Hyriopsis schlegeli,* was most suitable for the purpose, and the culture was set up at Lake Biwa in Japan, where it has developed considerably over the last two decades. Initially, pearls were obtained with a fairly large internal cavity (half the total diameter), but as the method has been improved, it has become possible to produce pearls with minimal cavities, known as "scars." Further attempts have recently been made in both India and China, in freshwater, and in Australia, where the same type of salt-water mollusks are used as with traditional methods. Because of the environment in which these pearls are produced, they are known in the trade as "freshwater pearls," without specifying that they are cultured. But noncultured freshwater pearls are very uncommon.

Appearance Nonnucleated cultured pearls are generally somewhat egg-shaped, with one pole more pointed than the other, sometimes being slightly compressed, almost in the shape of a bean. On other occasions, the shape is nearly spherical, but still one pole will be more pointed than the other. Much less typical forms are a flat, button shape, or still more rarely, a shape like a demijohn with no neck, i.e. rounded bodies with a vaguely pentagonal main cross-section, and, of course, rounded edges. When these pearls are used as part of a string, they are normally drilled crossways to their axes of rotation, except for those that are button-shaped. Their luster is generally very good, almost metallic at the acute pole, diminishing slightly further away from it. They have a very compact but translucent appearance. The color is usually silvery white, almost like that of Australian cultured pearls, but a bit warmer. They are often small, like a rather chubby grain of rice and in any case, never large, the maximum size being about 6 or 7 millimeters.

Distinctive features The features mentioned above are characteristic and distinctive, and with a little experience

one can recognize a string of nonnucleated, cultured pearls by simple examination under a lens, and usually even by eye. But it may be hard to pronounce on a single pearl, in which the typical features are not very clear. As always, in case of doubt, radiography can be used, as can diffraction diagrams, because when freshwater pearls are exposed to X rays, they exhibit particularly strong fluorescence and phosphorescence.

Occurrence   Most of these pearls come from Lake Biwa in Japan; but this type of freshwater culture has also started recently in India and China. The Australian saltwater variety is extremely rare at present.

Value   Thanks to their luster, compactness, pleasing color, and absence of foreign or artificial components, and despite the handicap of their shape, these pearls are worth at least as much as cultured pearls with a nucleus; in fact, well-shaped specimens are worth quite a bit more, although their price is still of the same order of magnitude.

Simulants   Glass imitations, closely resembling the small grain-of-rice-shaped pearls, are made for use in cheap jewelry.

Brooch with gold, brilliants, emeralds, enamel, and river pearls. Parma, private collection.

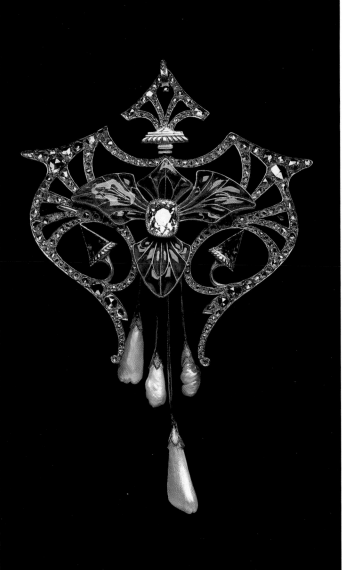

2.5–4

2.4–2.7

1.65 \ 1.49

35 CORAL

$CaCo_3$, or calcium carbonate in the form of calcite, is the main constituent of calcareous corals; minor constituents are $MgCo_3$, or magnesium carbonate and proteinaceous organic substances, which act as binding agents. A horny, proteinaceous substance whose composition varies according to the species is, on the other hand, the basic constituent of horny corals. Most of the coral used since antiquity as an ornamental material comes from the calcareous skeletons of colonies of marine organisms of the phylum *Cnidaria*, order *Corgonacea*, genus *Corallium*.

The most famous of these organisms is *Corallium rubrum*, which lives in the waters of the Mediterranean and, despite its name, provides not only red, but orange, pink, and white coral. Similar to this are *Corallium elatius*, C. *japonicum*, and C. *secundum*, which mainly live off the coasts of Japan, China, Indochina, the Philippines, and other archipelagos of the Indian and Pacific Oceans. Other corals are occasionally used for ornamental purposes as well. They are the calcareous skeleton of *Heliopora coerulea* of the order *Coenothecalia*, which produces what is known as blue coral, and the horny, proteinaceous skeleton of corals of the orders *Gorgonacea, Zoanthinaria,* and *Anthipatharia,* which supply so-called black coral.

Crystal system   Calcite, which is the main component of calcareous corals, crystallizes in the trigonal system. The proteinaceous substances of the horny corals are noncrystalline.

Appearance   The skeletons of corals vary in color: from bright to dark red, slightly orange-red, pink, and white, for *Corallium rubrum* of the Mediterranean; from red to orange red to orange pink with areas of white for C. *japonicum;* and from medium to deep pink, sometimes with alternate, concentric layers of lighter and darker color and a whitish portion corresponding to the axis for C. *elatius;* C. *secundum* has alternate, wavy lines of light and dark pink; while coral skeletons of the genera *Gorgonia, Eunicella, Gerardia,* and *Parantipathes* are blackish on the inside, with slightly more translucent, brown areas; and *Heliopora coerulea* is cold, almost gray-blue. The outer surface is compact and fairly regular, opaque, in most cases, except for blue coral, which is very porous, and the horny, black coral of the genus *Parantipathes,* which has numerous small surface protuberances, like gooseflesh.

Characteristic features are differences in translucency, or the arrangement of the streaks of color crosswise or lengthwise to the branches. On cross sections, observable by cutting through a branch, a concentric ring structure is always visible to some extent, sometimes with very faint rays cutting across it; this is very similar to the growth rings and medullary rays of tree trunks. Sometimes, coral also has a different-colored marrow or medulla (generally white), or an axial canal. All this produces a series of longitudinal alignments, closely resembling the grain of wood, which are visible on polished, outer surfaces or on longitudinal sections. Both cross and longitudinal sections of the ramifications display features very similar to those observed if a branching tree is cut into sections. These features are strictly determined by the organic structure and

Seabed with Corallium rubrum.

growth pattern of coral colonies and their skeletons. They also explain why, up to the early eighteenth century, coral was believed to be a vegetable, a type of small, submarine tree.

Physical properties   These are often hard to measure, except for the density, which shows clear differences, especially between calcareous and horny corals. For the first, the density is usually between 2.60 and 2.70 g/cm^3, but may be even lower, starting from 2.35 g/cm^3, when the coral contains large amounts of the organic component which binds the inorganic parts together. Blue coral also has a low density of about 2.46 g/cm^3. The refractive indices, which are hard to measure, are about n_ε 1.49, n_ω 1.65, thus being approximately the same as for calcite. At 2.5–4, the hardness is slightly higher than that of calcite. The organic substance helps give the coral good tenacity, enabling it to be fashioned and polished to a high degree. For horny corals, the density varies from 1.33 to 1.42 g/cm^3 or thereabouts, and the refractive index ranges from 1.54 to 1.56. Although they only have a hardness of 2.5–3, these corals take an equally good polish. They also have a certain degree of elasticity and can be heated and bent into bangles.

Genesis   In all cases, coral consists of the branching skeletons of animals which live in colonies planted on the seabed at depths varying from tens to hundreds of meters. They are typical of warmish to very warm seas.

Occurrence   Banks of coral are found in the Mediterranean, along the coasts of China, Vietnam, and Japan; near the Philippines, along some of the many Pacific archipelagos; and along parts of the African coastline.

Coral colonies occupy large areas especially in the Pacific, but also near the coast of South Africa, in the Red Sea, and to the east of Australia. These latter colonies, however, consist of madrepore, which has little in common with the corals used as ornaments.

35.1 Red Coral

The oldest known findings of red coral date from the Mesopotamian civilization, i.e. from about 3000 BC. For centuries, this was the coral *par excellence,* and at the time of Pliny the Elder it was apparently much appreciated in India, even more than in Europe. The name is derived from the Latin *corállium,* related to the Greek *korállion.*

Appearance   The red coral from the Mediterranean (*Corallium rubrum*) has very faint concentric rings. It is easier to see the longitudinal structures. The type from the seas near Japan has more clearly visible organic structures. The thin branches were and still are polished, pierced, and threaded, unaltered, into necklaces. Larger pieces are cut into spherical or faceted necklace beads, pear shapes for pendant jewelry, or cabochons. This coral is very compact and easily acquires a good polish, although this may deteriorate in time as the material is not very durable. It is also used for carved pieces and small figurines, in both oriental and western art styles.

The most highly prized varieties of coral are those that are a uniform, strong, bright red. Specimens that are too light

or too dark, or have an orange tinge or unevenly distributed color, are less valuable. Some basically red Japanese corals have a white axial portion. This is, of course, regarded as a defect, where it is not eliminated in the cutting process.

Distinctive features   Two basic facts must be remembered in distinguishing coral from its imitations:

1) The specimen should have the organic structure characteristic of coral;

2) On contact with a drop of hydrochloric acid (the readily available muriatic acid), the piece should display the strong effervescence characteristic of calcite.

The most frequent imitations are of glass. These have longitudinal striations similar to those of coral, but do not react to hydrochloric acid. Another common simulant is made from a compact, artificial agglomerate mainly of calcite, which lacks any trace of organic structure. As mentioned, the hardness is about 3.5, therefore well below that of glass. The organic substance in coral also gives it very good tenacity, far superior to that of the constituent mineral alone. Because of its organic content, the density varies quite widely, but is usually about 2.60–2.66 g/cm^3.

Occurrence   Red coral is gathered in the Mediterranean (mainly near Sardinia and Sicily), the Eastern Mediterranean, the Red Sea, and the seas around Japan.

Value   When made into polished and/or faceted necklace beads, it has roughly the same value as that of certain prized ornamental stones, such as good quality turquoise and lapis lazuli, The color, homogeneity of each piece (individually and as part of a necklace) and polish are very important. When the coral is made into carved pieces and figurines, the quality of the work is obviously very important. Furthermore, it should be remembered that large pieces are hard to find.

Simulants and synthetics   Very small pieces of coral or branching twigs are imitated by special glass which simulates the typical longitudinal structures; but clearly fused surfaces, the presence of air bubbles, and immunity to attack from hydrochloric acid uncover these imitations quite easily, especially if they are viewed through a lens or binocular microscope. Nowadays, a coral-colored agglomerate consisting mainly of calcite and called synthetic coral is also manufactured. This reacts to hydrochloric acid in the same way as true coral but lacks the characteristic structures of the organic version. As with other gems and ornamental materials of organic origin, the term synthetic is not very meaningful.

Parure in red coral (1830). Musée des Arts Décoratifs, Paris.

35.2 **Pink (and white) coral**

Not often seen on the market a few decades ago, pink coral is now widely available; large quantities of it come from the Orient.

Appearance The Mediterranean type (a special variety of the more common red coral) is very compact and, like red coral, takes a good polish, with barely visible organic structures and a fairly uniform, soft pink to white color. The oriental variety often has more clearly visible organic structures, sometimes emphasized by the presence of a white center or concentric color zoning. It is often very pale, with shaded areas or patches of pink or orange pink. On other occasions it has concentric zones of color from very bright pink to light pink or whitish; but it may be a beautiful uniform pink, very similar to Mediterranean coral. Sometimes, the rings of the trunk are genuine discontinuities or cracks and there may be other extensive radial or variously oriented cracks, making the whole structure more brittle and therefore less valuable. Costliest of all are the most compact, easily polished varieties, without cracks or cavities, of a perfectly uniform soft pink color, without any trace of orange. When pink coral has all these characteristics, combined with an antique pink color, and with the merest hint of violet, it is known as *pelle d'angelo* or "angel's skin." It is meaningless to describe patchily colored coral as "*pelle d'angelo* type" or "part *pelle d'angelo*," as the very existence of patches or discontinuities rules out such a definition. The inferior varieties often have poor polish, cracks, and, as a rule, some artificial color. Objects manufactured from pink coral include polished, spherical necklace beads, roughly carved but rarely faceted pieces, necklaces, pendants, cabochons, and other items of jewelry, and figurines.

Distinctive features As with red coral, the most important distinctive features are the typical organic structures (clearly visible in evenly colored corals, but much less apparent in the others) and reaction to hydrochloric acid. Minute examination is necessary to distinguish it from the pink shell used for the same purpose. The structure of the latter is different, consisting of almost flat or slightly curved parallel layers, never concentric rings; but the reaction to hydrochloric acid is identical. With pink coral, it is very important to establish whether the color is natural or whether, as often happens nowadays, the color of almost white coral has been heightened by the use of dyes.

Traces of dye may be visible in small, superficial cavities, or one may be able to see, by splitting one bead of a necklace, that the outer surface and that of a preexisting crack are more deeply colored than the newly fractured one. These are the main methods of detecting the presence of artificial colorants.

Occurrence Very limited quantities of pink coral come from the Mediterranean; considerable quantities, although mainly of inferior quality, come from the Far East, especially Japan. The *pelle d'angelo* variety, which is not common, may come from the Mediterranean, the Gulf of Chihli (in China), or from Japan.

Above: Carving in pelle d'angelo *pink coral.*
Below: Pink and white coral beads.

296

Value Good quality pink coral of a uniform and attractive color is worth at least as much as red coral. Most of the pink coral on the market is, however, of inferior quality and has been artificially colored. It is therefore much less valuable and is worth perhaps a quarter of the red variety. White coral also has quite a low value, given its poor ornamental qualities.

Simulants As already mentioned, pink coral can be imitated by similarly colored shells, which, apart from having a different structure, have a slightly higher density of about 2.85 g/cm^3 (compared with 2.63–2.70 g/cm^3 for pink coral). But the main problem with this type of coral is the common practice of using dyes to improve coral that is mainly white, contains a few streaks of pale color, or is distinctly patchy. In some cases it is difficult and costly to detect this type of fraud. Perhaps for this reason, pink coral has fallen sadly into disrepute, except for the better varieties obtained from reliable sources.

35.3 Blue Coral

This material, unusual in appearance and color, and of limited use, is obtained from the skeleton of *Heliopora coerulea*, a type of coral which lives mainly in the seas around the Philippines.

Appearance The most striking characteristic of blue coral is its color, which is bright blue or gray blue, sometimes with zoning in the form of concentric circles or even horizontal stripes. The most readily observable organic structures are two sets of channels parallel to the axis: one set is thin and barely visible, though numerous. The other is more prominent, less numerous, and larger, with dark walls; these channels are placed at regular intervals between the other channels. Due to the cavities, marks, and discontinuities where the channels emerge, blue coral never takes a polish comparable to that of red coral. Therefore, its use as an ornament is limited and mainly dependent on its color. It is made into spherical, cylindrical, spindle or barrel-shaped necklace beads, but does not lend itself to other uses.

Distinctive features The color and clearly visible organic structures make it quite easy to recognize.

Occurrence Blue coral comes mainly from the Philippines, where it is generally fashioned as well. Like other local materials such as black coral, shell, and porous white madrepore coral it is made into inexpensive necklaces.

Value Very low, partly because it is difficult to fashion and polish. It is essentially a curiosity on the western market.

Simulants It is not imitated at present, probably because it is little known.

Two examples of necklaces made from white coral.

35.4 **Black Coral**

This consists of the skeletons of polyp colonies, mainly of the genera *Gorgonia, Eunicella, Gerardia,* and *Parantipathes;* but unlike those that make up red, pink, and blue coral, these skeletal remains are of a horny nature, not calcic.

Appearance The color is black, but sometimes has minute, short, brownish yellow, slightly translucent streaks. It can acquire quite good luster if polished, but this will be of a horny character, similar to that of some plastics. It is used in cylindrical pieces which are drilled along the axis or horizontally to it, as necklace beads. It can be bent if heated and made into bangles. Cheap rings, carved items, and figurines up to ten centimeters tall are also made from larger pieces.

Distinctive features If cut crossways to the axis, the characteristic concentric rings, like those of tree trunks, are visible. These sometimes have marked discontinuities between one and the other, almost as though they were becoming detached. Faint radial structures and thin longitudinal structures, yellowish brown in color and slightly translucent, may also be visible. Sometimes, these limited areas of yellow-brown translucency show small protuberances on the underlying surface, as would have been present on the outer surface had it not been polished (in black coral of the genus *Parantipathes*). It is no use testing black coral with hydrochloric acid, as it does not contain calcium carbonate; but it should be remembered that the density is about 1.36 g/cm^3, which is much lower than that of red and pink corals. Due to its proteinaceous character, black coral emits a smell of burning horn if touched with a piece of red-hot wire. It is warm to the touch, like plastic, has a relatively low hardness of between 2 and 3, and is slightly elastic.

Occurrence It is gathered near the Hawaiian islands, in the Great Barrier Reef of Australia, in the Red Sea, on the west coast of Africa, the Antilles and, occasionally, in the Mediterranean.

Value Distinctly low, much lower than that of the main types of coral. As an ornament it is characteristic of many different cultures, but in the West it is mainly regarded as a curiosity, although appreciable quantities were seen on the market a few years ago.

Simulants It does not appear, at present, to be imitated.

Two examples of necklaces made from black coral.

36 IVORY

Mainly $Ca_5 (F,OH,Cl) (PO_4)_3$

2.50–2.75

1.80

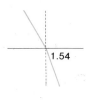

1.54

Ivory figurine (Oriental).

This material is largely obtained from the tusks of African and Indian (Asiatic) elephants, but also from the teeth or tusks of the hippopotamus, walrus, and other mammals. Like bones, it consists mainly of calcium phosphate in the form of oxyapatite and a small quantity of calcium carbonate, bound together by large amounts of the proteinaceous organic substance dentine to form a compact, elastic, tenacious whole.

Appearance   Tusks, which are the continuously growing incisors of the elephant, have a very long, slightly curved, roughly conical shape with an internal cavity which is also conical, petering out part-way along. When viewed in cross-section, the organic structure displays thin, slightly translucent, intersecting curved lines, similar to the marks left on a flat surface by a milling machine. The color, off-white with a faint yellow tinge, turns yellower with age. Aging sometimes also produces small cracks, mostly lengthwise, probably due to dehydration and alteration of the organic substance. The tusks of the male African elephant average two meters in length and may weigh 30 to 40 kg; those of the Asiatic elephant are somewhat small and less heavy. Much of the ivory formerly used in China came from fossil remains of mammoths, with very large, strongly curved tusks which were well preserved and still perfectly workable.

Physical properties   The hardness of 2.50–2.75 makes it fairly easy to fashion with ordinary metal tools. It also has considerable elasticity and tenacity, with the result that ivory objects are very strong and durable. The average density is about 1.79–1.80 g/cm³. It is hard to measure the refractive index, because of its lack of transparency, but this is normally about 1.53 or 1.54.

Genesis   As mentioned, it is of organic origin, being the typical material of mammals' teeth.

Occurrence   Most ivory comes from elephants, particularly the African elephant which lives mainly on the savannahs. Cameroon, Gabon, Zaire, Ghana, Sierra Leone, Tanzania, and Mozambique are thus particularly rich in ivory. Ivory also comes from India, Burma, Thailand, and other parts of Southeast Asia. The fossil ivory used in ancient China apparently came from Siberia and perhaps China as well.

36.1 Ivory

The name comes from the Latin *ebur,* of identical meaning. It has always been used as an ornamental material, but at various times over the centuries was much more highly prized than it is today. The zenith of its popularity was probably around the thirteenth century—strangely, both in Europe and in China, despite their completely different cultures.

Appearance   The cream to yellowish white color is characteristic (and is in fact known as ivory color); it turns a

drab yellow-brown with age. The longitudinal grain is always visible in bright light, due to the difference in translucence between one part of the tusk and another, and this displays the distinctive pattern of intersecting curves in cross section. It easily takes a good polish, although more crudely worked pieces (e.g., some low quality African craft objects) may display scratch marks from the planes used to fashion them. In thicknesses of a millimeter or a little more (as in the slats of some cooling fans as used by ladies) it is fairly elastic. It is tenacious without any tendency to splinter. The ornaments and luxury items, past and present, made of ivory are too numerous to mention. They include round-beaded necklaces and bangles, easily produced from the hollow basal portion of the tusk; carved pieces in bas-relief, for use both as pendant jewelry and the outer panels, for instance, of boxes and containers, and ceremonial weapon handles. Sculptures of human figures are also common. In Africa especially, entire tusks are carved without interfering with their basic shape and size, the completed piece designed to stand upright. Complete tusks are also fashioned in China, Japan, and India, but these are normally intended to be viewed horizontally and depict landscapes or everyday scenes, with an abundance of vegetation, houses, and pagodas, shown in minute detail. Small sculptures or other objects are also put together from numerous, juxtaposed pieces of ivory fixed to a thin wooden support, not visible in the finished article. This produces works of art exceeding the size of a single tusk and having the appearance of single-color "mosaics."

Oriental art forms also include complex-shaped containers, with minutely worked, carved walls and intricately pierced details. In the West, ivory has mainly been used for sculptures, boxes, and containers with bas-relief decorations, elaborate weapon handles, fans, and even inlays for furniture.

Distinctive features   Ivory's chief characteristic is its fine grain, distinguished from the background only by a slight increase in translucency, best seen in strong light, although barely visible, if at all, on the natural outer surface of the tusks, where this has been preserved. This readily distinguishes it from bone, which has a heterogeneous network of markings, although this is only visible under a microscope. Plastic imitations of ivory have, at the most, thin superficial furrows which crudely imitate the longitudinal grain and these melt and scorch visibly if touched with the tip of a thin piece of red-hot wire. Ivory also turns black, and gives off a smell of burning protein when burned, but the prevalence of the organic component gives it far greater resistance than any type of plastic. If necessary, measurement of the density is also very useful for distinguishing ivory from its imitations.

Occurrence   As mentioned above, most ivory comes from various parts of Africa (mainly Cameroon, Gabon, Zaire, Ghana, Sierra Leone, Angola, Tanzania, Mozambique, and Zimbabwe) and Asia (mainly India, Thailand, and Burma).

Above: Ivory bangle.
Below: Ivory statu-
ette (African).

Value   The price of ivory has risen again recently, but as with jade, very much depends on the quality of the workmanship, which can be outstanding because of the intrinsic

qualities of the material. When the workmanship is excellent, the value of ivory may equal that of other prized ornamental materials, including jade. But when the work is more commonplace, its value is much lower, although it will still be higher than that of small, mass-produced objects in, say, nephrite jade.

Simulants   Ivory was and is widely imitated by all types of plastics. Among the moulded objects produced are some which are far too large to have come from a single piece of ivory, as, for instance, small tables with a carved central pedestal. Sometimes, complete carved tusks have been made out of these plastics, which are very hard to distinguish from the real thing, at least with the naked eye. Many umbrella and walking-stick handles made earlier in the twentieth century are also of plastic, as are dressing table sets of the same period. All these imitations generally have a lower density than that of ivory, but much higher than that of transparent plastics, inert mineral powders having been incorporated in them to add to their credibility.

Above: Ivory chessman (twelfth century French). Museo del Bargello, Florence. Below: Tusk carved in the form of a ship (Oriental).

37 AMBER

Amber is a fossil resin of trees that lived tens of millions of years ago. Its chemical composition varies because it is a mixture of organic compounds, including succinic acid and succinic resins, originating from the polymerization of terpenes and resinous acids.

Crystal system Noncrystalline.

Appearance From transparent to translucent to semi-opaque, yellow to honey, brown or reddish brown, it sometimes has a dusty, friable reddish-brown, light brown, or gray crust, due to alteration. It is found in variously shaped nodules—swollen blobs, due to an accumulation of drops, "icicles," runs, or large lumps, like those formed by the resin of present-day trees, although in far greater masses. When present in alluvial sand or gravel, amber no longer has the opaque coating and is often rounded into pebbles or grains.

Physical properties Amber is singly refractive, with an index of about 1.54, and has a very low density of around 1.06–1.08 g/cm^3, so that it floats in a concentrated solution of kitchen salt. It has a hardness of around 2.5, but is reasonably tenacious and workable, even though it splinters when cut, showing signs of brittleness. It softens and starts to decompose at 150° and melts at about 250°C. On contact with the usual red-hot piece of wire, it gives off an aromatic smell as it decomposes, almost like the resin of present-day pine trees.

Genesis Amber originated from species of now-extinct plants, capable of producing enormous quantities of resin, which fell to the ground or filled large cracks and holes in the trunk and bark.

Subsequently, over a geological time span, it lost most of its more volatile components, then polymerized and hardened. The normal processes of erosion and sedimentation subsequently caused it to be deposited in deltaic sands on the shores and bed of what is now the Baltic Sea, or in other continental alluvial deposits, where it is found today.

Occurrence It is mainly found along the Baltic coasts of the Soviet Union and Poland, and in the Dominican Republic in the Antilles. Other European sources include Czechoslovakia, Romania, and Sicily. It is also found in the United States, Canada, and Chile; and in Burma.

Above: Block of amber.
Below: Amber pendant with insect inclusions.

37.1 Amber

The name has come down, probably through French, from the Arabic *anbar*. The Romans called it *succinum,* as it was rightly believed to be from tree sap. Its use as an ornamental material dates from Neolithic times. It was brought to the foothills of the Alps from the Baltic coast. The distances that had to be covered to obtain it, enormous for those days, give an idea of its importance.

Appearance It is typically yellow to honey-colored, or yellow brown to brown, with good transparency, revealing glimpses of opaque brown to black frustules on the inside, almost disc-shaped surfaces with types of radial veins and sometimes animal remains, especially of arthropods

(mainly insects, arachnids, and miriapods). Small gnats, wasps and ants are sometimes clearly recognizable, because whole and perfectly preserved in every detail. Some amber, however, is quite "cloudy"—from translucent to semiopaque—and lemon yellow to orange yellow or brown in color.

The semiopaque brown color is the least valuable. The opaque varieties are sometimes treated to make them transparent. Amber takes an excellent polish and is used in irregular, polyhedral pieces, similar to slightly elongated tetrahedra, polished and threaded into necklaces, and in spherical or oval disc-shaped and globular pieces with polyhedral faceting, likewise threaded into necklaces, bracelets and other types of jewelry. Pieces several centimeters in size (though not easy to find) are sometimes used as well, because having such a low density, this material is very light. In the recent past, it was used, in the West, the Arab world, and the Far East, for carved items, figurines, small perfume bottles, cigarette holders and pipe parts, brooches, buckles, and pendants. The semitransparent or opaque varieties are often used for carving and engraving.

Distinctive features There is another semifossil natural resin, of limited value and importance, called copal, which looks very much like amber at first sight. Numerous artificial, plastic materials are also widely employed as excellent, inexpensive substitutes for amber. To be sure of distinguishing them, the following procedure should be used. First, a quick check of the density should be made, using a very concentrated solution of kitchen salt in water. Only amber, copal, and polystyrene float in this; all other types of plastic sink, unless they have large cavities inside, which will be clearly visible. Next, two common organic liquids are used: benzole, which dissolves polystyrene fairly rapidly, making it go soft and "stringy," and ethyl alcohol (ordinary denatured alcohol), which softens the surface of copal in less than half a minute, so that if the specimen is rubbed against a piece of white cloth, it leaves a distinct mark, the friction also producing visible signs of abrasion. In this way, amber can be quite rapidly and positively identified, because it is not attacked by either benzole or alcohol. Partial immersion in alcohol also helps make another distinction: pieces are often found which have the basic characteristics of amber, but in fact consist of an agglomeration of numerous small fragments of amber (offcuts or pieces that were too small to begin with) that have been heated and compressed. In this case, a type of mosaic is visible with a lens on polished surfaces, because the contiguous pieces have slightly different hardnesses and show different relief when polished. Immersion in alcohol for between half a minute and two minutes causes the parts that have been softened by heat to turn slightly opaque, still further emphasizing the mosaic effect. Amber's famous ability to develop an electric charge and pick up pieces of paper if rubbed is not a useful means of distinction, as copal and nearly all plastics have the same property.

Occurrence In the past, most amber came from the southern coastal areas of the Baltic, which are now part of Poland and the Soviet Union. Other areas, such as Romania and Sicily, were much less important: Amber usable for

Above: Amber necklace.
Below: Amber tankard (sixteenth century German).
Museo degli Argenti, Florence.

Carving in amber.

ornamental purposes has also been found in Burma—home of many of the principal gemstones—and large quantities of very fine amber have also been obtained for more than a decade from the Dominican Republic.

Value Nowadays it is quite low, or at any rate, much lower than it must have been many centuries ago. Obviously, antique and/or finely worked pieces are an exception to this rule, but they are not often seen.

Simulants Ever since production of plastics began several decades ago, they have nearly all been used to imitate amber. Large amounts of old-fashioned jewelry, therefore, are in circulation which are believed to be amber but are, in fact, plastic. In the Orient (mainly India and China) various sculpted or engraved objects have been produced, some of them quite large, which are now coming onto the market as old or antique, but which are made of plastic fashioned like amber. Many modern pieces of silver jewelry of Arabic or African origin are now set with pieces of plastic instead of amber. Copal is sometimes used for these as well. Although less valuable because it is unstable and liable to deteriorate, it is at least a natural material. The tremendous confusion on the market and the difficulty of distinguishing amber readily from many types of plastic, not to mention agglomerated amber and copal, have greatly diminished the respect this material enjoyed in the past.

INTRODUCTION

The very high cost of precious stones, which is, in part, due to their rarity, has long encouraged attempts, first, to imitate them and later to reproduce them. Imitation, which is still practiced today and could well continue into the future, involves the production of very cheap materials that are to some extent similar to precious stones. The classic example is glass, both colorless and colored.

The second possibility, that of producing gems synthetically, only arose at the end of the seventeenth century, when the exact chemical nature of the various precious stones began to be known. Reproduction involves the development of materials which are increasingly similar, even in their smallest details, to the natural ones, so much so that it is sometimes difficult to tell them apart.

A third and final category concerns artificial materials, which have no counterpart in nature. These are the product of research into materials which possess the physical and chemical properties of precious stones, or even accidental by-products of work on new crystalline materials needed for modern technology, obtained, for example, during synthesis of crystals for laser generation. This may be described as the final phase, not just because it is very recent (post-World War II), but because it is the only other way in which human activity can be employed to satisfy the growing demand for a material which is, by definition, rare: the precious stone.

The prices of these nonnatural materials vary a great deal depending on the cost of producing them. For instance, synthetic rubies and sapphires, which can be mass produced, have ridiculously low prices (of the order of a few dollars per carat, ready faceted); but synthetic emeralds, which are much more complex and costly to produce, fetch hundreds of dollars per carat. Finally, given the extreme difficulty of transforming graphite into diamond, synthetic diamonds at present cost much more than natural ones, although it has been possible for some time to manufacture small diamonds for industrial uses only, at fairly competitive prices.

"Composite" stones are a special case, midway between imitations and synthetics. Composites are produced by joining different materials in an effort to achieve an overall appearance similar to that of a precious stone. The most typical examples are doublets and triplets (Fig. 32). These are separate pieces superimposed and glued together. Doublets, which were widely used in the past, consisted of a portion of colored glass surmounted by a thin layer, usually of red garnet, which is relatively hard, with a high refractive index. Triplets had three layers, with just the central one of colored glass. Nowadays, however, the center portion more often consists of colored cement. A typical past, and present, imitation of emerald consists of a triplet with two pieces of colorless synthetic

Alchemist's laboratory from a painting by Jan van der Street (seventeenth century). Palazzo Vecchio, Florence.

The structure of doublets and triplets.
a. Doublet: thin layer of natural stone (usually red garnet), plus colored glass. b. Doublet: thin layer of natural stone (usually pale green corundum with obvious inclusions), plus strongly colored synthetic stone (synthetic sapphire or ruby). c. Triplet: colorless synthetic

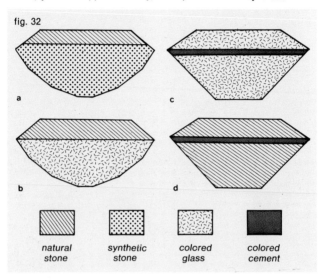

fig. 32

natural stone   synthetic stone   colored glass   colored cement

spinel or colorless quartz and beryl, held together by a layer of green cement.

Glass

This is the most common form of imitation, because of its low manufacturing cost, but it is also generally the most easily recognizable. Glass is always optically isotropic, therefore always singly refractive, and nonpleochroic; it always has conchoidal fracture, never cleavage, conducts heat less than crystalline substances and therefore feels "warmer" to the touch than precious stones, although the difference is much smaller than in other materials such as plastic.

Ordinary glass, which is the product of the melting and subsequent cooling of silica, potash or soda, and lime, has an appreciable hardness, of about 5.5, although this is low compared with that of the principal gemstones. It has modest optical qualities with low values for the refractive index and dispersion. The hardness increases quite considerably, to 7, in borate glass, in which the silicon is partially replaced by boron, but the other, already modest characteristics are still further reduced. Lead glass, on the other hand, in which all or part of the calcium is replaced, has excellent optical properties (this is what is known commercially as "crystal"), but a hardness of less than 5. Beryl glass produced by the fusion of low quality beryl has occasionally been used as well. This has quite a good hardness of 7, but its other properties are somewhat different from those of the gems being imitated.

The orders of magnitude for the most important properties are as follows:

	H	$d(g/cm^3)$	n
Borosilicate	7	2.3–2.4	1.47–1.51
Common glass	5.5	2.4–2.5	1.50–1.52
Lead glass	4.5–5	2.9–6.3	1.54–1.69
Beryl glass	7	2.2	1.46

Synthetic stones

The knowledge of the chemical composition of precious stones gradually acquired during the eighteenth and early nineteenth centuries provided the theoretical basis for reproduction in the laboratory of gems which had hitherto only been imitated with glass or enamel.

The difficulty in synthesizing gems, however, lies not so much in reproducing the natural materials chemically, even with their typical colors, as in reproducing all their characteristic features including, if necessary, perfect transparency and freedom from visible inclusions. Early reproductions were often

Synthesis of ruby (and corundum in general) by the Verneuil method.

fig. 33

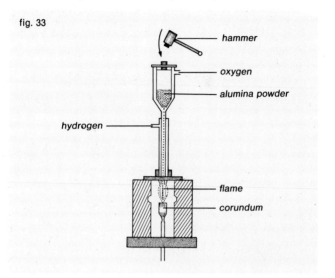

not usable because they contained many impurities. This was what happened, for example, with the very first attempt, made in 1837, by the Frenchman Gaudin, who obtained crystals of ruby by fusion of potassium aluminium sulphate and potassium chromate at a temperature of about 2000°C.

The way ahead was nevertheless clear for the reproduction of ruby and sapphire, in particular, which are the colored varieties of corundum (aluminium oxide), because of this mineral's chemical simplicity. Around the turn of the century (1891–1904), the Frenchman August Victor Lewis Verneuil perfected the flame fusion method, by inventing a furnace, inside which very fine alumina powder containing about 2 percent chromic oxide, is fused at a temperature of about 2000°C, by a flame produced by combining two currents of gas: hydrogen and oxygen. The molten powder drops by the force of gravity onto a support where it grows, in successive stages, into a single crystal of rather bulbous shape, known as a *boule* (drop, ball, pear), of perfectly transparent ruby, suitable for cutting (Fig. 33).

The Verneuil furnace is still used today, but the production of synthetic corundum has greatly improved, some 500 million carats, in a great variety of colors, now being produced each year.

Synthetic spinel is produced in exactly the same way, the best results being achieved with an excess of alumina over magne-

Verneuil furnace for the synthesis of ruby (and other forms of corundum).

sia, rather than the 1:1 ratio of its chemical formula: $MgAl_2O_4$. This chemical diversity produces slight differences in the physical properties, namely, a small increase in the refractive index and density and clear birefringence, which is anomalous, given the crystal's cubic symmetry. Synthetic spinels also come in many different colors, from light aquamarine to deep blue, green to pink, yellow to colorless. It was much used in the pre-World War II years as a substitute for diamond. The light blue variety is the most widely used. It is used to simulate aquamarine, and is plentiful on the market. The red variety is very rare because it is hard to produce.

The production of emerald is much more complex. The first method devised, the Espig process, only became known about twenty years ago, although the first experiments dated from World War I. This is an ingenious process involving the fusion of two constituents, beryllium oxide and aluminium oxide, by means of a flux (lithium molybdate). The density of this molten material, which also contains small quantities of chromic oxide as a colorant, is kept at about 2.9 g/cm^3 to allow the third constituent, silica, to float on top. In this way it can dissolve very gradually in the melt, causing a reaction between the three components, which produces emerald crystals (Fig. 34). These were the *Igmeralds,* very small quantities of which were produced by German industry in the five years prior to World War II.

Synthesis of emerald by the flux fusion or flux-melt process.

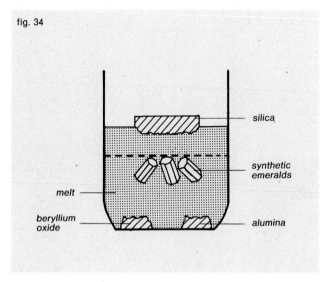

fig. 34

silica

synthetic emeralds

melt

beryllium oxide

alumina

Two different procedures are now used, the details of which have not fully been made public for fear of competition. The first, known as the flux fusion or flux melt process, copies the Espig method: the flux consists of lithium molybdate and lithium vanadate, and the reagents are silica, which floats on the melt, and beryllium and aluminium oxides, which remain at the bottom of the crucible; chromium salt is used as a coloring agent. This is apparently the method employed by the United States firm Chatham, one of the main producers of synthetic emerald. The other big manufacturer, Gilson, in France, claims to use the same system, but with low quality beryl as a raw material and chromium as a colorant. The beryl dissolves in the flux, recrystallizing onto seed plates.

The second process, known as the hydrothermal process, was mainly used by Linde in the United States, but this company has since surrendered the rights and equipment to others, after its large output proved difficult to market. This method uses autoclaves, or electrically heated, pressure-sealed containers, inside which a strongly acid, aqueous environment is created. At temperatures of between 500–600°C., the reagents, silica at one end of the container and beryllium and aluminium oxides at the other (in addition to the usual chromium), dissolve and intermingle, crystallizing as emerald on seed crystals arranged at the center of the autoclave. This second system is closer to the natural mode of formation, but is perhaps more complicated, because it has to be done in sealed containers at very high pressures. This precludes adding reagents or making any other modifications to the chemical composition once the process is under way. Whether the flux fusion or the hydrothermal method is used, the extremely slow growth rate of these crystals——several months——together with the complexity of the entire process, makes the cost of the synthetic material quite high. The selling price of the synthetic material may be as much as one-fifteenth or even one-tenth that of the natural product.

Modern technology is capable of producing synthetic beryls of various colors, apart from emerald: pale green with nickel; gray-green with manganese; light blue with copper; bright pink with cobalt; deep blue with iron. But these varieties are not in demand, and their production cost is the same as that of emerald, so they are of no commercial interest.

A particular variant of the hydrothermal method of synthesis is used to produce large quantities of synthetic quartz. Quartz is one of the most common minerals in nature, and its price is accordingly low. Only the colored varieties such as violet amethyst and yellow citrine have any appreciable value as gems. But not even the price of these stones could justify the cost of synthesis, were it not for the fact that the manufacture of quartz crystals, particularly colorless ones, has become an important industry in its own right. Modern technology uses enormous quantities of quartz as a piezoelectric material in oscillators, microphones, clocks and watches, and cigarette lighters. These applications, moreover, require untwinned crystals, which are quite easy to produce synthetically.

An autoclave, up to or over 3 meters high, containing an aqueous solution, generally with sodium carbonate or hydroxide is used for this process. Small fragments of quartz of no commercial value are placed on the bottom, as the source material. The rest of the container is occupied by a "cage" supporting numerous small seed crystals of quartz. When the temperature is raised to about 400°C., the crushed quartz dissolves and crystallizes onto the seeds in the upper portion, which is a few tens of degrees cooler.

This process is known as hydrothermal transport and recrystallization. Iron produces the yellow color typical of citrine quartz or, in smaller, accurately gauged quantities and subsequently irradiated with gamma rays, the structural defects known as color centers which yield the typical violet color of amethyst. The cost of synthetic citrine and amethyst is little (if at all) lower than that of the natural stones. The advantage is in the much greater uniformity of color obtainable in a single large piece. A crystal weighing one kg, for example, can be produced from which enough material can easily be obtained to make a necklace with identically colored beads and no flaws; whereas to achieve the same effect with natural amethyst would necessitate a laborious process of selection.

Richly colored quartzes of a type not found in nature can also be produced, particularly green, (cobalt) blue, and brown specimens, which are very attractive, but obviously synthetic.

Opal has also been produced synthetically. It is similar in chemical composition to quartz, except that the silica is combined with an appreciable quantity of water and, above all, it is not crystalline. Once the intimate arrangement of particles in this stone had been established with an electron microscope, efforts were made to reproduce it in the laboratory. Opal consists of perfectly ordered, tiny spheres of silica, about one-tenth of a micron in size. The order is similar to that of the crystalline state, but with the difference that here it is not at the atomic level, but in spheres about 1000 times bigger.

Opal synthesis was pioneered by the Australian Gaskin, but mass production was only achieved about ten years ago by Gilson in France. The procedure, which copies the natural process of formation, consists of producing tiny spheres of silica as even in size as possible. These are allowed to settle in water in very tall cylinders, to form perfectly uniform rows of spheres (Fig. 35). They are then rapidly heated to about 600°C. to eliminate most of the water and cause cementation of the spheres. Opal, depending on the size of the spheres and their degree of homogeneity, may, as mentioned, be colorless, white or black, but is also found with brilliant, iridescent colors, as in noble opal. The same varieties as the natural ones can be produced synthetically, at one-twentieth to one-fifth of the cost.

It is still not possible to produce synthetic diamonds which are suitable as gems for less than the price of natural ones. But the inherent interest of producing in the laboratory the most simple (chemically) precious stone, justifies a brief mention of past and present efforts.

At the end of the seventeenth century, Averani and Targioni of the Accademia del Cimento in Florence demonstrated that diamond burns without leaving ash, and in France at the end of the eighteenth century, Lavoisier, starting from the assumption that the gas produced by combustion of diamond was carbon dioxide, concluded that diamond was one of the forms of the carbon element, chemically identical to the familiar and widespread graphite and similar to household coal. Since that time, scientists have been trying to change the very common crystalline form into the very rare one, which has such outstanding characteristics.

Apart from numerous past attempts that lacked much scientific foundation, the first serious experiments were performed at

fig. 35

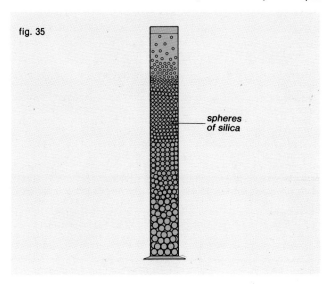

spheres
of silica

the end of the nineteenth century. In particular, the Scotsman J. B. Hannay claimed to have produced synthetic diamond by decomposition of hydrocarbons with metallic lithium at high temperatures and pressures in welded iron tubes. There is considerable doubt as to the success of these experiments, although a very rare form of diamond crystal is on display at the British Museum, claiming to be "Hannay diamonds."

At about the same period, the Frenchman Henri Moissan thought of obtaining diamond by rapid cooling of a carbon solution in molten iron. Having been brought to a temperature of 3000°C. in an electric furnace, the crucible was dropped into cold water, thereby producing enormous pressure inside the melt, by contraction of the outer crust. This operation should have made the carbon crystallize as diamond, but its success has never been proved.

Despite other attempts, some of them highly original, such as the use of a gun to achieve the very high pressures presumed to be necessary, it was not until 1955 that a group of Americans, led by Hall, obtained the first sure success by reaction between graphite and iron sulphide at 1600°C. in a special press called a girdle, capable of producing pressures in the order of 70,000 times atmosphere. It appears to be iron, or rather, iron with various other metals, above all nickel, which acts as a catalyst, or permits polymorphous transformation of

Plant for the production of small diamonds from graphite subjected to a pressure of over 200,000 x atmosphere and a temperature of 2600° C.

graphite into diamond. The production of small diamonds for industrial use is now a very active industry, able to compete in price and quantity with the diamonds obtained from mines. But production of diamonds of gem quality and size is much more difficult; and the cost of the synthetic versions is still greater than that of the natural stones, despite the fact that new methods have been devised, according to which carbon from a carbon-metal melt is deposited very slowly onto diamond seed crystals.

Artificial stones
The inherent difficulty in obtaining synthetic diamonds, at any rate at competitive prices, is responsible for the development of artificial stones, thus described because they have no counterpart in nature. While there are many different colored precious stones, and low or modestly priced synthetic forms of the more expensive ones, such as ruby and emerald, have been developed to meet a growing demand on the market, there are very few colorless natural precious stones, apart from diamond. The two closest to diamond are zircon and colorless corundum, neither of which has outstanding qualities. Corundum has appreciable hardness, but unexceptional optical properties, with fairly low refractive indices and dispersion. Zircon has superior optical properties, but is much less hard and strongly birefringent, the marked double refraction producing hazy outlines. A stone that can be considered midway

Production of cubic zirconia by crystallization from a melt according to the "skull melt" process.

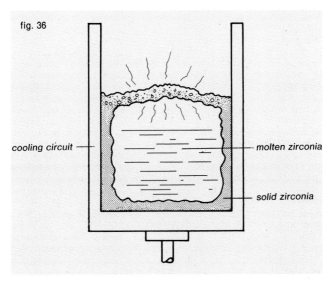

fig. 36

cooling circuit — molten zirconia

— solid zirconia

between a synthetic and an artificial product is rutile, or titanium dioxide. Rutile is always colored in its natural state, because it contains numerous impurities, but practically colorless crystals can be produced in the laboratory by the Verneuil method. Synthetic rutile, sold under the name of "titania," has a high refractive index, but modest hardness and very strong birefringence, which reduces its value. Furthermore, its exceptional dispersion renders it positively iridescent, instead of colorless, making it "impossible" as an imitation of diamond.

The case of colorless spinel is to some extent similar, in that virtually all the natural varieties are colored. It has the advantage over rutile of being a bit harder and singly refractive, but its other optical properties are very modest.

Truly artificial stones are the product of the last thirty years and they have been developed not only in an attempt to imitate diamond, but above all, as by-products of the preparation of large crystals for modern technology, such as laser generators, piezoelectric material, and material for computers.

The crystals of some salts such as *tantalate, lithium niobate,* and *strontium titanate* have excellent characteristics and the last, in particular, is quite often used for the gem market. Only its low hardness, combined with considerable brittleness, has limited the success of this stone, which has the advantage over synthetic rutile of being singly refractive, but like rutile has such strong dispersion as to appear iridescent rather than colorless. Strontium titanate, which is prepared by the classic Verneuil method, or by crystallization from a melt, can be produced in different colors, from yellow to red to black, by adding very small quantities of certain metals.

A group of artificial products also aiming to imitate diamond consists of certain members of the garnet family, not existing in nature—silicates of various metals like magnesium, aluminium, iron, calcium, chromium, and manganese. Only colored varieties of garnet occur naturally, the most highly prized of which are the fiery red *pyrope* and green *demantoid*. Many members of this group have been produced in the laboratory, all of them, obviously, with the same crystal structure, but with the most varied chemical compositions. Two members of interest to the gem trade are YAG and GGG, which are the initials for yttrium aluminium garnet ($Y_3Al_5O_{12}$) and gadolinium gallium garnet ($Gd_3Ga_5O_{12}$). These silica-free garnets, which are quite different from anything found in nature, because of the preponderance of silicon, have a number of useful characteristics. YAG has been the most successful, because of its hardness, combined with good optical properties and low cost, while the superior optical characteristics of GGG cannot compensate for its low hardness and higher cost. Both are prepared by the Czochralsky process, according to which molten material is deposited very slowly onto a seed crystal. After an initial success, above all for YAG, these artificial garnets now appear to be on the decline, because of the arrival of new products with still better characteristics. One of these is cubic zirconia (CZ), which has been on the market for just a few years. It is a cubic form of zirconium dioxide. Unlike other colorless stones used as diamond simulants, which have excellent optical characteristics but low hardness or vice-versa, cubic zirconia has good hardness, refractive index, and dispersion values and is singly refractive. It is far from easy to produce, because the cubic form is only one of the crystalline forms of zirconium oxide, namely, the high temperature (over 2300°C.) variety, which has to be stabilized by the addition of suitable elements (such as yttrium) in order to persist at normal temperatures. The method of producing these crystals is somewhat complex and was named the "skull" process by its Russian inventor, Osiko. An externally cooled crucible is used, inside which radio waves melt the material at the center only, a solid outer crust of oxide being left next to the walls (the "skull"). Very slow cooling of the melt leads to the formation of good-sized crystals (Fig. 36).

Gem Descriptions

38 **SYNTHETIC DIAMOND**

C

Elementary carbon. The first serious attempts at producing synthetic diamonds were made at the end of the nineteenth century by Hannay in Britain and Moissan in France, with uncertain, but probably negative, results. The first sure successes were achieved in 1953 in Sweden, 1955 in the United States, and probably about the same time in the Soviet Union. Production is now estimated to exceed 100 million carats a year, equal to about two-thirds of the industrial diamonds used.

Crystal system   Cubic.

Appearance   Always in minute, polyhedral crystals, with well-developed octahedral, cubic or even rhombic dodecahedral faces, from a few hundredths of a millimeter to about a millimeter in size, this being predetermined as far as possible by adjusting the environment and period of growth. Around 1970, stones weighing about one carat each uncut were also produced experimentally in the United States, using other, smaller diamonds as a raw material. Colored specimens in blue, yellow, and gray were also obtained. These diamonds, with clearly defined, cubic or octahedral faces, were of a suitable size and quality for use as gems.

Physical properties   Identical to those of natural diamonds: hardness 10; density 3.52 g/cm^3; refractive index, about n 2.42; perfect octahedral cleavage.

Production   Synthetic diamonds (for industrial uses) are now manufactured by many companies worldwide: in the United States, the Soviet Union, Japan, China, India, Holland, Finland, South Africa, Sweden, and Ireland (the industries in the last three countries mentioned are related to the De Beers group).

38.1 **Synthetic diamond**

Very few gem quality synthetic diamonds have been produced, their cost being extremely high. Some of them are housed at the Smithsonian Institution in Washington. Unless one is involved in their production, the chances of coming across a specimen are slim.

Appearance   A few of these diamonds have been cut into ovals or brilliants, weighing 0.25–0.40 carats. With others, the spontaneous facets have merely been polished to make them perfectly transparent, maintaining their slightly flattened cubic shape, with small, octahedral faces. Some are colorless or almost so; others, yellow, light blue, or grayish.

Distinctive features   One cannot generalize from so few examples, but the inclusions are apparently different from those of natural diamonds.

Cost   They are not found on the market, having been produced solely for research purposes. But they apparently cost much more than good quality natural diamonds of similar characteristics.

Synthetic diamond crystals.

330

9

4

1.77 | 1.76

39 SYNTHETIC CORUNDUM
Al_2O_3

Aluminium oxide. This is the most common synthetic product used as a substitute for natural gems, and it has been widely employed for technical purposes as well; for example, for the "jewels" in watches.

Crystal system Trigonal, like the corresponding mineral. In most cases, the synthetic product does not have well-developed crystallographic faces.

Appearance The vast majority of synthetic corundums produced by the Verneuil flame fusion method are pear- or sausage-shaped, thinning down into a short peduncle at one end. Specimens produced by other methods of fusion (mainly the Czochralsky process, also known as "pulling from the melt") are uncommon and have a squat, cylindrical shape with horizontal striations, terminating in a cone at one end, or a very long, cylindrical, rod shape. But the most recent (costly and therefore little used) flux melt and hydrothermal processes produce crystals, singly or in groups, which are very similar to the natural ones. A complete range of colors, as well as colorless, can be obtained. Colors may be red to pink, orange, yellow, green, blue, violet, and gray-green turning to violet-red.

Physical properties Identical to those of natural corundum: hardness 9; density about 4.0 g/cm³; refractive indices about $n_ε$ 1.760, $n_ω$ 1.769.

Production This is concentrated in certain countries with highly developed chemical industries, notably Switzerland, France, Germany, Italy, Czechoslovakia, the Soviet Union, Japan, and the United States.

39.1 Synthetic ruby

This was the first synthetic gem to be manufactured on an industrial scale and quantities have steadily increased to the present day, the Verneuil method being the most widely used.

Appearance Synthetic ruby is usually bright red, differing very little from the natural stone, the physical properties of which are also faithfully reproduced. It is given the same oval, round or pear-shaped mixed, faceted cuts or is made into cabochons. But it is also cut into special shapes, often weighing 5–15 carats; for instance, rectangular with a smooth, convex upper surface and faceted lower surface, or with the top part convex, but consisting of numerous, juxtaposed square facets and the bottom part faceted; or oval, again with a smooth, convex upper surface and faceted lower surface. These cuts are characteristic of synthetic rubies. They are found in large stones that are highly transparent, being completely free of inclusions, and are often used for large, old-fashioned rings for men or set into religious objects. Beads 2–3 to 7–8 millimeters in diameter are also typical; of a perfectly even, bright red color and uniform diameter, they are made into necklaces and bracelets. These pieces of jewelry could not possibly be made of natural rubies. On the rare occasions when natural rubies

Above: Boules of synthetic corundum, produced by the Verneuil method. Below: Oval cut synthetic ruby (left) and pear-shaped cut (right).

332

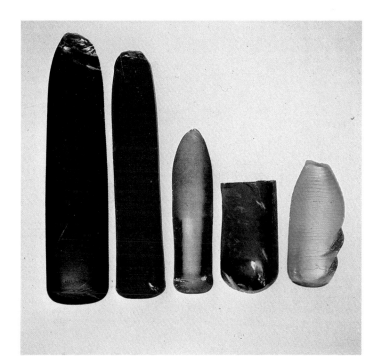

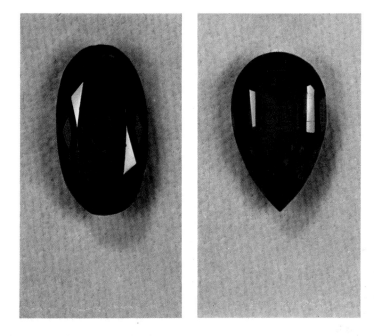

are used for this purpose, they are generally of mediocre color, full of inclusions, and of graduated diameters. Fine quality natural ruby is much too valuable to be treated in this way.

Distinctive features These are almost exclusively internal: generally speaking, this material is quite limpid. Provided one can find the right direction, thin (noncrystallographically oriented) curved lines, characteristic of growth by deposition of successive layers of molten material, will be visible under a lens, or better still a microscope, and sometimes, small gas bubbles and "swarms" of minute, opaque foreign bodies (unmelted alumina powder) can be seen. In the past, a network of internal cracks was sometimes produced by a sudden change of temperature to compensate for the suspicious absence of inclusions. The resulting stones appeared vaguely similar to some natural rubies with numerous inclusions.

Cost Extremely low, bearing no relation to that of their natural counterparts; in fact, most of the cost of ordinary synthetic rubies is in the cutting. The rare synthetic rubies produced by the flux melt or hydrothermal processes are much more expensive, costing little less than the better secondary gems. Hence, manufacture of these is not normally economical. But given their resemblance to natural stones and the possibility of some of them being sold as "good," there is a market for them. While sale of these stones invariably starts out perfectly above board, it sometimes ends in a highly profitable fraud after a few changes of hands, because of the high value of natural rubies of similar characteristics.

39.2 **Synthetic sapphire**

Production of this synthetic gem started a few years later than ruby, greater difficulties being encountered in reproducing the color.

Appearance The color of medium-light faceted stones often looks darker at the edges, due to an optical effect. It may also be colder and grayer than natural sapphires. It is cut into all the shapes used for the natural stones, both faceted and cabochon. The cabochon cut is, in fact, the one that best suits it. Synthetic sapphires cut *en cabochon* are the most convincing and hardest to distinguish from natural stones.

Distinctive features The color, sometimes with an unusual shade and color zoning, and the absence of blue-green pleochroism may distinguish synthetic sapphire from some, but not all, natural sapphires, given their variability. Here, too, the main distinctive features are internal and only visible under a lens or microscope: broad bands rep-

Above: Synthetic ruby.
Below: Synthetic sapphire.

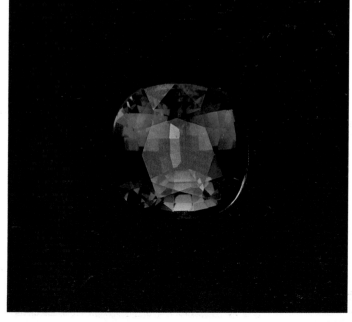

resenting curved growth lines emphasized by a different depth of color are much more clearly visible than those of synthetic rubies if the stone is examined against the light. Sometimes gas bubbles and minute foreign bodies either separately or in "swarms" follow the growth curves.

Cost As with synthetic ruby, the cost is very low and mainly accounted for by the cutting process.

39.3 **Synthetic star ruby and sapphire**

This variety of corundum has also been manufactured synthetically for a few decades. Titanium oxide is added to the alumina. It is then precipitated out as tiny crystals along the corundum crystal lattice by a process of very slow cooling, giving rise to the star effect.

Appearance These stones are invariably cut into round or oval cabochons, which generally have a star with six very obvious, if thin, rays. They normally have very limited transparency. The usual colors are bright red (ruby), or equally bright blue (sapphire), although blue-gray and dullish red stones have been produced.

Distinctive features The star is very obvious and clearcut, more so than in most natural gems. The curved growth lines characteristic of synthetic corundum are nearly always clearly visible. Sometimes, these are faintly visible in the form of concentric circles on the unpolished lower surface of the stone as well. One of the leading manufacturers also used to engrave the company's initial, a squat letter "L," on the underside of cabochons.

Above: Synthetic star ruby, 1.80 ct. (left) and synthetic star sapphire, 2.20 ct. (right)
Center: Pink synthetic corundum (left) and yellow (right).
Below: Violet synthetic corundum.

Cost Low, although a bit higher than that of normal synthetic rubies and sapphires, as the method of producing them is more complex.

39.4 **Colorless and other varieties of synthetic corundum**

Early attempts with ruby proving relatively straightforward, synthetic corundum soon began to be produced in many different colors, not so much to imitate other types of natural corundum (some of these colors do not occur naturally), as to provide a highly effective, inexpensive ornamental material or even to imitate gems of quite a different mineralogical nature.

Appearance The varieties most often seen are colorless, pink, various shades of yellow including brown- or orange-yellow, and violet. More rare are gray-green stones that turn reddish in artificial light. The colorless variety was used in the past to imitate diamond; the pink is a good imitation of pink sapphire; the yellows have mainly been used to imitate topaz, although they are not very similar; and the amethyst violet variety is normally—for some inexplicable reason—called synthetic alexandrite, despite the fact that it looks quite different from alexandrite chrysoberyl. The variety which changes color *is* intended to be an imitation of alexandrite, but it is not a very convincing one. These stones are given more or less all the types of cut used for colored stones, particularly those they are designed to imi-

tate, but the round, mixed cut is more often seen than with natural stones.

These stones are often quite large (easily 5–15 carats or more), except for the colorless variety, which generally appears in small stones, which are harder to distinguish from diamond. All the varieties of synthetic corundum have the characteristic fine luster of natural corundum, although this is not always shown to advantage in poorly cut stones.

Distinctive features   These synthetic corundums, which are all produced by the Verneuil method, usually display characteristic growth curves, although these may be barely visible, if at all, in the yellow and orange-yellow varieties. They lack, of course, the typical inclusions of their natural counterparts. Where they are used to imitate a gem of a different mineral type, this can immediately be detected by measurement of the physical properties.

Cost   Very low, even for fine specimens.

40   STABILIZED CUBIC ZIRCONIUM OXIDE (Cubic Zirconia or CZ)

ZrO_2

Cubic zirconium oxide, stabilized by the addition of 15–18 percent yttrium oxide (Y_2O_3) or 5–8 percent calcium oxide (CaO). It is an artificial product, not corresponding to any natural gemstone.

Crystal system   Cubic.

Appearance   Cubic zirconia is produced by the skull melt process and looks like an association of somewhat irregular crystals produced by the cracking of a homogeneous, transparent mass, with a light, opaque crust (the wall of the "skull"). It is perfectly transparent and usually perfectly colorless as well, but it may be a faint, brownish yellow, due to impurities. It can also be obtained in different colors, such as yellow, violet, red, and pink.

Physical properties   It has a hardness of about 8.5, which is good, but less than that of corundum. The density is about 5.65 g/cm^3 or 5.95 g/cm^3, depending on the stabilizer used. The refractive index is about 2.17, therefore too high to be measured by ordinary jewelers' refractometers, but nonetheless a bit lower than that of dia-

mond. On the other hand, the dispersion of 0.065 is higher than that of diamond.

Production   This involves the use of very advanced technology. At present, it is only produced in the United States, Switzerland, and the Soviet Union.

40.1 Djevalite, phianite, cubic zirconia

These names refer mainly to the colorless variety used as a substitute for diamond. Cubic zirconia looks very similar to diamond and is now much the most widely used diamond simulant.

Appearance   It is perfectly transparent and colorless, highly lustrous, and when cut into brilliants or related pear-shaped, oval or marquise fancy cuts is extremely similar to diamond, while step-cut stones look a bit duller. Its good hardness, plus the fact that it is isotropic, means that it can be cut with great precision, giving sharp facet edges, like those obtainable with diamond.

Distinctive features   To the practiced eye, brilliant cut stones show slightly higher dispersion (or fire) than diamond in bright light. Because the refractive index is a bit lower than that of diamond, total internal reflection is limited in cut stones; thus, if they are viewed from above and tilted gradually, a dark area will be visible at a certain point through the table facet, corresponding to some of the pavilion facets which, instead of reflecting the light, are letting it through. Sometimes, the girdle has a distinctive, diagonally striated, transparent appearance, unlike that of a diamond. In the case of a loose stone, particularly one of some size, e.g., 9–10 millimeters in diameter, one can feel the density of this material, which is almost double that of diamond, merely by weighing it in the hand. Cubic zirconia is also hard, but less so than corundum, against which it can be tested if need be. This must be done cautiously, however, under a microscope, to avoid undue damage to the stone.

Cost   Very low, mainly due to the cutting process; about the same as that of modern synthetic spinels and corundums.

Above: Round brilliant of cubic zirconia.
Below: Colorless cubic zirconia, 2.30 ct., set in a ring.

41 SYNTHETIC SPINEL

MgAl₂ or MgO•Al₂O₃

8

3.64

1.73

Magnesium aluminium oxide. In fact, the synthetic product nearly always has a different composition, which may vary from $MgO•2Al_2O_3$ to $MgO•3Al_2O_3$, or even $MgO•4Al_2O_3$. It was obtained by accident, using the Verneuil process, by adding MgO as a stabilizer to Al_2O_3, in an attempt to produce more realistic-looking synthetic sapphires than were originally possible. It only came into use in 1920.

Crystal system Cubic, like the corresponding mineral.

Appearance Like the corundums produced by the Verneuil method, it is in the shape of a pedunculated pear or sausage, although it sometimes shows indications of cubic faces, giving it a squarish cross-section with rounded corners. It can be obtained in a wide range of colors of different intensities, such as yellow, greenish yellow, light green, blue-green, sky blue, bright blue, dark green turning to reddish violet, and colorless.

Physical properties Synthetic spinel has a slightly higher refractive index (about 1.73) than natural noble spinel. The density is about 3.64 g/cm³. It has anomalous birefringence (probably due to excess alumina).

Production Generally the same as the countries which produce synthetic corundum: France, Germany, Switzerland, Italy, Czechoslovakia, the Soviet Union, Japan, and the United States. In some cases, the two are manufactured under the same roof.

41.1 Light blue synthetic spinel

This is much the most common type of synthetic spinel and is the main stone used to imitate aquamarine beryl.

Appearance The color varies from soft pale blue to deep blue, but when viewed against a white ground, it often has a grayish or violet-gray tinge. It is perfectly transparent with strong luster. It is mainly given faceted, step cuts, not always with truncated corners. Mixed round, oval, and pear-shaped cuts are used as well. Because synthetic spinel is hard but not brittle, extravagant types of cuts are also possible, quite a frequent example being one that is roughly star-shaped. Another unusual cut often used on synthetic spinel is the "scissors" cut, which is rectangular in shape, an elongated cross linking the corners of the crown. See fig. 31, page 72. Stones of all sizes are found, from a fraction of a carat to 15–20 carats in weight.

Distinctive features The color, due to cobalt, and therefore different from that of the natural gem, can easily be distinguished by an expert. Single refraction combined with a blurred, cross-hatched pattern due to anomalous birefringence, which is very obvious in polarized light, is distinctive of this and all synthetic spinels. It has greater luster than the aquamarine it is intended to imitate. A star or scissors cut in a light blue stone is a warning sign, although not a sure indication, that the stone is synthetic.

Cost Very low and mainly due to the cutting process.

Above: Variously colored boules of synthetic spinel. Below: Light blue synthetic spinel to imitate aquamarine.

41.2 **Colorless and other varieties of synthetic spinel**

Synthetic spinel, already mentioned, is produced in a vast range of colors, designed to imitate one or another of the better-known gems. Any such resemblance is always approximate, although these stones sometimes have interesting characteristics in their own right.

Appearance Yellow to yellow-green synthetic spinels (used to imitate chrysoberyl) are a lemon yellow shade which generally turns greener in bright light, due to fluorescence. The light green specimens (to imitate aquamarine) are a cold, wan color, which also turns greener in bright light. The blue-green ones (to imitate zircon) have quite an appropriate color, midway between bright blue and paint-box green and very similar to that of the natural gem. The blue ones (used to imitate sapphire) have a striking cobalt-blue tint not found in natural sapphires. Those which change color from dark green to reddish violet (used to imitate alexandrite) are a very deep, often almost blackish color, quite different from that of alexandrite. They have considerable luster, sometimes better than that of the gems they are designed to imitate. All the faceted cuts are used and these are quite easily executed due to the good characteristics of the material.

Distinctive features If blue synthetic spinel is viewed from the table facet in strong tungsten light, the facet edges of the pavilion display curious striae of red fluorescence. The fact that it is singly refractive differentiates the synthetic from most of the gems it is used to imitate. Thus greenish blue and colorless spinel, which are used to imitate zircon, do not show the obvious doubling of the facet edges of the latter. When colorless spinel is used to imitate diamond, it looks much less lustrous with very limited dispersion, and is therefore quite readily distinguished. Furthermore, in polarized light, the blurred, cross-hatched appearance (due to anomalous birefringence) will immediately identify it. Only in some cases is it possible to see under a microscope the curved growth lines associated with the Verneuil process. Minute gas bubbles are sometimes present as well, often being tadpole-shaped or elongated and contorted.

Cost The price is always very low and mainly depends on the cut.

Above: Light blue synthetic spinel (left) and yellow-green (right).
Center: Synthetic blue spinels to imitate zircon (left) and sapphire (right).
Below: Pink synthetic spinel (left) and colorless (right).

344

42 YAG (YTTRIUM ALUMINIUM GARNET)

$Y_3Al_2(AlO_4)_3$

Aluminate of yttrium and aluminium, with a garnet-type structure. It is an artificial product with no natural counterpart.

Crystal system   Cubic.

Appearance   It is produced by the Czochralsky process according to which crystals in the form of cylindrical rods about 4–5 centimeters in diameter and 20 centimeters long are "pulled" from the melt. It is perfectly transparent and colorless, but green, yellow and blue forms have also been produced by adding small quantities of other elements.

Physical properties   It has a hardness of slightly more than 8. The density is about 4.55 g/cm³. The refractive index of 1.83 is quite high, but much less than that of diamond and cubic zirconia. The dispersion of 0.028 is far lower than that of diamond.

Production   It is mainly produced in the United States.

42.1 YAG (colorless)

This was the chief substitute for diamond in the 1960s. It has now been replaced by other products, mainly cubic zirconia.

Appearance   Perfectly transparent and colorless and singly refractive like diamond, it is usually seen cut into brilliants; more rarely, it is given a step cut. Its luster is about the same as that of colorless zircon and greater than that of corundum and spinel. Being hard but not brittle, it is easily given a high polish and sharply defined edges. But low dispersion makes these stones look a bit lifeless, particularly those with a step cut.

Distinctive features   Because YAG's refractive index is quite a bit lower than that of diamond, if a brilliant cut stone is viewed from above and tilted gradually, a characteristic dark area will appear in the table facet (opposite the observer), corresponding to certain facets of the pavilion which let the light through instead of reflecting it. Furthermore, if the stone is viewed from the table facet (with a lens or microscope) the distinct reflections of the table and crown facets will not be visible as they are with diamond. Also, if step cut stones are placed upside down with the table facet resting on a printed page, the letters will be visible through it. The girdle is not finished like that of diamond; it is not cylindrical and is usually striated, as if it had been filed; yet, despite this rough finish, it looks fairly transparent. A hardness test using a corundum-tipped pencil (9), which is midway between the two, will readily distinguish YAG from diamond.

Cost   One of the lowest, equal to that of the least expensive synthetics. The cost of the raw material is, in fact, very low and it is much quicker and easier to cut than diamond, being softer and without any tendency to brittleness.

Above: 4.8 cm bar of colorless YAG. Below: Round brilliant of colorless YAG, 2.10 ct.

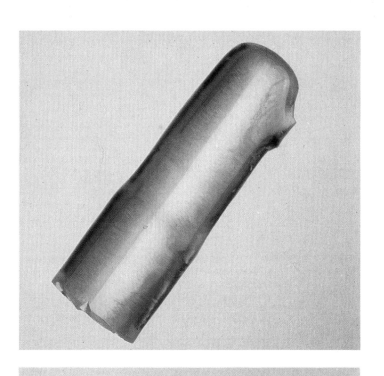

43 SYNTHETIC BERYL

$Be_3Al_2Si_6O_{18}$

8

2.65

1.56 | 1.56

Silicate of beryllium and aluminium. Because of the value of emerald, efforts were made to synthesize beryl after corundum and spinel. The task proved far from easy, and mass production was only achieved around the 1950s. The basic procedures used have already been described. They are typically slow: it may take several weeks to obtain crystals of an acceptable size. They could be made to grow more rapidly, but the resulting crystals would be fractured, with numerous, highly characteristic inclusions, obviously making them less transparent and much more easy to distinguish from natural emerald. Synthetic beryl is normally only produced in the emerald green variety; colorless, pink, pale blue, and yellow crystals have occasionally been produced for research purposes, but they are not available on the market.

Crystal system Hexagonal.

Appearance This depends on the method used. The flux melt process produces isolated, hexagonal, prismatic crystals or groups of prismatic crystals. Crystals have been obtained weighing 1000 carats or more, but growth usually stops much sooner. The prismatic crystals are very hard to distinguish, at first sight, from natural ones. The hydrothermal method produces crystals of more complex appearance, because to hasten their growth a bipyramidal seed crystal is used.

At one time, this second process was only used to deposit a thin layer of synthetic emerald (a few tenths of a millimeter) onto a seed consisting of a colorless, or almost colorless, piece of natural beryl (a variety of very low value) which had already been given a step cut. The stone was then carefully polished to give it the necessary luster without removing the coating, which was entirely responsible for the color. In both the flux and hydrothermal processes chrome is used to reproduce the green of natural emeralds.

Physical properties These are much the same as for natural beryl. Nearly all synthetic emeralds produced by the flux melt process have slightly lower refractive indices ($n\varepsilon$ 1.560, $n\omega$ 1.563) and birefringence (0.003 or 0.004) than natural beryl. The density is also a bit lower, ranging from 2.64 to 2.66 g/cm³. However, the physical properties of synthetic emeralds produced by the hydrothermal process generally match those of natural emeralds perfectly—particularly the comparatively rare types with a thin, synthetic coating.

Production Having started up independently in Germany, the United States, and later Austria, this is now concentrated in the United States and France, but has apparently begun in Japan and the Soviet Union as well.

Above: Synthetic emerald, 1.80 ct. Below: Ring with synthetic emerald and small brilliants.

43.1 Synthetic emerald

The (emerald) green variety is the only one which is manufactured synthetically on an industrial scale. Production has been attempted by a number of companies, some of which have subsequently abandoned the task as uneconomical.

Appearance It is usually quite a strong emerald green, with a bluish tinge, and, as with natural emeralds, the step or trap cut is normally used, mixed oval or pear-shaped cuts being rarer. Cut stones are generally quite limpid, although stones of this quality take longer to grow. All in all, their outward appearance is very similar, if not identical, to that of their natural counterparts.

Distinctive features It was mentioned in the discussion on physical properties that accurate measurement could reveal differences between the refractive indices, birefringence, and density of natural emeralds and the synthetic ones produced by the flux melt process. The stones are normally distinguished, however, by their inclusions. In the case of hydrothermal synthetic emeralds, these are not very different from some inclusions in natural emeralds, but they are "oddly" arranged in relation to the growth lines and are also positioned like mirror images of one another on either side of a thin central plate constituting the seed onto which the synthetic product was grown. Emeralds produced by the flux melt process contain variable quantities of swirling, veillike inclusions consisting of whitish residues of flux material trapped in cracks that developed during their formation. But it is admittedly not easy to distinguish between synthetic and natural emeralds without a good microscope, a lens alone often proving inadequate.

Cost The cost of stones with few inclusions is quite high, equal to certain prized secondary gems, but much lower than that of natural emeralds. Stones with copious inclusions are worth somewhat less, but are still among the highest-priced synthetic stones.

Above and below: Two synthetic emeralds of different shapes.

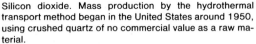

44 SYNTHETIC QUARTZ
SiO_2

7

2.65

1.55 | 1.54

Silicon dioxide. Mass production by the hydrothermal transport method began in the United States around 1950, using crushed quartz of no commercial value as a raw material.

Crystal system Trigonal, like the corresponding mineral.
Appearance In well-formed crystals, although these are usually flattened in relation to two prominent rhombohedral faces, giving them a distinctive elongated shape, somewhat similar to that of a flat brick or ingot. Normally transparent and colorless, synthetic quartz can easily be given a yellow or violet tint like the corresponding varieties of natural quartz; it can also be brown, bright green, and shades of blue, which have no natural equivalent.
Physical properties The same as for the mineral: hardness 7; density 2.65 g/cm³; refractive indices $n\omega$ 1.544, $n\varepsilon$ 1.553.
Production Large amounts are produced in the United States, Great Britain, and the Soviet Union. The colored varieties, which can be used as ornamental materials, are from the Soviet Union.

44.1 Amethyst, smoky, citrine, brown, green and blue synthetic quartz

The above colors are produced by adding small quantities of other substances such as iron, cobalt, and aluminium, and in the case of amethyst and smoky quartz, by subsequent treatment with high energy radiation.

Appearance The amethyst, citrine, and blue varieties are virtually the only ones used for ornamental purposes. For the color of the first two, see the description of the natural varieties. Blue quartz is produced in both a soft, aquamarine-type color and vivid cobalt. Gems are given faceted step or oval, round or pear-shaped mixed cuts, but also made into cabochons and spherical necklace beads. The amethyst and citrine varieties are widely employed, but the blue variety is much less popular, and the other colors are used still less.

Distinctive features The amethyst and citrine versions look extremely similar to the natural stones and can only be distinguished from them under a microscope or lens when they contain obvious, typical inclusions. The blue variety is a strange, garish color not normal in gemstones. The brown and green varieties are also distinctive colors, similar if anything to some tourmalines, although they are distinguishable from these by their weaker pleochroism and different physical properties.

Cost Very low, as with most synthetics, except for amethyst, which costs little less than the natural variety.

45 GGG (GADOLINIUM GALLIUM GARNET)

$Gd_3Ga_2(GaO_4)_3$

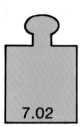

Galliate of gadolinium and gallium, with a garnet-type structure. It is an artificial product with no natural counterpart.

Crystal system   Cubic.

Appearance   It is mainly produced by the Czochralsky method of crystallization from a melt, in cylindrical bars a few centimeters in diameter and up to 30 centimeters long, or in large, pedunculated pear shapes up to 10 centimeters in diameter. It is perfectly transparent and colorless or with a yellow tinge. In time, it may turn brownish in the light.

Physical properties   It has a hardness of 6.5, which is less than that of YAG and CZ or cubic zirconia. It has a very high density of 7.02 g/cm^3, which is double that of diamond and also higher than that of the most recent imitations. The refractive index of 2.02 is above the range of ordinary refractometers. The dispersion is 0.045, which is roughly the same as that of diamond.

Production   Because of certain special characteristics it displays, it was and still is mainly produced for use in various branches of electronics, especially in the United States.

45.1 GGG

Having very similar characteristics to diamond, in some respects more so than YAG, GGG partially replaced the latter as a diamond substitute in the 1970s, despite its much higher cost. But it has in turn been superseded by cubic zirconia, which has still better characteristics and is a lot cheaper.

Appearance   Transparent and colorless (or with a yellow-brown tinge), it is seen almost exclusively in the form of brilliants. It bears a strong resemblance to diamond, but since the stone is not very hard, the facet edges often have small chips on them.

Distinctive features   The refractive index is higher than that of YAG, a similar, more widely distributed product, but still less than that of diamond. Here, too, the effects on total internal reflection are such that if a stone is tilted gradually, a dark, transparent area is visible from the table facet, corresponding to certain pavilion facets, which let the light through instead of reflecting it. The girdle is usually different from that of diamond; less clearly cylindrical and with a striated appearance, as if it had been smoothed with a file. Its density is so high that, in the case of a loose stone 8 to 10 millimeters in diameter, it can be appreciated simply by weighing it in the hand.

Cost   Higher than that of modern synthetic stones, but less than most costly synthetics like emeralds. It is hardly ever seen on the market nowadays.

1.50 ct. GGG with brilliant cut.

46 SYNTHETIC RUTILE

TiO_2

Titanium dioxide. This is produced by a special variant of the Verneuil method, using extra oxygen.

Crystal system Tetragonal, like the corresponding mineral.

Appearance In the shape of a pedunculated pear or sausage (therefore without obvious crystal faces), generally about 3 centimeters in diameter and no more than 10 centimeters long. It is transparent and usually pale yellow, but can also be bright blue or red; it is not possible to produce a perfectly colorless form.

Physical properties It has a hardness of 6, which is of course quite low. The density is 4.25 g/cm³. The refractive indices are $n\omega$ 2.61, $n\varepsilon$ 2.90, thus it is intensely birefringent. The dispersion is also exceptionally high: at 0.28, it is the highest of any stone used for ornamental purposes. It has prismatic cleavage and is brittle.

Production Appreciable quantities were manufactured in the United States during the 1950s, but production is now very limited.

46.1 Synthetic rutile (or titania)

This was widely used to imitate diamond in the United States in the 1940s and 1950s, but was soon ousted by the appearance of more satisfactory imitations on the market.

Appearance It has very strong luster and is always given a brilliant cut. Normally, it is slightly cloudy rather than perfectly transparent. It has a faint yellowish tinge, but because of its very high dispersion looks positively iridescent in bright light. Under a lens, its very strong birefringence produces an obvious doubling of the facets and edges which is more striking, for instance, than that of zircons. Because the stone is not very hard, the facet edges are not sharp, and it feels slippery.

Distinctive features Strong birefringence, combined with very high dispersion, low hardness, and a yellow tinge make it easy to recognize.

Cost Higher than that of other diamond simulants such as cubic zirconia or YAG, but lower than that of the most costly synthetics, such as emerald.

Brilliant cut synthetic rutile; detail enlarged to emphasize its high dispersion.

47 SYNTHETIC STRONTIUM TITANATE
SrTio$_3$

Strontium titanate, produced by a variant of the Verneuil method, using extra oxygen. It is wholly artificial, with no natural counterpart.

Crystal system   Cubic.

Appearance   In the shape of a pedunculated pear or sausage, generally no more than 2.5 centimeters in diameter and about 10 centimeters long. It is transparent and colorless.

Physical properties   It has rather a low hardness of 5.5, and is somewhat brittle. The density is 5.13 g/cm^3. The refractive index is 2.41, which is almost equal to that of diamond. It has exceptional dispersion, of 0.19, which is only exceeded by synthetic rutile.

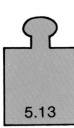

Production   Considerable quantities were manufactured in the United States around 1955, but production is now very limited, as it has been replaced by other synthetic materials.

47.1 Fabulite (synthetic strontium titanate)

This is one of several fanciful names coined for this artificial product issued on the market beginning in 1955. It appeared at the time to be a first-rate imitation of diamond, but after only a few years has been rendered almost obsolete by products with better characteristics (above all, hardness), which look more like diamond and cost less.

Appearance   It has considerable luster, equal to that of diamond, when the facets and edges have not been damaged by use. Because of its exceptional dispersion, it looks highly iridescent in strong light. In diffuse light, it is perfectly colorless. It is singly refractive like diamond. The facet edges are often visibly damaged due to its brittleness and low hardness. It is always cut into brilliants.

Distinctive features   When viewed with a lens from above in strong light the iridescence is characteristic, being more obvious than in diamond and little less than that of synthetic rutile. Not being strongly birefringent, it can immediately be distinguished from the latter. Obvious surface damage, particularly to the facet edges, is indicative of its low hardness. For the same reason, the facet edges are not sharp and the stone feels slippery to the touch.

Cost   Higher than that of other, more recent, and better imitations of diamond, but less than that of the most expensive synthetics, such as emerald.

Above and below:
examples of fabulite.

48 SYNTHETIC TURQUOISE

$CuAl_6 (OH)_8 (PO_4)_4 \cdot 4H_2O$

Hydrated phosphate of copper and aluminium. This is manufactured from artificial raw materials, by a sintering process similar to that used for ceramics. It is fairly similar to natural turquoise in chemical composition and crystal structure, although the water content is lower, perhaps as a result of the production process.

Crystal system Triclinic, but as this product is an aggregate of minute grains, the individual crystals can never be distinguished.

Appearance In bars or "ingots" obtained from a mould, of a uniform, bright blue color very similar to that of the natural gem. It is also produced with a network of blackish veins.

Physical properties It has a hardness of 5.5 to 6, like the (rare) very good quality natural turquoise. It has a density of 2.60 to 2.75 g/cm^3. As often happens with microcrystalline materials, only one refractive index is measurable; it is around 1.60.

Production At the moment, synthetic turquoise is only produced in France.

48.1 Synthetic turquoise

The synthetic turquoise produced is used exclusively as an ornamental material.

Appearance It is usually very homogeneous, and a striking, light blue color. It takes a good polish like good quality natural turquoise, only very thin pieces are translucent. It is always cut into cabochons or spherical or polished pieces for necklaces. It is also produced with blackish veining, like some natural turquoise.

Distinctive features It has the physical properties of good quality natural turquoise. Its hardness is, therefore, much greater than that of nearly all natural turquoise available on the market. Under a microscope, or even a lens, a minute cellular pattern like hexagonal mesh is visible in one direction only, and this is the surest means of distinction. Unlike most natural turquoise nowadays, it is not treated with paraffin.

Cost Quite low, several times lower than that of natural turquoise of similar quality and even a lot less than that of poor-quality natural turquoise.

Above: Uncut synthetic turquoise, 80 mm.
Below: Cabochon of synthetic turquoise, 18 ct.

49 SYNTHETIC OPAL
$SiO_2 \bullet nH_2O$

4.5–5

2–2.1

1.45

Noncrystalline hydrous silicon dioxide. This is produced by a lengthy and difficult process and, in most cases, corresponds exactly to natural opal. Sometimes, however, the particles of silica are impregnated with plastic instead of silica gel, the resulting product thus having a different composition, despite being identical in appearance.

Crystal system   Noncrystalline.

Appearance   Although it is always sold as ready-cut stones, it is presumably manufactured in small sheets a few millimeters (probably 6 or 7) thick. It has lively iridescence, like that of precious opal. The other varieties of opal are of no commercial interest and are therefore not manufactured.

Physical properties   The density varies from 2.00 to 2.14 g/cm^3, but can be as low as 1.95 for pieces impregnated with plastic. The refractive index is about 1.45. The hardness of 4.5 to 5 is a bit lower than that of natural opal. It has even greater porosity than natural opal, although this is eliminated in the types impregnated with plastic.

Production   Initially, it was only produced in France, but it is now manufactured in Japan as well.

49.1 Black and white synthetic opal

Synthetic opal came on the market in 1974 and is produced in the two basic varieties of ornamental value, with a light or dark ground.

Appearance   It matches the appearance of noble or precious opal precisely, with patches of iridescence on a milky white or deep blue to smoke gray or blackish ground. Naturally, the contrast between the background and colored patches produced by light diffraction is stronger in the dark variety (see the section on natural opal). It is generally cut into oval or round cabochons; more rarely, into less regular shapes, the thickness not usually exceeding 5 millimeters. Recently, however, polished, spherical necklace beads with a diameter of 7–8 millimeters and more have been manufactured, proving that it can be produced in greater thicknesses.

Distinctive features   It is very hard to distinguish from natural opal. Only under a microscope can one see a difference in the patches of color, which have a minutely tesselated appearance like lizard skin, never seen in the natural variety. As a result, the edges of the colored patches are also minutely sinuous and indented.

Cost   The white opal is less expensive than the black, which costs as much as some natural secondary gems, but less than the most expensive synthetic products.

White and black synthetic opal.

50 SYNTHETIC LAPIS LAZULI

The chief constituent is lazurite, or silicate of sodium and aluminium containing sulphur, $Na_8S(AlO_2)_6(SiO_2)_6$, but the synthetic product also contains an abnormally large amount of sodalite. It is manufactured from an agglomeration of artificial raw materials by a process similar to that used for ceramics and apparently corresponds only very approximately to the composition of natural lapis lazuli, which is in any case somewhat variable, being a rock.

Crystal system Cubic, for both lazurite and sodalite.

Appearance In bars obtained from a mould, of a uniform deep blue color with an almost violet tinge. Some are dotted with minute, evenly distributed pyrite crystals.

Physical properties It has a hardness of 4.5, therefore a bit lower than that of natural lapis lazuli. The refractive index is about 1.50. The density is 2.38–2.46 g/cm³, thus slightly lower than that of natural lapis lazuli, although roughly the same as that of its chief constituent, lazurite. It is distinctly porous.

Production At the moment, it is only produced in France.

50.1 Synthetic lapis lazuli

This is not yet widely available on the market.

Appearance A uniform, deep blue color with a hint of violet, which is uncommon in the natural material. It easily takes a fine polish and is also produced scattered with minute fragments of pyrite. It is made into cabochons and, above all, spherical or polyhedral polished necklace beads.

Distinctive features It never contains the patches and veins of light-colored minerals often visible in natural lapis lazuli. Because this product is an artificial agglomerate of tiny, relatively homogeneous particles, rather than a collection of small crystals which have developed together, interpenetrating to some extent, granulometry reveals a minute, uniform structure. Furthermore, when synthetic lapis lazuli contains pyrite, microscopic examination reveals that this consists of small, ground fragments evenly mixed with the other constituents. It reacts to hydrochloric acid by an even stronger emission of hydrogen sulphide than natural lapis lazuli. The combination of unusually low density and high porosity is quite distinctive.

Cost Decidedly low, much like that of other inexpensive synthetic ornamental materials.

Above: 70 mm bar of synthetic lapis lazuli.
Below: Cabochon of synthetic lapis lazuli, 6.53 ct.

SYNOPTIC TABLES

The following tables list the principal natural, synthetic, and artificial stones in decreasing order of magnitude for hardness, density, and refractive indices and subdivided by color. Where there is a wide variation in values the upper and lower limits are given (e.g., 3.80–4.20). For birefringent substances, the maximum and minimum indices are shown thus: (e.g.) 1.66;1.91. In the case of hardness, a figure of 7.5.8, for example, indicates a value between the two, whereas 4–5.5 indicates variability within those limits.

List of the principal natural and artificial stones in descending order of HARDNESS:

	H	d(g/cm³)	n
Diamond	10	3.52	2.42
Corundum	9	4.0	1.76; 1.77
Cubic zirconia (artificial)	8.5	5.7–5.9	2.17
Chrysoberyl	8.5	3.72	1.74; 1.75
YAG (artificial)	8.25	4.55	1.83
Synthetic spinel	8	3.64	1.73
Noble spinel	8	3.6	1.71
Blue and colorless topaz	8	3.56	1.61; 1.62
Yellow-brown and pink topaz	8	3.55	1.63; 1.64
Beryl	7.5.8	2.7	1.57; 1.60
"High" zircon	7.5	4.7	1.96; 2.01
Rhodolite (garnet)	7–7.5	3.74–3.94	1.76
Pyrope (garnet)	7–7.5	3.65–3.87	1.73–1.75
Andalusite	7–7.5	3.13–3.20	1.63; 1.64
Cordierite	7–7.5	2.59	1.53; 1.55
Spessartine (garnet)	6.5–7.5	4.16	1.80
Tsavolite (green grossular garnet)	6.5–7.5	3.58–3.69	1.74
Almandine (garnet)	6–7.5	3.95–4.20	1.76–1.83
Tourmaline	7	3.02–3.20	1.62; 1.64
Quartz	7	2.65	1.54; 1.55
Olivine	6.5–7	3.34	1.65; 1.69
Jadeite jade	6.5–7	3.34	1.66; 1.67

	H	d(g/cm^3)	n
Spodumene	6–7	3.18	1.65; 1.68
Demantoid (garnet)	6.5–7	3.84	1.88
Hessonite (garnet)	6.5–7	3.5	1.74
GGG (artificial)	6.5	7.02	2.02
Zoisite	6.5	3.11–3.40	1.69; 1.70
Chalcedony	6.5	2.61	1.53
Hematite	6.5	5.2–5.3	2.94; 3.22
Pyrite	6–6.5	5.0–5.2	. . .
Labradorite (feldspar)	6–6.5	2.65–2.75	1.56; 1.57
Albite moonstone (feldspar)	6–6.5	2.62–2.65	1.53; 1.54
Adularia moonstone (feldspar)	6–6.5	2.56	1.52; 1.53
Rhodonite	5.5–6.5	3.4–3.7	1.73; 1.74
Opal	5.5–6.5	2.1	1.45
Synthetic rutile	6	4.25	2.61; 2.90
"Low" zircon	6	3.93–4.07	1.79; 1.81
Noble orthoclase (feldspar)	6	2.56	1.52; 1.53
Amazonite (feldspar)	6	2.57	1.52; 1.53
Diopside	5.5.6	3.27–3.31	1.68; 1.71
Turquoise (gem quality)	5–6	2.65–2.90	1.61
Nephrite jade	5–6	2.9–3.4	1.61
Strontium titanate (artificial)	5.5	5.13	2.41
Lapis lazuli (gem quality)	5–5.5	2.7–2.9	1.50
Serpentine	2–5	2.3–2.6	1.55; 1.56
Pearl	2.5–4.5	2.68–2.78	. . .
Synthetic lapis lazuli	4.5	2.38–2.46	1.50
Malachite	4	3.8	1.66; 1.91
Rhodochrosite	4	3.4–3.7	1.60; 1.82
Coral (calcareous)	3.5–4	2.65	. . .
Ivory	2.5–2.75	1.8	1.54
Amber	2.5	1.07	1.54

List of the principal natural and artificial stones in descending order of DENSITY:

	d(g/cm^3)	H	n
GGG (artificial)	7.02	6.5	2.02
Cubic zirconia (artificial)	5.7–5.9	8.5	2.17
Hematite	5.2–5.3	6.5	2.94; 3.22
Pyrite	5.0–5.2	6–6.5	. . .
Strontium titanate (artificial)	5.13	5.5	2.41
"High" zircon	4.7	7.5	1.96; 2.01
YAG (artificial)	4.55	8.25	1.83
Synthetic rutile	4.25	6	2.61; 2.90
Almandine (garnet)	3.95–4.20	6–7.5	1.76–1.83
Spessartine (garnet)	4.16	6.5–7.5	1.80
"Low" zircon	3.93–4.07	6	1.79; 1.81
Corundum	4.0	9	1.76; 1.77
Rhodolite (garnet)	3.74–3.94	7–7.5	1.76
Pyrope (garnet)	3.65–3.87	7–7.5	1.73–1.75
Demantoid (garnet)	3.84	6.5–7	1.88
Malachite	3.8	4	1.66; 1.91
Chrysoberyl	3.72	8.5	1.74; 1.75
Rhodonite	3.4–3.7	5.5–6.5	1.73; 1.74
Rhodochrosite	3.4–3.7	4	1.60; 1.82
Tsavolite (green grossular garnet)	3.58–3.69	6.5–7.5	1.74
Synthetic spinel	3.64	8	1.73
Noble spinel	3.6	8	1.71
Blue and colorless topaz	3.56	8	1.61; 1.62
Yellow-brown and pink topaz	3.55	8	1.63; 1.64
Diamond	3.52	10	2.42
Hessonite (garnet)	3.5	6.5–7	1.74
Zoisite	3.11–3.40	6.5	1.69; 1.70
Nephrite jade	2.9–3.4	5–6	1.61
Olivine	3.34	6.5–7	1.65; 1.69
Jadeite jade	3.34	6.5–7	1.66; 1.67
Diopside	3.27–3.31	5.5.6	1.68; 1.71
Andalusite	3.13–3.20	7–7.5	1.63; 1.64

	d(g/cm^3)	H	n
Tourmaline	3.02–3.20	7	1.62; 1.64
Spodumene	3.18	6–7	1.65; 1.68
Lapis lazuli	2.7–2.9	5–5.5	1.50
Turquoise (gem quality)	2.65–2.90	5–6	1.61
Pearl	2.68–2.78	2.5–4.5	. . .
Labradorite (feldspar)	2.65–2.75	6–6.5	1.56; 1.57
Beryl	2.7	7.5.8	1.57; 1.60
Quartz	2.65	7	1.54; 1.55
Coral (calcareous)	2.65	3.5–4	. . .
Albite moonstone (feldspar)	2.62–2.65	6–6.5	1.53; 1.54
Chalcedony	2.61	6.5	1.53
Serpentine	2.3–2.6	2–5	1.55; 1.56
Cordierite	2.59	7–7.5	1.53; 1.55
Noble orthoclase (feldspar)	2.56	6	1.52; 1.53
Adularia moonstone (feldspar)	2.56	6–6.5	1.52; 1.53
Amazonite (feldspar)	2.56	6	1.52; 1.53
Synthetic lapis lazuli	2.38–2.46	4.5	1.50
Opal	2.1	5.5–6.5	1.45
Ivory	1.8	2.5–2.75	1.54
Amber	1.07	2.5	1.54

List of the principal natural and artificial stones in descending order of magnitude for REFRACTIVE INDEX/INDICES:

	n	H	d(g/cm^3)
Hematite	2.94; 3.22	6.5	5.2–5.3
Synthetic rutile	2.61; 2.90	6	4.25
Diamond	2.42	10	3.52
Strontium titanate (artificial)	2.41	5.5	5.13
Cubic zirconia (artificial)	2.17	8.5	5.7–5.9
GGG (artificial)	2.02	6.5	7.02
"High" zircon	1.96; 2.01	7.5	4.7
Malachite	1.66; 1.91	4	3.8

	n	H	d(g/cm³)
Demantoid (garnet)	1.88	6.5–7	3.84
YAG (artificial)	1.83	8.25	4.55
Almandine (garnet)	1.76–1.83	6–7.5	3.95–4.20
Rhodochrosite	1.60; 1.82	4	3.4–3.7
"Low" zircon	1.79; 1.81	6	3.93–4.07
Spessartine (garnet)	1.80	6.5–7.5	4.16
Corundum	1.76; 1.77	9	4.0
Rhodolite (garnet)	1.76	7–7.5	3.74–3.94
Chrysoberyl	1.74; 1.75	8.5	3.72
Pyrope (garnet)	1.73–1.75	7–7.5	3.65–3.87
Hessonite (garnet)	1.74	6.5–7	3.5
Tsavolite (green grossular garnet)	1.74	6.5–7.5	3.58–3.69
Rhodonite	1.73; 1.74	5.5–6.5	3.4–3.7
Synthetic spinel	1.73	8	3.64
Noble spinel	1.71	8	3.6
Diopside	1.68; 1.71	5.5–6	3.27–3.31
Zoisite	1.69; 1.70	6.5	3.11–3.40
Olivine	1.65; 1.69	6.5–7	3.34
Spodumene	1.65; 1.68	6–7	3.18
Jadeite jade	1.66; 1.67	6.5–7	3.34
Yellow-brown and pink topaz	1.63; 1.64	8	3.55
Andalusite	1.63; 1.64	7–7.5	3.13–3.20
Tourmaline	1.62; 1.64	7	3.02–3.20
Blue and colorless topaz	1.61; 1.62	8	3.56
Nephrite jade	1.61	5–6	2.9–3.4
Turquoise (gem quality)	1.61	5–6	2.65–2.90
Beryl	1.57; 1.60	7.5–8	2.7
Labradorite (feldspar)	1.56; 1.57	6–6.5	2.65–2.75
Serpentine	1.55; 1.56	2–5	2.3–2.6
Quartz	1.54; 1.55	7	2.65
Cordierite	1.53; 1.55	7–7.5	2.59
Ivory	1.54	2.5–2.75	1.8
Amber	1.54	2.5	1.07
Albite moonstone (feldspar)	1.53; 1.54	6–6.5	2.62–2.65
Chalcedony	1.53	6.5	2.61

	n	H	$d(g/cm^3)$
Adularia moonstone (feldspar)	1.52; 1.53	6–6.5	2.56
Amazonite (feldspar)	1.52; 1.53	6	2.57
Noble orthoclase (feldspar)	1.52; 1.53	6	2.56
Lapis lazuli (gem quality)	1.50	5–5.5	2.7–2.9
Synthetic lapis lazuli	1.50	4.5	2.38–2.46
Opal	1.45	5.5–6.5	2.1

List of the principal natural and artificial stones subdivided by COLOR (in descending order of magnitude for refractive indices).

Colors: various shades of RED and PINK

	n	H	$d(g/cm^3)$
"High" zircon	1.96; 2.01	7.5	4.7
Almandine (garnet)	1.76–1.83	6–7.5	3.95–4.20
Rhodochrosite	1.60; 1.82	4	3.4–3.7
Spessartine (garnet)	1.80	6.5–7.5	4.16
Corundum (ruby and pink sapphire)	1.76; 1.77	9	4.0
Rhodolite (garnet)	1.76	7–7.5	3.74–3.94
Pyrope (garnet)	1.73–1.75	7–7.5	3.65–3.87
Hessonite (garnet)	1.74	6.5–7	3.5
Rhodonite	1.73; 1.74	5.5–6.5	3.4–3.7
Noble spinel	1.71	8	3.6
Spodumene (kunzite variety)	1.65; 1.68	6–7	3.18
Jadeite jade	1.66; 1.67	6.5–7	3.34
Topaz	1.63–1.64	8	3.55
Tourmaline (rubellite variety)	1.62; 1.64	7	3.06
Beryl (morganite and bixbite)	1.58; 1.57	7.5·8	2.7
Quartz	1.54; 1.55	7	2.65
Chalcedony	1.53	6.5	2.61
Fire opal	1.45	6	2.1
Coral	. . .	3.5–4	2.65

Colors: ORANGE, YELLOW, BROWNISH YELLOW, BROWN, GREENISH YELLOW

	n	H	d(g/cm^3)
Synthetic rutile	2.61; 2.90	6	4.25
Diamond	2.42	10	3.52
Zircon	1.96; 2.01	7.5	4.7
YAG (artificial)	1.83	8.25	4.55
Corundum	1.76; 1.77	9	4.0
Chrysoberyl	1.74–1.75	8.5	3.72
Hessonite (garnet)	1.74	6.5–7	3.5
Synthetic spinel	1.73	8	3.64
Olivine	1.65; 1.69	6.5–7	3.34
Jadeite jade	1.66; 1.67	6.5–7	3.34
Topaz	1.63; 1.64	8	3.55
Andalusite	1.63; 1.64	7–7.5	3.13–3.20
Tourmaline	1.62–1.64	7	3.02–3.20
Beryl	1.57; 1.60	7.5·8	2.7
Serpentine	1.55–1.56	2–5	2.3–2.6
Citrine quartz	1.54; 1.55	7	2.65
Amber	1.54	2.5	1.07
Albite moonstone (feldspar)	1.53–1.54	6–6.5	2.62–2.65
Chalcedony	1.53	6.5	2.61
Noble orthoclase (feldspar)	1.52–1.53	6	2.56
Common opal	1.45	6	2.1
Pyrite	. . .	6–6.5	5.0–5.2

Color: GREEN

	n	H	d(g/cm^3)
Diamond	2.42	10	3.52
"High" zircon	1.96; 2.01	7.5	4.7
Malachite	1.66; 1.91	4	3.8
Demantoid (garnet)	1.88	6.5–7	3.84
YAG (artificial)	1.83	8.25	4.55
"Low" zircon	1.79; 1.81	6	3.93–4.07
Corundum	1.76; 1.77	9	4.0
Alexandrite chrysoberyl	1.74; 1.75	8.5	3.72

	n	H	d(g/cm³)
Tsavolite (garnet)	1.74	6.5–7.5	3.58–3.69
Synthetic spinel	1.73	8	3.64
Diopside	1.68; 1.71	5.5·6	3.27–3.31
Olivine	1.65; 1.69	6.5–7	3.34
Spodumene (hiddenite variety)	1.65; 1.68	6–7	3.18
Jadeite jade	1.66; 1.67	6.5–7	3.34
Andalusite	1.63; 1.64	7–7.5	3.13–3.20
Tourmaline	1.62; 1.64	7	3.02–3.20
Nephrite jade	1.61	5–6	2.9–3.4
Beryl (emerald and aquamarine)	1.57; 1.60	7.5·8	2.7
Serpentine	1.55; 1.56	2–5	2.3–2.6
Synthetic quartz	1.54; 1.55	7	2.65
Chalcedony	1.53	6.5	2.61
Amazonite (feldspar)	1.52; 1.53	6	2.57

Colors: LIGHT BLUE, DARK BLUE, BLUE-GRAY

	n	H	d(g/cm³)
Synthetic rutile	2.61; 2.90	6	4.25
Diamond	2.42	10	3.52
"High" zircon	1.96; 2.01	7.5	4.7
Corundum	1.76; 1.77	9	4.0
Synthetic spinel	1.73	8	3.64
Noble spinel	1.71	8	3.6
Zoisite (tanzanite variety)	1.69; 1.70	6.5	3.11–3.40
Jadeite jade	1.66; 1.67	6.5–7	3.34
Tourmaline	1.62; 1.64	7	3.02–3.20
Topaz	1.61; 1.62	8	3.56
Turquoise	1.61	5–6	2.65–2.90
Beryl (aquamarine)	1.57; 1.60	7.5·8	2.7
Labradorite (feldspar)	1.56; 1.57	6–6.5	2.65–2.75
Synthetic quartz	1.54; 1.55	7	2.65
Cordierite	1.53; 1.55	7–7.5	2.59
Chalcedony	1.53	6.5	2.61
Adularia moonstone (feldspar)	1.52; 1.53	6–6.5	2.56

	n	H	d(g/cm³)
Amazonite (feldspar)	1.52; 1.53	6	2.57
Lapis lazuli	1.50	5–5.5	2.7–2.9
Synthetic lapis lazuli	1.50	4.5	2.38–2.46
Opal	1.45	5.5–6.5	2.1
Coral	. . .	3.5–4	2.65

Color: various shades of VIOLET

	n	H	d(g/cm³)
Zircon	1.96; 2.01	7.5	4.7
Almandine (garnet)	1.76–1.83	6–7.5	3.95–4.20
Corundum	1.76; 1.77	9	4.0
Rhodolite (garnet)	1.76	7–7.5	3.74–3.94
Synthetic spinel	1.73	8	3.64
Noble spinel	1.71	8	3.6
Zoisite (tanzanite variety)	1.69; 1.70	6.5	3.11–3.40
Jadeite jade	1.66; 1.67	6.5–7	3.34
Topaz	1.63; 1.64	8	3.55
Amethyst quartz	1.54; 1.55	7	2.65
Cordierite	1.53; 1.55	7–7.5	2.59

COLORLESS or OFF-WHITE stones

	n	H	d(g/cm³)
Synthetic rutile	2.61; 2.90	6	4.25
Diamond	2.42	10	3.52
Strontium titanate (artificial)	2.41	5.5	5.13
Cubic zirconia (artificial)	2.17	8.5	5.7–5.9
GGG (artificial)	2.02	6.5	7.02
"High" zircon	1.96; 2.01	7.5	4.7
YAG (artificial)	1.83	8.25	4.55
Corundum	1.76; 1.77	9	4.0
Synthetic spinel	1.73	8	3.64
Jadeite jade	1.66; 1.67	6.5–7	3.34
Tourmaline	1.62; 1.64	7	3.02–3.20

	n	H	d(g/cm^3)
Topaz	1.61; 1.62	8	3.56
Nephrite jade	1.61	5-6	2.9-3.4
Beryl	1.57; 1.60	7.5·8	2.7
Serpentine	1.55; 1.56	2-5	2.3-2.6
Quartz	1.54; 1.55	7	2.65
Ivory	1.54	2.5-2.75	1.8
Albite moonstone (feldspar)	1.53; 1.54	6-6.5	2.62-2.65
Adularia moonstone (feldspar)	1.52; 1.53	6-6.5	2.56
Chalcedony	1.53	6.5	2.61
Opal	1.45	5.5-6.5	2.1
Pearl	. . .	2.5-4.5	2.68-2.78
Coral	. . .	3.5-4	2.65

BLACKISH or GRAYISH stones

	n	H	d(g/cm^3)
Hematite	2.94; 3.22	6.5	5.2-5.3
Corundum	1.76; 1.77	9	4.0
Star diopside	1.68; 1.71	5.5·6	3.27-3.31
Jadeite jade	1.66; 1.67	6.5-7	3.34
Tourmaline	1.62; 1.64	7	3.02-3.20
Nephrite jade	1.61	5-6	2.9-3.4
Labradorite (feldspar)	1.56; 1.57	6-6.5	2.65-2.75
Quartz	1.54; 1.55	7	2.65
Chalcedony	1.53	6.5	2.61
Adularia moonstone (feldspar)	1.52; 1.53	6-6.5	2.56
Opal	1.45	5.5-6.5	2.1

Natural and synthetic stones with marked BIREFRINGENCE (recognizable with the aid of a lens).

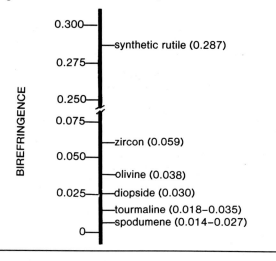

Colorless natural and synthetic stones with the highest DISPERSION or "fire."

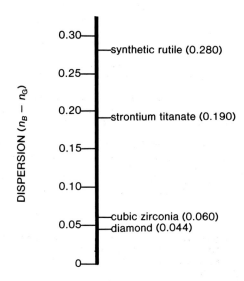

GLOSSARY

Adularescence   Cloudy appearance exhibited by certain curved, semitransparent or transparent gems, creating an impression of a diffuse, mobile reflection or sheen. Characteristic of adularia moonstone.

Alluvium   Continental sediments due to transport and deposition of gravel, sand, and clay by running water, rivers, and streams.

Artificial   Said of a precious stone produced in the laboratory with the hardness, optical properties, and composition of a gemstone, but not existing in nature.

Asterism   Luminosity in the form of a four- or six-pointed star, displayed by particular stones, due to the presence of a radiating pattern of needlelike inclusions.

Biaxial Having two optic axes. Birefringent crystalline substances of monoclinic, orthorhombic, and triclinic symmetry.

Birefringence   1. Double refraction (see below). 2. The strength or degree of double refraction expressed as the difference between the high and low indices.

Cabochon   Convex cut used for opaque or strongly colored transparent stones.

Carat   A unit of weight used in gemology, corresponding to 0.200 grams and divided into 100 "points," abbreviated to ct.

Chatoyancy   Iridescent luminosity producing a thin bright line similar to that displayed by cats' eyes, due to the presence of similarly oriented filiform (threadlike) inclusions.

Cleavage   In crystalline substances, breakage along planes parallel to possible crystallographic faces.

Conchoidal fracture   Breakage which leaves a conchoidal shell-shaped surface.

Contact   Thermal metamorphism associated with igneous intrusions, i.e. an increase in temperature without an increase in pressure.

Crystal   A homogeneous body in the form of a geometric solid bounded by polyhedral faces, the nature of which is an expression of the orderly and periodic arrangement of its constituent atoms.

Cutting   Operation which transforms a rough stone into an ornamental one, endeavoring to bring out its optical properties and eliminate any flaws.

Density   The ratio of the weight of a substance to its volume, expressed in g/cm^3, and numerically equal to the specific gravity.

Deposit   An accumulation of one or more minerals suitable for extraction.

Dike   A body of igneous rocks of appreciable length but limited thickness, often filling a fracture or fault plane.

Dispersion   The separation of white light into its constituent colors by refraction or diffraction.

Double refraction   Ability of certain crystals to split incident light into two rays with different refractive indices.

Eruption An outpouring of lava, dust, and gas at the earth's surface.

Extrusive A term applied to igneous rock which has flowed out at the surface of the earth.

Feathers or veils Residual inclusions along the surface of a crack produced in a crystal during its formation, so called because they look like feathers or veils (see also *lace*).

Fluorescence Temporary emission of radiations of different wavelength (i.e. color) by a substance struck by light rays.

Fracture Breakage with an irregular surface.

Genesis The processes responsible for the formation of minerals and rocks.

Hardness The resistance offered by a substance to actions which tend to modify its surface (scratching, abrasion, penetration).

Hard stones Lapis lazuli, jadeite jade, nephrite jade, the various forms of chalcedony (agate, onyx, cornelian, sard, chrysoprase, jasper, etc.), turquoise, and all other nontransparent stones. The semitransparent, uniform emerald green variety of jadeite jade (known as imperial jade) is an exception, being closer in value and use to the principal gemstones.

Hydrothermal Process by which minerals are formed from hot, aqueous solutions.

Igneous Rocks formed from the crystallization of a silicate melt.

Inclusion Gaseous, liquid, or solid material of various natures incorporated in a crystal during its growth.

Intrusive A body of igneous rock which has forced itself into a pre-existing rock along some definite structural feature such as a joint.

Labradorescence Patchy or diffuse iridescence due to the interference of light by reflection from parallel inclusions. Characteristic of labradorite.

Lace Liquid inclusions trapped along the surface of a crack produced in a crystal during its formation and partially healed by such fluids. The pattern of the residual liquid is similar in appearance to lace, or the veins on an insect's wing.

Lenticular masses Mineral deposits similar to dikes, but with a less regular, more massive shape, vaguely similar to that of a large, strongly convex lens.

Magma Molten silica containing volatile substances in solution, present beneath the surface in certain areas of the earth's crust.

Magmatic Process according to which minerals are formed by a crystallization from magma.

Metamict Partially or wholly amorphous because of the destruction of the crystalline structure by emissions from radioactivity (e.g., of zircon).

Metamorphism (geological) Process of transformation undergone by rocks when they are subjected to temperatures and/or pressures different from those of the environment in which they were formed. This changes the nature of some minerals, or even just their form, without necessarily changing the chemical composition of the rock as a whole. If the metamorphism is merely due to subsidence of the earth's crust, it is known as regional metamorphism. If it is due to intrusion of magmatic or igneous (i.e., high temperature) rocks, it is known as contact or thermal metamorphism.

Metamorphism (mineralogical) When a mineral may be chemically changed by chemical processes.

Metasomatism Chemical transformation which certain rocks undergo in a metamorphic environment, due to the transmigration (loss or gain) of certain chemical constituents, resulting in a change in their mineralogical composition, e.g., calcic limestones to dolomite.

Mineral A structurally homogeneous solid of definite chemical composition, formed by natural processes.

Mineralogical species Basic unit of classification of minerals, according to the dual criteria of chemical composition and crystal structure.

Mineralogical variety Different examples of the same species, which regularly differ in shape and, above all, color.

Optic axis Direction of single refraction in a doubly refractive crystal.

Pegmatites Dikes or lenselike bodies of igneous rock, caused by the cooling of residual liquors from a magma. Usually contains large individual crystals and many minerals which are rare in ordinary magmatic rocks.

Piezoelectricity Ability of some crystalline substances (e.g., quartz) to produce electric charges when compressed, and conversely to oscillate if a suitable electric charge is applied to them.

Pleochroism A difference in light absorption (and therefore color) in the various directions of vibration of a nonmonometric crystalline substance; in particular, the word dichroism is used for dimetric crystals and trichroism for trimetric ones.

Pneumatolytic Adjective describing minerals formed by crystallization under pressure of magmatic fluid, which has the combined characteristics of a gas and a liquid.

Point A unit of weight used in gemology, corresponding to one hundredth of a carat, or 0.002 grams.

Primary (deposit) A type of deposit containing minerals which have crystallized in situ.

Principal gemstones Diamond, emerald, ruby, and sapphire. These four gems alone account for about 90 percent of the value of the gem trade.

Refraction An optical phenomenon which causes a light ray to deviate at the boundary between two substances, owing to the fact that the light travels through them at different velocities.

Refractive index Ratio of the velocity of light in a vacuum (in practice, air) and in a substance, measurable in terms of the ratio of the sines of the angle of incidence and the angle of refraction at the interface between the two media.

Regional Adjective describing metamorphism which affects large cubic masses of the earth's crust. These areas are subjected to considerable increases in temperature and pressure, as a result of subsidence to depths of thousands of meters.

Rock A natural association of minerals both coherent (e.g., granite) and incoherent (e.g., sand).

Secondary (deposit) A mineral deposit caused by action of atmospheric agents on a primary deposit and generally carried far from the latter.

Secondary gems   Beryl of colors other than emerald green, chrysoberyl, spinel, topaz, corundum of colors other than red and dark blue, garnets, tourmaline, zircon, amethyst, and all the other more or less transparent gems. Alexandrite chrysoberyl and black opal are notable exceptions, their value being much closer to that of the principal gemstones.

Sedimentary   Processes (such as denudation) which form rocks from materials derived from existing rocks.

Silk   Term used to describe a close network of long needle-like inclusions, usually of rutile, in corundum. These inclusions give the gem a silky luster.

Single refraction   Property characteristic of all vitreous substances, monometric crystals, and, in certain directions, even nonmonometric crystals, according to which a light ray entering the substance from air is associated with a single wave and a single refractive index.

Star   See *asterism.*

Symmetry   Property displayed by crystals according to which if a series of operations is performed (reflection, rotation, inversion), an identical arrangement of faces and edges is obtained to the one at the point of departure.

Synthetic   Said of a precious stone produced in the laboratory, which exactly reproduces the chemical composition and physical characteristics of the natural stone.

Tenacity   Resistance to forces of fracture or breakage. The opposite of brittleness.

Twin   Union of two or more individual crystals according to precise crystallographic rules called twinning laws.

Uniaxial   Adjective describing birefringent crystalline substances of the dimetric group which have only one optic axis.

Veins   Bodies of mineral matter where length greatly exceeds width.

Volcanic   Synonymous with *extrusive* (see above).

BIBLIOGRAPHY

Aloisi, P. *Gems*. Florence: Le Monnier, 1932.

Andergassen, W. *Il diamante oggi*. Rome: Paleani, 1982.

Anderson, B. W. *Gem Testing*. London: Newnes Butterworth, 1974.

Bauer, M. *Edelsteinkunde*. Leipzig: Chr. Herm. Tauchnitz, 1909.

Bruton, E. *Diamonds*. London: N.A.G. Press Ltd., 1974.

Cavenago-Bignami Moneta, S. *Gemmologia*. Milan: Hoepli, 1980.

Elwell, D. *Man-made Gemstones*. Chichester: Ellis Horwood Ltd., 1979.

Gübelin, E. *International World of Gemstones*. Zurich: ABC edition, 1974.

Liddicoat, R. T., Jr. *Handbook of Gem Identification*. Los Angeles: Gemological Institute of America, 1972.

Nassau, K. *Gems Made by Man*. Radnor, PA: Chilton Book Co., 1980.

O'Leary, B. *A Field Guide to Australian Opals*. Adelaide: Rigby Ltd., 1977.

Pagel-Theisen, V. *Prontuario del diamante*. Milan: Master.

Schlossmacher, K. *Edelsteine und Perlen*. Stuttgart: Schweitzerbartsche Verlagsbuchhandlung, 1954.

Sinkankas, J. *Gem Cutting*. New York: Van Nostrand Reinhold, 1962.

Sinkankas, J. *Gemstone & Mineral Data Book*. New York: Winchester Press, 1972.

Sinkankas, J. *Van Nostrand's Standard Catalog of Gems*. New York: Van Nostrand Reinhold, 1968.

Smith, G. F. Herbert. *Gemstones*. London: Chapman & Hall, 1977.

Webster, R. *Gems*. London: Newnes Butterworth, 1975.

ANALYTICAL INDEX

(*numbers in italics refer to illustration*)

Picture credits